Breaking Ground

The Inside Story of Chicago's Greek Nursing Home Movement

Breaking Ground

The Inside Story of Chicago's Greek Nursing Home Movement

John P. Psiharis

Greek American Press

Chicago, Illinois

Published by Greek American Press
An Imprint of Psihco, LLC., Chicago, Illinois

Website: GreekAmericanPress.com

First Edition

Published in the United States of America

Library of Congress Control Number: 2024904248

ISBN: 979-8-9890724-2-2 (print)
979-8-9890724-3-9 (eBook)

This book is also available as an eBook

Elaine Thomopoulos and John Psiharis at Greek-American Community Services office, 3911 North Monticello Street, Chicago, IL. Circa 1987.

Cover pictures:

Front cover: The Greek American Rehabilitation and Care Centre. Wheeling, Illinois. September 13, 2018. Photo by John Psiharis. John Psiharis collection.

Front cover inlay: An artistic rendering of the Greek American Nursing Home under construction. "A Dream Comes True," benefit dinner invitation. November 25, 2001. John Psiharis collection.

Back cover: A 1993 meeting of the Executive Committee of the Greek-American Nursing Home Committee held at Greek-American Community Services, 3940 N. Pulaski Rd., Chicago, Illinois. Pictured (L-R): John Rassogianis, Toni Panos, John Psiharis, Elaine Thomopoulos, Dr. Theodosis Kioutas, Thalia Jameson, Christine Burbulis, and James Mezilson. John Psiharis collection.

To all who played a part in the accomplishments chronicled within, and to those who will carry the torch into the future, I dedicate this book to you.

Hellenism in the Heartland

The "Hellenism in the Heartland" series, published by Greek American Press, chronicles the legacy of Greek-American Community Services (GACS) and the early histories of its two related organizations, the Greek-American Nursing Home Committee (GANHC) and the Coalition of Limited English Speaking Elderly (CLESE). It also offers a glimpse into Hellenic life in Chicago during this era (1980s-2000s); a time of increased cultural appreciation and awareness, renewed ethnic pride, and unprecedented achievement.

Authored by John Psiharis, who was GACS co-founder, president, and executive director; with the active involvement of Dr. Elaine Thomopoulos; who served as GACS co-founder, vice president, administrator, and cultural arts program director; this series includes photos, ephemera, detailed timelines, and who's who listings for each organization. John and Elaine's experiences, recollections, and files, provide a comprehensive history of GACS and insider accounts of how the GANHC achieved what some thought impossible, the fulfillment of the community's long-held dream of establishing a Greek-American nursing home.

The first in this series, ***Working to Preserve Our Heritage: The Incredible Legacy of Greek-American Community Services,*** meticulously details the dynamic history of GACS, which in its day, celebrated, promoted, and preserved Greek American cultural heritage though far-ranging public programs in the arts and humanities, touched the lives of thousands through its social services, introduced adult day care as a viable care option for the community, helped build better interethnic understanding and cooperation, and gave birth to the committee that established Chicago's Greek-American Nursing Home. The early years of the Coalition of Limited English Speaking Elderly (CLESE), an organization GACS played a key role in launching, are also described.

Breaking Ground: The Inside Story of Chicago's Greek Nursing Home Movement, the second in the series, recounts the groundbreaking efforts of the GANHC to establish a Greek American nursing home. This book, in intimate detail, tells the story of how this monumental project came to fruition. John and Elaine's involvement as co-founders and board members throughout this time provides a unique vantage point for this narrative.

The third, ***Hellenes in the Windy City: The Greeks in Chicago - 1980-2000,*** co-written by John Psiharis and Elaine Thomopoulos, is a snapshot of Greek life in Chicago during the time of GACS, including profiles, photos, and ephemera of some of the more prominent individuals and organizations of the era. A 2025 release is planned.

NOW AVAILABLE

WORKING TO PRESERVE OUR HERITAGE: THE INCREDIBLE STORY OF GREEK-AMERICAN COMMUNITY SERVICES

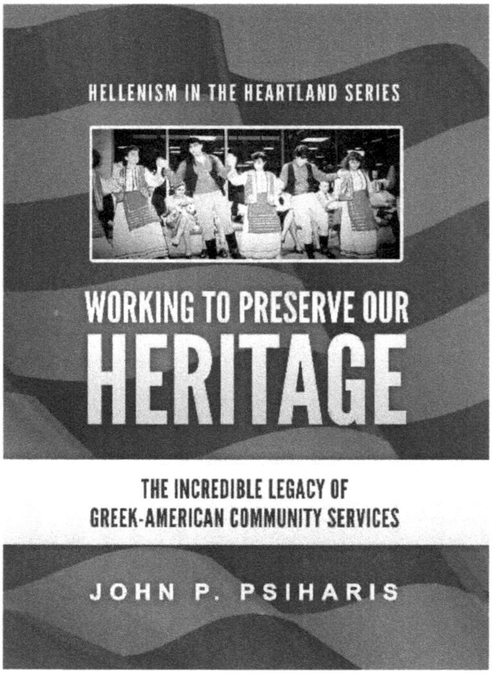

On a cold and snowy evening in December 1982, motivated by the lofty Hellenic ideals of *philotimo* and *philoxenia,* a diverse and dynamic group of Greek Americans launched a groundbreaking movement that forever changed the landscape of Chicago's Greek community.

Forty years later, John Psiharis, with substantial involvement from Dr. Elaine Thomopoulos. the co-founders of Greek-American Community Services, recount how this determined group of Greek-Americans helped ignite a renaissance in Chicago's Greek Community and counts amongst its achievements the establishment of a Greek-American nursing home, an impressive portfolio of groundbreaking cultural programming, enhanced multi-cultural cooperation, and a legacy of service in helping those in need.

Extensive research and insider accounts offer a glimpse into the behind-the-scenes stories and inner workings of this trailblazing organization lauded as "a leading example of the very best our community has to offer." Enhanced with 210 images and pictures, the book provides a who's who encompassing 180 entries, a chronological history for GACS, and a chapter about the early years of the Coalition of Limited English Speaking Elderly, an organization GACS helped launch.

COMING SOON

HELLENES IN THE WINDY CITY: THE GREEKS IN CHICAGO 1970-2000

The 1970s through 2000s were momentous times for some 240,000 Greek Americans living in Chicagoland. After decades of working to establish themselves in the U.S., the fruits of their labors were becoming apparent. Greeks had become the highest educated and second wealthiest ethnic group in the U.S.

It was a time of progress, promise, assimilation, ethnic pride, and accomplishment. In Chicago, Greek Americans owned countless restaurants and stores as well as many other businesses of all types and sizes. They excelled in medicine, law, government, academics, and the sciences. Churches and organizations were integral to Greek American society. It is noteworthy that this era gave birth to two massive Chicago-based community projects, the National Hellenic Museum, and the Greek American Rehabilitation and Care Centre.

John Psiharis and Elaine Thomopoulos, co-founders of Greek-American Community Services and the Greek-American Nursing Home Committee, join forces as co-authors, to chronicle Chicago's Greek community during this pivotal time in its history. Pictures and ephemera add to this story as do extensive listings of business owners, professionals, politicians, academics, artists, and others of the era. Biographies of some individuals and organizations that were influential in the community at this time are also included.

Contents

Part 3

GANHC Who's Who

Part 4

Part 5

About the Co-Founders

John Psiharis was co-founder, president, and executive director of Greek-American Community Services from inception through 2002 and served on the Greek-American Nursing Home Committee from inception through 2006. He was a founding member and two-time past president of the Coalition of Limited English Speaking Elderly.

John's professional activities have included serving as coordinator of community services for the Community Advocacy Network of Lutheran Social Services of Illinois, senior services director at the Hyde Park Neighborhood Club, and executive director of the Bosnian and Herzegovinian American Community Center. He is currently the executive director of the Irving Park Community Food Pantry; a position he has held since 2008.

John was appointed by three Chicago mayors (Washington, Sawyer, and Daley) to serve as a member of the Chicago Community Development Advisory Committee and completed a three-year term as chairman of the Chicago Department of Cultural Affairs City Arts-Social Services Grants Committee. He was a board member of the Chicago Council for Justice for Cyprus and twice elected community representative to the William Howard Taft High School Local School Council, from which he is an alumnus. He holds a Bachelor of Arts in Human Services degree from the National College of Education (National Louis University) and pursued graduate studies in public administration at Roosevelt University.

John is founder and CEO of Psihco, LLC. and publisher of its Greek American Press imprint, and is co-owner of Big Helpers, Inc., a Chicago-based award-winning business he co-founded. He was a consultant to the Loyola University of Chicago School of Education, Metropolitan Asian Family Services, America's Disabled, Fuji Television Network of Japan, and several other organizations and businesses of various types and sizes.

In addition to the "Hellenism in the Heartland Series," John's writings have appeared in *Ergon,* the *Greek Press*, *Greek Star*, *Hellenic Chronicle*, *The National Herald*, and *WindyCityGreek.com*. He has written chapters in *Organizing a Volunteer Program Serving the Elderly, The ABCs of ADCs,* and *Modern Greece*. He is the author of *Working to Preserve Our Heritage: The Incredible Legacy of Greek-American Community Services* (2023) and *Breaking Ground: The Inside Story of Chicago's Greek Nursing Home Movement* (2024).

Elaine Thomopoulos was co-founder, vice president, and administrator of Greek-American Community Services from inception through 1990. She was also a consultant to the Cultural & Arts Program and held the position of Cultural & Arts Program director on a part-time basis from 2000-2002. Elaine was a member of the Greek-American Nursing Home Committee from inception through 2004 and served as second vice president through much of that time.

Elaine earned a Ph.D. in psychology from the Illinois Institute of Technology and was the first director of social services for the Hellenic Foundation. She served as project director of both the Community Advocacy Network and its Assyrian Project for the Elderly, programs of Lutheran Social Services of Illinois. Elaine was a consultant to the Assyrian Universal Alliance Foundation and Chicago project director of "Innovative Approaches to Dissemination of Caregiver Information through Ethnic and Religious Groups," a joint project of the American Jewish Committee Institute and Catholic University.

Elaine was the project director for the "Greek-American Women of Illinois" project sponsored by the Greek-Women's University Club and funded by the Illinois Humanities Council, and the Berrien County Historical Association's "Greeks of Berrien County, Michigan Project," which was funded by the Michigan Humanities Council.

Her writing endeavors included serving as managing editor of the special issues "Books" and "Scientists" for *The National Herald,* a Greek American newspaper. She has also published articles about Greeks and Greek Americans in scholarly journals, as well as newspapers and magazines.

Elaine was the editor of *Organizing a Volunteer Program to Serve the Elderly* and *Greek-American Pioneer Women of Illinois.* She is the author of *Images of America: St. Joseph and Benton Harbor*, *Resorts of Berrien County*, *The History of Greece,* and *Legendary Locals of St. Joseph and Benton Harbor.* Most recently she was editor of *Modern Greece*, published in 2021.

Acknowledgments

I extend my deep appreciation to Dr. Elaine Thomopoulos. Elaine's memories and contributions of photos, documents, ephemera, editing prowess, and advice were instrumental to this project. It has been great to once again to work together with her on this book and other projects. I especially enjoyed our Thursday lunches at the Greek Islands, coffees and delicacies at Artopolis, and visits to the National Hellenic Museum to work on this and other projects. Even though work on this book has come to an end, I look forward to our continuing collaboration in future endeavors.

I also posthumously recognize John Rassogianis for his help with this project. John was integral to GACS and GANHC throughout the years covered in this book. John's recollections added an extra dimension, and his contributions, photos, and editing help are much appreciated. John passed away in October 2022, shortly before this book was completed. Although he did not see the finished product, John was able to read, edit, and contribute to much of the original manuscript. I am grateful to have had the opportunity to collaborate with him one last time.

Many of the photos included in this book are from my collection of photos, documents, press clippings, and memorabilia, including items given to me over the years by Frieda Aravosis, Alex Cantos, Tessie Cantos, Bessie Choporis, Ann Prusinski, and John Rassogianis. Other documents, press clippings, and ephemera are from Elaine's collection. John Rassogianis provided additional photos.

A big thank you to Jeremy Bucher, collections manager, Margaret Frasier, former collections manager, and the National Hellenic Museum, for their support of this project and access to the museum's archives related to Greek-American Community Services and the Greek-American Nursing Home. Of particular assistance were archival records, documents, and photos from the *Greek Star, Greek Press*, James Michael Mezilson, Theano Papazoglou Margaris, Ann Prusinski, and Elaine Thomopoulos collections.

Thank you to Elaine Columbus for sharing photos and news clippings related to a fundraising benefit for the GANHC she co-chaired.

Thank you to Elaine Columbus, Barbara Javaras, and Theresa Tzakis for helping to identify people in various photographs; and to Craig Shutt and Toni Enderle for lending their Photoshop skills to improve the quality of several photos in this book.

I extend my gratitude to Ricardo Rodriguez, who is also my business partner with Psihco, LLC, and CEO of Big Helpers, for his support and guidance during this years-long effort. His advice, ideas, talents, skills, and encouragement are greatly appreciated.

I extend my love and appreciation to my past and present feline family members who kept me company and provided needed affection, attention, and distraction throughout this years-long process: Dickens, * Dison, Hero, Morris, * Shell, Soafire, * Thomas, Tornado (Tornie), * and Zora.

Much of the collective archives that Elaine and I have related to Greek-American Community Services, the Greek-American Nursing Home Committee, the Greek-American Rehabilitation and Care Centre, and the Coalition of Limited English Speaking Elderly will be turned over to the National Hellenic Museum after this project ends so that these items may be available into the future.

Foreword

The idea for this series of books first came about when I discovered several envelopes with photos in a box that I hadn't seen in quite some time. As I looked through the snapshots and thought about the people and stories behind each picture, I realized that in the coming years, few would know who these people were, or their part in the story of Greek-American Community Services (GACS) and the Greek-American Nursing Home Committee. Much of what they worked so hard to achieve would be unknown to future generations. In large and small ways, they unselfishly gave their time, talent, and treasure, and in so many other ways, to this legacy.

Several weeks later, I attended a meeting at the Greek-American Rehabilitation and Care Centre (GARCC). It was my first visit to the facility in several years, and I was impressed by how far they had come. As I contemplated the Wall of Honor on prominent display in the lobby, I again realized that the stories of those who were recognized on this Wall will be lost to those in the coming decades who will assume responsibility for the GARCC. I expect that future generations will continue to benefit from the GARCC but will never know the challenges encountered and sacrifices made by so many to realize the long-held dream of opening the nation's second Greek American nursing home. The first Greek nursing home, the Hellenic Nursing Home for the Aged in Canton Massachusetts, opened in 1973 and is run by the Hellenic Women's Benevolent Association. It is now known as the Hellenic Nursing Home and Rehabilitation Center.

Nationally, there were three Greek-operated retirement homes. The oldest, St. Michael's Home, currently located in Long Island, New York, was established in 1958 and is owned and operated by the Greek Orthodox Archdiocese of America. Hollywood House, operated by the Hellenic Foundation, opened in 1973 and catered to seniors in Chicago. The building was sold to the Heartland Alliance for Housing in 2007. They provided affordable housing to lower-income seniors.

On June 6, 2023, the Alliance and all its properties, representing some 800 units of affordable housing, including Hollywood House, went into receivership. The organization blamed restrictions on rent collections during the COVID pandemic and price inflation related to labor, utilities, and other expenses. Their buildings had a sizable number of building code violations as well. The American Hellenic Educational Progressive Association (AHEPA) opened a senior housing facility in St. Louis and eventually established properties in other parts of the country.

I created a Facebook page as a means of sharing these photos and the stories behind them but soon realized that this was not enough. Facebook only allowed brief descriptions of photos that were a snapshot in time and not the story of the organizations or their accomplishments.

It became apparent that these memories needed to be preserved and set into context for the story to be properly told. Further, this is not just the story of GACS; it is also a glimpse into Chicago's Greek community during the latter part of the twentieth century. As a co-founder of both organizations, executive director of GACS throughout much of its existence, and a member of the GANHC board from inception through 2006, I grew to realize that there was no one more appropriate to tell this story and that if I did not do this, no one else could or would.

Elaine Thomopoulos was also there from day one. She was co-founder of both organizations and at various times served as GACS vice president and administrator when we shared leadership of the organization from inception through 1990 and continued to lend her support after leaving the administrator role. In later years, she served as a consultant and director of the Cultural & Arts Program. Elaine was a board member and second vice president of the GANHC from inception through 2004. Since we were involved in different facets of these organizations, Elaine and I each had unique experiences and memories to contribute to this project. Forty years after the founding of GACS, I am overjoyed to have had this opportunity to connect with Elaine once again and to be able to share the story and legacy of GACS in such a comprehensive manner!

John Psiharis tutors unknown girl during a tutoring session. *Hellenic Foundation Newsletter,* April 1978. Elaine Thomopoulos collection.

I first met Elaine in the late 1970s when I was 12 years old and volunteered at the Hellenic Foundation, while Tessie Cantos, my aunt who raised me, worked as the job placement counselor and office manager. Elaine was the director of social services. I helped to coordinate a health education lecture series, health fairs, and a summer youth tutoring program as both a volunteer and later as a part-time staff member.

In 1982, Elaine left the Hellenic Foundation and became project director of the Community Advocacy Network (CAN), a program of Lutheran Social Services of Illinois (LSSI) focused on helping senior citizens access needed benefits or services through trained volunteers. CAN operated the Assyrian Project for the Elderly, teen-chore and telephone reassurance programs, community workshops, in-service training, and other programs. I followed Elaine to CAN. Tessie remained at the Hellenic Foundation for several years after that.

In 1983, as a CAN volunteer, I began to help with fundraising and then was hired part-time to be the coordinator of development where I helped organize fundraising events such as Hike/Bike-a-thons, house party benefits at Elaine's house, and a membership drive. I then became the coordinator of community services at CAN.

As Elaine and I worked together at CAN, we had occasional conversations about the Greek community and the social service and cultural needs within it. The Hellenic Foundation was doing a good job of meeting many of the community's needs, but there were areas of concern that were not being addressed. At a certain point, a vision of what would become GACS emerged.

Over lunches at Demetrios, Mr. James, Mr. Steer, Alps, and several Chinese and Thai restaurants that were near the CAN office, the concept took shape. In the coming weeks, we contacted people we thought would be interested and invited them to an exploratory meeting to discuss this in greater detail. I arranged with Pol Gavaris, proprietor of the Elysion Restaurant, to use the back room of his restaurant for a meeting on December 14, 1982. It was the first of several meetings that resulted in the founding of Greek-American Community Services and set into motion what became the Greek-American Rehabilitation & Care Centre in Wheeling, Illinois.

In 1985, the nursing home effort spun off from GACS into its own organization, the Greek-American Nursing Home Committee (GANHC), with many of us serving on both boards. In 2002, 19 years after the founding of GACS, the nursing home opened its doors.

Over the coming years, GACS offered an impressive array of cultural programming that lived up to the motto of "Working to Preserve Our Heritage." Be it film festivals, conferences, and traveling museum exhibits or lectures, classes, and demonstrations, the acclaimed GACS Cultural & Arts Program reached across the state and touched the lives of thousands who attended or participated in the many programs that were offered.

Concern for the elderly was apparent early on with the establishment of a volunteer-friendly-visiting program, English-as-a-Second Language (ESL) classes, and community education lectures held during the St. Demetrios

Young at Heart senior citizens group meetings. GACS coordinated Greek community participation in a groundbreaking needs assessment of Chicago's ethnic elderly. Services were enhanced when the Community Advocacy Network (CAN), initially a program of Lutheran Social Services of Illinois, merged with GACS in 1987 and added to the services the organization offered to seniors.

In 1990, GACS launched Northwest Chicago Senior Care, first located at Alvernia Place and subsequently at 3940 N. Pulaski. At the time, it was the only adult day care center on Chicago's northwest side and the first in the nation focused on serving the Greek elderly. GACS briefly launched a chore/housekeeping program, helped usher in Chicago's Benefits Eligibility Checklist (BEC), and assisted thousands to receive assistance in paying their utility bills. Although they did not come to fruition, GACS explored, considered, or initiated planning for a meals-on-wheels program, a Golden Diner's congregate dining program, and several other initiatives.

Along the way, GACS worked with most Greek organizations and established dialogues and close working relationships with several ethnic communities in Chicago including Assyrians, Black people, Chinese, Hispanics, Italians, Jews, Koreans, Latinos, Polish, Ukrainians, Vietnamese, and others.

Additional efforts to collaborate with ethnic communities were apparent with the creation of the Coalition of Limited English Speaking Elderly (CLESE), of which GACS played a key role and was a founding member. The GANHC was also a member organization. CLESE grew into an unprecedented coalition of leaders of organizations representing most ethnic groups that resided in the metropolitan Chicago area. The collaborative spirit and common purpose of CLESE members led to major improvements in service provision to limited and non-English speaking elderly.

In later years, GACS encountered financial difficulties because of continued past due payments from the state, limitations in fundraising due to the GANHC capital campaign kicking into high gear and the impending opening of the nursing home, and a concurrent effort to raise money for the construction of the National Hellenic Museum. It was under these circumstances that the GACS Board made the difficult decision to close its doors. Eventually, the owed funds were received, and outstanding bills were paid.

Although disheartened, there was no time to rest. All eyes were focused on the impending opening of the nursing home. After years of blood, sweat, and tears, the home was about to become a reality.

With zero dollars and little experience, this group set out to accomplish what many thought was not possible; building a Greek American nursing home for the elders of our community that treated them with dignity and respect and honored their culture, heritage, life experiences, preferences, and language. It would be a home that would care for them irrespective of one's ability to pay.

After years of laying the groundwork, fundraising, and considering several suitable locations; we thought we found the ideal place, North Park Village on Chicago's northwest side. Despite several years of intensive efforts, the project became a victim of Chicago's "pay to play" politics. The land the city originally offered was substituted for a piece of property that held leaking underground fuel tanks that posed a toxic environmental hazard. The land that the GANHC had initially been offered and bid on went to a politically connected developer.

As they say, everything happens for a reason. After the North Park Village fiasco, the committee cast a wider net into the suburbs where it was believed we would receive better consideration. Soon, we came across the eight-acre site in Wheeling, Illinois where the Greek American Rehabilitation and Care Centre is now located.

Buying the land was the easy part. The GANHC needed to secure the Certificate of Need (CON) from the state, obtain zoning approvals, establish and nurture community support, launch a multi-million-dollar fundraising campaign, arrange financing, finalize designs, hire contractors, manage the construction process, hire staff, identify residents, and of course, open and operate a nursing home.

Along the way, there were victories and setbacks as we navigated uncharted waters. Each milestone that was achieved presented a new round of opportunities and challenges. Through it all, the GANHC galvanized support for what was an unparalleled community-wide effort that united generations of Greek Americans for a common purpose.

It had been a long-term vision to establish a Greek Village on the GANHC campus in connection with the nursing home. We envisioned a community that encompassed skilled nursing care, assisted living, independent living, adult day care, a senior center, intergenerational programming, and meals-on-wheels prepared from the nursing home kitchen, with opportunities for joint activities and programming within this spectrum. We foresaw purchasing the surrounding land as it became available to create this campus. I'm delighted that in 2018, the GARCC moved a big step closer to fulfilling this dream when it purchased the former Wheeling Senior Center and an adjacent professional medical center building. A vision for what is becoming the Bouras International Campus is evolving that in addition to the nursing home and its services, may include assisted and independent living options, adult day care, and a senior center. Outpatient rehabilitation, occupational, speech, and restorative therapy are currently available and based in the Paterakis Center. A childcare center catering to both employees and the surrounding community is now in operation.

This book includes individual and shared recollections that Elaine Thomopoulos, John Rassogianis, and I had, as well as a detailed chronological history of the GANHC. There is also a listing of key people and supporters of this project during this time. Four decades have passed, and I find that for certain events or people, there are vivid memories and for others, they are foggy at best. Extensive research helped fill in the details and, in some cases, unlocked other memories or events.

In researching and writing this book, Elaine and I have scoured our collective files related to GACS, GANHC, and CLESE and reviewed hundreds of photos, documents, press clippings, notes, board and committee meeting minutes, appointment calendars, correspondence, and publicity materials that helped to tell the story. A few matters, conversations, or details deemed confidential at the time are not included but may be touched upon in the book based on information that was subsequently available in the public domain or discussed during an open board of directors meeting. No client names were used, except for those that had been mentioned in public or the media at the time.

Many of the photos were taken by Instamatic, Polaroid, pocket, or disposable cameras that were not of the quality that we are accustomed to today. Additionally, over the years, the condition of some of the photos deteriorated. When possible, the photos were enhanced to improve their quality. With each of these photos, a determination was made that the documents, people, or activities depicted in the picture were of enough significance to be included, even if the photo was not top-notch.

One conundrum encountered repeatedly was the spelling of names. Some names were spelled in more than one way and years later it is difficult to confirm the correct spelling. Examples of this include: Yannis and Yiannis, Yorgos and Yiorgos, Kosta and Costa, Dimitrios and Demetrios, Spiro, Spyro, and Spero, Rigas and Regas, Soteria and Sotiria, and the list goes on. In quoted texts, the names are spelled as they appeared in the newspaper article or document being cited. When possible, letterheads, correspondence, ad books, and online searches were used to determine the spelling used in the narrative. Unfortunately, with an undertaking of this nature, it is inevitable that despite these painstaking efforts, errors will occur.

Other discrepancies are now apparent with the benefit of hindsight. For example, Crystal Palace Banquets is variously listed as being in Des Plaines, Park Ridge, and Mount Prospect. As of this writing, Crystal Palace is in Mount Prospect. I have included the location as it was provided in the source material. There are instances where there is conflicting information concerning titles, dates, and venues of various events. Again, I have relied on the source material being cited.

Although every effort was made to be as accurate and comprehensive as possible, there are gaps. For instance, most of my copies of GACS meeting minutes and other files are gone and no other copies have surfaced; thus, a wealth of information that would have been helpful may be lost forever. My files related to the early years of the GANHC are also gone. Elaine couldn't locate her copies either. For the GANHC, this is particularly evident between 1988 and 1994. These years were busy times for the GANHC as it was considering or working on the Foster and Pulaski, Dunning, North Park Village, and Rosehill cemetery properties. Theresa Tzakis, a GANHC board member since 1986 and secretary for a period, does not have her records anymore. Toni Panos, GANHC secretary prior to Theresa, no longer has her copies either. Today, Theresa continues as a member of the board and is active in the Centre's women's auxiliary. Having joined in 1986, she has the distinction of being the board's longest-serving member. Theresa and Eleni Bousis are the two remaining board members who joined before the nursing home opened.

We reviewed what the National Hellenic Museum had archived, and as of July 2022, they had little from the period we were looking for. It is worth noting that visiting the Museum was difficult in 2020, 2021, and early 2022, due to COVID-19 pandemic closings and restrictions so our ability to access their archives was limited. I faced similar restrictions (rightfully so) in being able to visit the nursing home during this period, which had an impact on my ability to access records and take updated pictures. Although additional details in certain areas would have been helpful, they do not detract from the overall story.

Listings in the "Who's Who" section are based on roles within the organization and in some cases, people may be listed more than once under different categories. Unfortunately, the passing of years has caused some details to fade. In those cases, I have included the name but may not be able to recall details about their involvement. Although the listings of donors, staff, and volunteers are extensive, they are not all-inclusive. The list is based on our collective memories so many years later and information available from files, media, and ephemera that Elaine and I had in our collections. Additional information was gleaned through research from a variety of sources. I have strived to be as accurate and inclusive as possible, but given gaps in available records or memories, some may have been missed. If that is the case, I apologize in advance. Many played a role in the story of the GANHC in large and small ways and they all deserve appreciation.

Philotimo

"*Philotimo*, at its core, is about goodness, selflessness, giving without wanting anything in return and the force that drives individuals to think about the people and the world around them." *(1)*

Philoxenia

"The Greek word *Philoxenia*, literally translated as a 'friend to a stranger,' is widely perceived to be synonymous with hospitality.

For Greeks, it is much deeper than that. It is an unspoken cultural law that shows generosity and courtesy to strangers.

Philoxenia today can be as simple as a smile, helping a stranded motorist, buying a meal for a homeless person, or opening your home to friends and family." *(2)*

(1) "Philotimo, One Greek Word Packed with So Much Meaning, It Can't Be Defined." *Greek City Times.* October 22, 2018. Accessed July 31, 2023. https://greekcitytimes.com/2018/10/22/philotimo-one-greek-word-packed-with-defined/.

(2) Kokkinidis, Tasos. "Philoxenia: The Ancient Roots of Greek Hospitality." *Greek Reporter.* July 6, 2023. Accessed July 31, 2023. https://greekreporter.com/2023/07/06/philoxenia-the-ancient-roots-of-greek-hospitality/.

Part 1

Charting the Course

(This section is reprinted from *Working to Preserve Our Heritage: The Incredible Legacy of Greek-American Community Services*).

On a cold and snowy evening in December 1982, a small and eclectic group of Greek Americans gathered over coffee in the back room of the Elysion Restaurant in Chicago's Budlong Woods neighborhood to discuss unmet needs within Chicago's Greek community. The conversation was lively and wide-ranging with an array of concerns and ideas being discussed.

It became apparent that the needs of our community's older adults were of primary concern. They had come to this country from the *patrida* (homeland) and worked hard to acclimate to their new surroundings, raise families, and earn a living. As they entered their golden years, they found themselves not only dealing with the usual problems of growing older but also those confronted by most immigrant elders. Seniors were culturally and socially isolated. Many spoke little or no English and were unfamiliar with American culture and customs. When in need of help, other than the Hellenic Foundation, there were few places that they could go to and find someone who spoke their language and shared their cultural values.

All agreed that the Hellenic Foundation was providing valuable services to the community, however, there were still areas of concern that were not being addressed. Key among them was the need for a nursing home that would focus primarily on the needs of the Greek elderly. Other areas of discussion were the need for an array of community services and cultural programs that focused on the Greek American community. The Hellenic Foundation did not offer cultural programming. Research in identifying the specific needs of the community was also deemed important since it would enable us to better understand and respond to areas of concern.

The initial guest list for this meeting included: Dr. Theodosis Kioutas, a medical doctor who was active within the Greek community; Thalia Jameson, a teacher at Chapin Elementary School; Helen Geocaris, wife of the highest-ranking Greek American elected official in Chicago (John Geocaris, 40th Ward Democratic ward committeeman); Jim Heliotes, a supervisor with the Chicago Department of Streets and Sanitation; Polyzoes "Pol" Gavaris, proprietor of the Elysion Restaurant; Charles Mouratides, editorial director, *Lerner Newspapers*; Jean Kaporis, a community elder who was actively involved in her church (Annunciation Cathedral); Ethel Kotsovos, a social worker who had worked for the Hellenic Foundation; Anna Manos, a legal secretary; and Toni Panos, a medical secretary who was active in several Greek organizations including the Daughters of Penelope. A snowstorm that evening reduced attendance.

Since this is the meeting that started it all, the complete minutes are reprinted below.

Greek-American Community Services of Chicago
Planning Committee Meeting

Tuesday, December 14, 1982, Elysion Restaurant, 2800 W. Foster Ave
The meeting was called to order at 6:45 p.m.

Present: John Psiharis. Elaine Thomopoulos, Dr. Theodosis Kioutas, Jim Heliotes, and Pol Gavaris.

John opened the meeting by proposing that an agency to serve the Greek American community should be organized. He sighted the lack of services being provided to Greek Americans and the need for our community to become united. He stated that the proposed agency would not duplicate the services already offered but would supplement them, and in no way compete with the Hellenic Foundation.

Dr. Kioutas thought that services were scant and agreed. Dr. Kioutas brought up cases to illustrate his point that the Greek elderly-especially those in nursing homes- do not have adequate services:

Mrs. H – moved from Hollywood House to Lake Land Nursing Home. Hollywood House could not care for her adequately. Now she is isolated at the nursing home and has no one to talk to or no way to communicate with the staff.

Mrs. D. – who had lived in Hollywood House – is currently in Illinois Masonic Hospital. She will have to move to a nursing home. She has spinal arthritis and cannot function on her own.

Dr. Kioutas felt that a nursing home should be considered as a goal for G.A.C.S.C.

Pol and Jim felt that Hollywood House was primarily for the richer Greeks and that no facilities existed for those who could not afford the high rents.

According to Elaine, the only other known agency helping Greeks in the U.S. (besides the Hellenic Foundation) is

H.A.N.A.C. in New York. She suggested that we should not limit services to Chicago.

The consensus is that we should not limit the board to being of Greek background but that our services be directed to the Greek American community. Pol felt that we should also get involved in cultural affairs.

John reported on his conversation with Father Kaloudis (Holy Trinity) who said that he was eager to help us and may be interested in providing us with office space. We would have to submit a written request to their Board. If they approve it, then the bishop would also have to approve it.

Dr. Kioutas suggested that we contact a few board members in advance to explain our ideas (Chris Demopoulos and Mike Pontikes). He also suggested that we ask Father Kaloudis to act as an advisor.

After discussion, it was the consensus of the group that we should wait until after we are incorporated before we talk to anyone. After incorporation, we should talk to the Hellenic Foundation about how we can work together. Jim added that Holy Trinity is in the 36th Ward.

John stated that we must first write bylaws before we can incorporate. Dr. Kioutas suggested that his wife Anna (an attorney) could help us with the legal wording.

John and Elaine were selected to write a rough draft of the bylaws, to be reviewed at our next meeting.

Other people to be asked to join include Sam Kostogiannes, nominated by Pol, and seconded by Jim. Approved. Pol will ask. Thalia Jameson, nominated by John, seconded by Elaine. Approved. John will ask. Other names mentioned as people who may be interested in this project include Chris Demopoulos, President, Holy Trinity (Dr. Kioutas and John), Gus Contos, C.P.A. (Jim and Pol). Peter Panagoulias, a professor (Dr. Kioutas and Pol).

Recommendations included the following:

1. Co-Chair people – rather than one officer will serve as chief executives.
2. Dr. Kioutas suggested that officers should have two successive two-year terms at most in the same position. John felt that there should not be a restriction if the officers are doing a good job.
3. Pol suggested that we include non-board members to serve on committees as consultants. If these people

perform well, they may be placed on the board. All agreed.

4. The purposes of the organization may include:
    i. Health and consumer education (lectures, health fairs, Tel-Med, etc.)
    ii. Legal Assistance
    iii. Immigration and Naturalization
    iv. Housing for Greeks
    v. Education (tutoring, etc.)
    vi. Social Services (not those done by the Hellenic Foundation)

All agreed that the agency should remain non-political.

Jim reported that according to the 1980 census, 23,000 Greeks reside in Chicago and that 1,500 registered voters live in the 40th Ward.

Pol allowed us to use the restaurant as the mailing address for correspondence.

The next meeting will be held on Friday, January 14 at 6:30 p.m.

The meeting was adjourned by John at 8:45 p.m.

According to Elaine's handwritten notes of the January 14, 1983, meeting:

The meeting convened at 7:15 p.m. In attendance were John Psiharis, Elaine Thomopoulos, Polyzoes Gavaris, Jim Heliotes, Sam Kostogiannes, and Steve Kapsalis. Absent: Thalia Jameson.

John opened the meeting by stating we needed to raise some funds to cover initial fees, such as filing fees and postage for the various applications needed for incorporation. Jim Heliotes suggested that once elections are held and a treasurer is selected, each board member should contribute $25.00. The motion was approved.

Sam suggested that we have seven officers: a president, two vice presidents, a secretary, an assistant secretary, a treasurer, and an assistant treasurer. The motion was approved.

The idea of having two co-chairmen rather than one principal officer was discussed and John was asked to look into it. Sam suggested that we look into designing a logo for GACS.

It was decided that the selection of new members of the planning committee will be accepted into the group only after his/her nomination is approved by all members of the planning committee. This should occur before the new member attends their first meeting.

> The remainder of the meeting was devoted to reviewing the by-laws submitted by John and Elaine. Dr. Kioutas said his secretary would be willing to type the second draft of the by-laws, and that John should call him Monday afternoon to make arrangements. His wife will then review for legal wording. The next meeting will be on Tuesday, February 8, 1983, at 6:30 p.m. Meeting was adjourned at 10:15 p.m.

By the end of the meeting, there was agreement that our group should move forward with these conversations and plan to establish a not-for-profit organization that would address these needs. The initial name considered was Greek-American Social Services. After Pol mentioned that the acronym would be GASS, we chose Greek-American Community Services instead. The hyphen between Greek and American was discussed and it was decided to keep it since our goal was to link these two cultures. It was also decided that our services, although Greek-focused, should be available to anyone who needed assistance. Dr. Kioutas spoke of it as a way of enhancing the image of the Greek Community within the broader community in the same way Catholic Charities, Council for Jewish Elderly, or Lutheran Social Services of Illinois did.

It was agreed that our scope would not be limited to the Chicago region. We planned to expand our footprint into other areas of the country when the opportunity arose.

During subsequent meetings, discussions continued, and initial participants invited others to join the conversation. The logistics of creating an organization became a primary topic. Although most of us were involved in various organizations in one fashion or another, few understood what needed to take place for us to become a full-fledged legal organization. A board of directors was created, and officers were elected. Bylaws would need to be written and incorporation papers filed.

Article I of the bylaws defined the purpose of the organization as follows: "Greek-American Community Services has been organized to operate exclusively for charitable purposes, in providing services to the Greek Communities including but not limited to:

1. Community Services
2. Social Services
3. Housing
4. Cultural
5. Research regarding Greece and its heritage and other programs designed to meet the growing needs of the Greek American

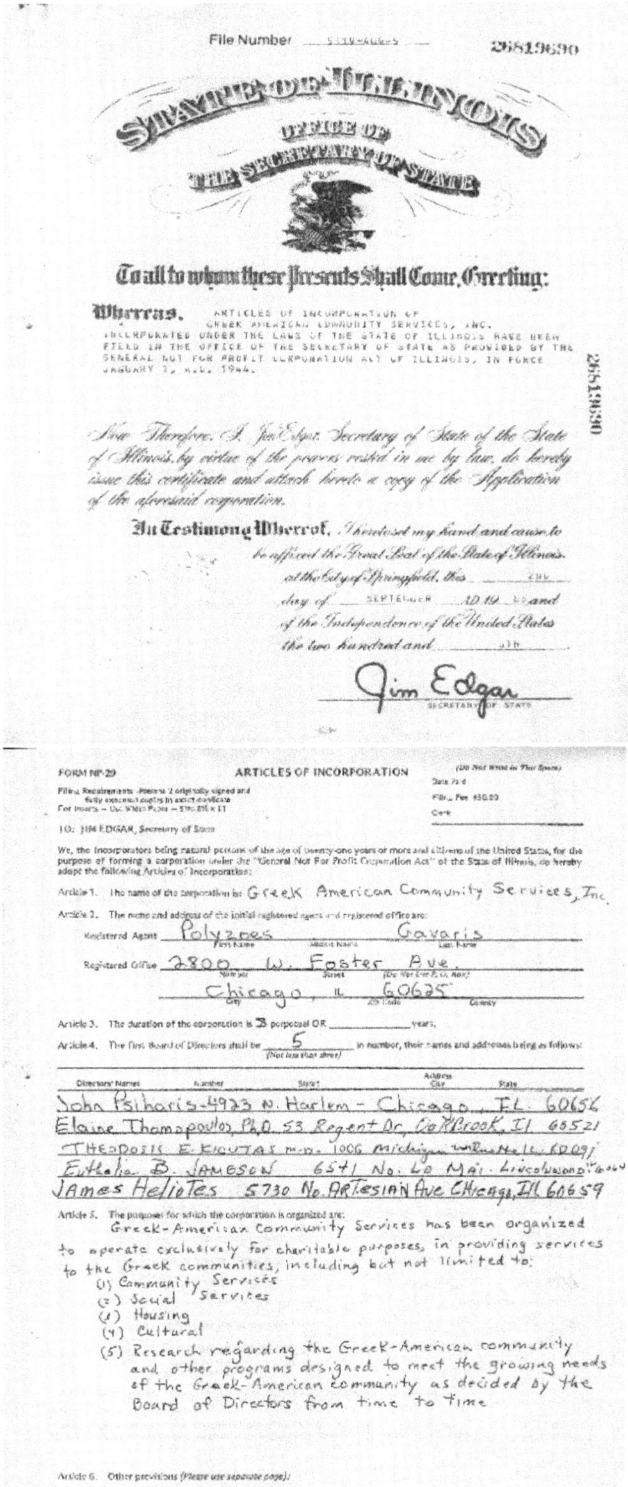

File Number 5319-406-5 26819690

STATE OF ILLINOIS
OFFICE OF
THE SECRETARY OF STATE

To all to whom these Presents Shall Come, Greeting:

Whereas, ARTICLES OF INCORPORATION OF GREEK AMERICAN COMMUNITY SERVICES, INC. INCORPORATED UNDER THE LAWS OF THE STATE OF ILLINOIS HAVE BEEN FILED IN THE OFFICE OF THE SECRETARY OF STATE AS PROVIDED BY THE GENERAL NOT FOR PROFIT CORPORATION ACT OF ILLINOIS, IN FORCE JANUARY 1, A.D. 1944.

26819690

Now Therefore, I, Jim Edgar, Secretary of State of the State of Illinois, by virtue of the powers vested in me by law, do hereby issue this certificate and attach hereto a copy of the Application of the aforesaid corporation.

In Testimony Whereof, I hereto set my hand and cause to be affixed the Great Seal of the State of Illinois, at the City of Springfield, this 2ND day of SEPTEMBER AD 19 83 and of the Independence of the United States the two hundred and 8TH

Jim Edgar
SECRETARY OF STATE

FORM NP-29

ARTICLES OF INCORPORATION

(Do Not Write in This Space)
Date Paid
Filing Fee $50.00
Clerk

Filing Requirements: Present 2 originally signed and fully executed copies in exact duplicate
For Inserts – Use White Paper – Size 8½ x 11

TO: JIM EDGAR, Secretary of State

We, the Incorporators being natural persons of the age of twenty-one years or more and citizens of the United States, for the purpose of forming a corporation under the "General Not For Profit Corporation Act" of the State of Illinois, do hereby adopt the following Articles of Incorporation:

Article 1. The name of the corporation is: Greek American Community Services, Inc.

Article 2. The name and address of the initial registered agent and registered office are:

Registered Agent Polyzoes (First Name) (Middle Name) Gavaris (Last Name)

Registered Office 2800 (Number) W. Foster (Street) Ave. (Do Not Use P.O. Box)

Chicago (City), IL 60625 (Zip Code) (County)

Article 3. The duration of the corporation is ☒ perpetual OR ______ years.

Article 4. The first Board of Directors shall be 5 (Not less than three) in number, their names and addresses being as follows:

Directors' Names	Number	Street	Address City	State
John Psiharis - 4923 N. Harlem - Chicago, IL 60656				
Elaine Thomopoulos, PhD. 53 Regent Dr, OakBrook, IL 60521				
THEODOSIS E. KIOUTAS M.D. 1006 Michigan [illegible] IL 60091				
Euthalia B. JAMESON 6541 No. LeMai. Lincolnwood IL 60646				
JAmes HelioTes 5730 No. ARTESIAN Ave Chicago, Ill 60659				

Article 5. The purposes for which the corporation is organized are:
Greek-American Community Services has been organized to operate exclusively for charitable purposes, in providing services to the Greek communities, including but not limited to:
(1) Community Services
(2) Social Services
(3) Housing
(4) Cultural
(5) Research regarding the Greek-American community and other programs designed to meet the growing needs of the Greek-American community as decided by the Board of Directors from time to time

Article 6. Other provisions (Please use separate page):

Greek-American Community Services Articles of Incorporation. September 2, 1983. Elaine Thomopoulos

6. Community as decided by the Board of Directors from time to time."

In February, officers were elected, and the bylaws were reviewed. I was elected president and Elaine became vice president; however, we worked in tandem as equals. Anna Manos agreed to serve as treasurer, and Helen Geocaris assumed the duties of secretary. John Geocaris offered us a desk in his ward office on Lawrence Avenue above the Family House restaurant, which was used as our initial address. Stationery was ordered from Liberty Press.

At the March 8 meeting, the Board voted to adopt the by-laws, and the Articles of Incorporation were signed for submission to the state of Illinois. A summer tutoring program was also discussed.

Once the documents were completed, they were submitted to the Illinois Secretary of State and the Cook County Recorder of Deeds. A complicated application to the Internal Revenue Service to request 501c (3) tax exemption would then need to be completed. A bank account was established at Commercial National Bank. The initial treasury was composed of $100 donations from each of us.

The minutes of the May 11, 1983, GACS Board meeting at the Elysion Restaurant, as submitted by Elaine:

> The meeting was called to order at 7:00 p.m. Members present included Pol Gavaris, Thalia Jameson, James Heliotes, John Psiharis, Elaine Thomopoulos, Toni Panos, and Anna Manos. Dr. Kioutas and Sam Kostogiannes were out of town. Pol Gavaris had to leave the meeting early. Pol reported that Steve Kapsalis is no longer interested in serving on the board. Elaine volunteered to contact Sam Kostogiannes to find out if he is still interested in serving on the board. It was noted that he has missed several meetings.
>
> John Psiharis moved that the Greek-American Community Services incorporate. Elaine Thomopoulos seconded the motion. The motion was passed unanimously.
>
> John Psiharis moved that Anna Manos be accepted as a new member of the board. Thalia seconded the motion. The motion passed unanimously.
>
> Elaine Thomopoulos moved that Terri Tzakis be accepted onto the Greek-American Community Services Committee if she is interested. She reported that Terri was recommended by Thalia Jameson and is active in *Soteria*. Thalia Jameson seconded the motion, and the motion was passed unanimously.

Thalia Jameson nominated Stella Adinamis Cuthbert. John seconded the motion which was passed unanimously. Sonia Arvanites was nominated by Elaine Thomopoulos and seconded by John Psiharis. The motion passed unanimously.

Bill Zane was nominated by Elaine Thomopoulos and seconded by James Heliotes. The motion passed unanimously.

Elaine Godellas was nominated by Elaine Thomopoulos and seconded by John Psiharis. The motion was passed unanimously.

Lou Mitchell was nominated by Toni Panos, second by John Psiharis. The motion was passed unanimously.

The Greek-American Community Services unanimously agreed that we should express our thanks to Pol Gavaris for the use of the Elysion Restaurant banquet room. It was agreed that meetings be held on Tuesday, Wednesday, or Friday and that if by chance the restaurant was ever not available, our alternate site would be the 40th Ward Office at the N/W corner of Maplewood and Peterson.

Elaine Thomopoulos suggested that copies of the board members' addresses and minutes of our meetings be distributed to the committee members.

Elaine Thomopoulos moved that we develop a prospective member application form. John Psiharis seconded the motion, which was passed unanimously. John Psiharis, Elaine Thomopoulos, and Anna Manos volunteered to design this form. John Psiharis was selected to collect money for incorporation. The meeting was adjourned at 8:30 p.m.

The GACS Nursing Home Committee was established during a June 28, 1983, meeting held at the Elysion Restaurant. According to the meeting minutes, the members present were Charles Mouratides, Jim Heliotes, Anna Manos, Elaine Thomopoulos, Toni Panos, and John Psiharis.

Elaine presented a detailed report on her visit to the Hellenic Nursing Home in Boston three years ago.

Charles Mouratides suggested being a liaison with existing nursing homes. Elaine pointed out the problem of control regarding administration. Jim Heliotes suggested contacting hospitals regarding the nursing home idea to rent facilities in hospitals. Elaine pointed out her contact about four years ago with Swedish Covenant Hospital and how expensive it is since Medicaid only pays part of the expenses. Elaine suggested the St. Peter and Paul Northside group and the Japanese American Service Committee who have already explored the idea.

> Possible hospitals to contact include Swedish Covenant, Ravenswood, Northwest, Thorek, Bethany, Edgewater, and Forkosh. Charles suggested exploring if they can offer "free care."
>
> Elaine Thomopoulos, John Psiharis, and Charles Mouratides will be on the Nursing Home Committee. John will ask Dr. Kioutas if he is interested in being on the committee and serving as chairman. The consensus was that we explore the nursing home as a goal.
>
> Other suggestions were: Preventive health programs as a possibility. John said that the Illinois Consultation of Ethnicity in Education offers consultation on how to set up speaking engagements and media coverage. Anna Manos volunteered to help with the tax-exempt forms.

The notice for the August 23 meeting, handwritten by Elaine, included the following: "John Yonan, Executive Director of the Assyrian Universal Alliance Foundation will speak about the proposed purchase of a nursing home by the Assyrian Foundation including how this is financed. He will also discuss the possibility of there being a Greek wing in this nursing home."

GACS was officially incorporated as a not-for-profit corporation within the State of Illinois on September 2, 1983. Once that was granted, we applied for 501(c)3 tax exemption. The IRS granted the final determination that we were exempt in January 1986.

A meeting notice that I sent for the October 11, 1983, board meeting stated "Our guest speaker will be Mr. William Smith, Jr., attorney at law, who is considered to be one of the top nursing home lawyers in the state. Mr. Smith serves as legal counsel to the Illinois Association of Homes for the Aged, the Evangelical Retirement Homes of Greater Chicago, and the Life Care Services of Des Moines, Iowa. He will discuss the legal and financial aspects of obtaining financing and running a nursing home. The agenda will include the following: Approval of minutes from the last meeting; guest speaker – Mr. William Smith, Jr; an update on articles of incorporation; discussion on touring nursing homes; discussion on tax-exemption papers; discussion on future plans; old business; new business. Dr. Kioutas joins Elaine and me in urging all Board members to attend this very important meeting. The input and presence of every board member are imperative to the success of GACS. It's time to move towards making our dream of a united Greek community a reality."

Harry Milakis, an experienced fundraiser with the City of Hope, helped GACS to develop a fundraising plan and joined the nursing home committee to lend his expertise to that project as well. During an early meeting, he helped synthesize our lofty vision into what became the GACS motto, "Working to Preserve our Heritage." An early Christmas fundraising appeal letter that Harry crafted included a bookmark emblazoned with the GACS name and motto bordered by the Greek key. Unfortunately, Harry passed away from cancer too soon, but his motto lived on throughout the years of GACS.

In the coming months, we continued the process of establishing the organization and began to look at ways we could put our mission into practice. In the coming years, these initial efforts would lead to groundbreaking achievements in the Greek American community.

Despite lackluster support from some in the community's "leadership," which made it more difficult to raise funds or move the organization's vision forward, Greek-American Community Services persevered and blossomed into a respected and successful organization that launched pioneering social services, innovative cultural programs and laid the groundwork for establishing the first Greek American nursing home in the Midwest and the second in the nation.

Throughout the two-plus decades that are the focus of this book, the stories of GACS and the GANHC provide a glimpse into Chicago's Greek community during a time of assimilation, ethnic pride, and increased cultural awareness. This is a testament to all who played a part in Greek-American Community Services and the Greek-American Nursing Home Committee through their generous donations of time, talent, and treasure, and in many other ways, that helped transform Chicago's Greek American community in the later years of the 20th century.

Part 2

Greek-American Nursing Home Committee

Nursing the Dream

During a June 23, 1983, GACS Board meeting at the Elysion Restaurant, the Greek-American Nursing Home Committee was established as a committee of GACS, and in my capacity as president, I appointed Dr. Theodosis Kioutas to serve as chairman and John Geocaris as co-chairman.

We focused on the nursing home project, and regular meetings were held. Through the Coalition of Limited English Speaking Elderly (CLESE), Elaine and I came to know Rev. Masaru Nambu, executive director of the Japanese American Service Committee (JASC). JASC provided home care, adult day care, and other social services and cultural programs. They too were working towards establishing a nursing home for their community and were further along in the process than we were.

We invited Rev. Nambu to speak with the board. He brought Abel Swirsky, a consultant for their nursing home project. Throughout several meetings, we were briefed on the extensive process needed to establish a nursing home, including a reality check in terms of finances. He recommended double the budgeted amount be set aside to cover operations and stressed the importance of the correct patient mix to remain profitable (private-pay vs Medicaid vs Medicare) and (skilled, intermediate, and short-term care). Among the difficulties they encountered were the need to compromise with neighbors including a 60-foot setback and accommodation for traffic. It was costly but essential for them to make these changes since the Planning Commission wouldn't approve unless the neighborhood was in favor. This information, as well as what was gleaned through visits to several ethnic nursing homes, helped provide us with a better understanding of the path forward.

Dr. Kioutas was a tenacious, effective, tireless, credible, and passionate spokesman for the cause. He was well-respected in the community and had many friends. Dr. Kioutas could easily speak to both the Greek immigrant and the Greek American communities about the need for a Greek nursing home, often citing examples of isolated elderly patients that he visited in nursing homes throughout the city. In doing so, he inspired support for this vision despite skepticism from some who did not expect that a project of this magnitude would ever come to fruition.

Many in the Greek community were jaded by past efforts to build a nursing home in Chicago and doubted our group's ability to accomplish this monumental goal. They felt that the Hellenic Foundation had misled the community about its plans to establish a nursing home. After years of fundraising and buying and selling properties, the result (aside from their social service programs) was Hollywood House, a senior citizens' apartment building for those who could live independently, rather than the nursing home that had been the original goal.

The Hellenic Women's Philanthropic Society "Soteria," was created to establish a Greek nursing home. Founded in the 1940s, funds were mostly raised in the 1950s and 1960s, and over the years, with interest, their treasury had grown to more than $270,000. They were in danger of losing their tax-exempt status if something wasn't done with the money.

Through the efforts of Thalia Jameson, Jean Kaporis, and Christine Burbulis, who were members of Soteria, the organization agreed to support the Greek-American Nursing Home Committee. In October 1986, Soteria voted to donate a portion of the funds upfront and hold the balance in reserve until a Certificate of Need was granted and financing was arranged. This support, at a time when the committee was working to reach out to the community, was instrumental in establishing GANHC as a viable and credible undertaking.

Toni Panos, Helen Geocaris, Eugenia Seifer, and Anna Manos were active in the Daughters of Penelope, a women's fraternal organization that grew out of the American Hellenic Educational and Progressive Association (AHEPA). Through their efforts at the chapter and district levels, the daughters agreed to support the nursing home and designated the project as a priority for their fundraising efforts.

The GANHC reached out to Peter and Dean Adinamis at Adinamis Funeral Homes, Galewood Chapels, Cumberland Chapels, and other funeral homes with Greek clientele to place donation cards in their lobby. This became a source of income going forward, with some designating the GANHC to receive memorial donations in their obituaries as well.

An early benefactor of GANHC was Dr. John Nicholson, a retired ENT doctor, and philanthropist. Dr. Nicholson bequeathed $250,000 for the building campaign and an additional $25,000 for administrative costs.

At about the same time, Helen Geocaris and I co-chaired a community reception that introduced the organization's plans to the general community. Through the generosity of Bill and Mary Kakavas, owners of Thirteen Colonies Banquets, the hall and related expenses for the event were gratis. The event was a success. Several hundred people were in attendance to hear about this endeavor. Some made donations or pledges towards the project, while others took the information back to their clubs, organizations, and churches. Equally important, the event provided a mailing list of people who were supportive of the project and wanted to help in the future. Bill and Mary were early benefactors of the nursing home and eventually joined the boards of both Greek-American Community Services and the Greek-American Nursing Home Committee.

A Schism from Within

As the Greek-American Nursing Home Committee moved forward in its work to identify a suitable location for the facility and begin to raise the funds needed to make it happen, some thought that the nursing home committee should spin off into its own organization separate from GACS. They were concerned that having the nursing home under the auspices of GACS would confuse the community and that some may be reluctant to donate to the project if their donation was going to GACS. Donors might misunderstand how their money was being used and assume their funds were instead supporting the community services and cultural programs offered by GACS. A not-for-profit organization that was specific to the purpose of building a nursing home would give donors confidence that their funds would only benefit the nursing home.

Others envisioned GACS as an umbrella organization that included the nursing home, community services, and cultural programs under one banner. The Council for Jewish Elderly, Japanese American Service Committee, Catholic Charities, Casa Central, and others were examples where social service programs and nursing homes co-existed under the same organizational umbrella, enhancing the overall size, reach, and impact of the organization and allowing for seamless service delivery and streamlined services, operations, management, and expenses.

At a meeting in early 1985, heated discussions were followed by a close vote to separate the two projects. As a result of this vote, Polyzoes Gavaris, John Geocaris, Jim Heliotes, and Peter Skouris resigned from the GANHC but remained with GACS. The Greek-American Nursing Home Committee was incorporated as its own 501 (c) (3) organization to establish a Greek

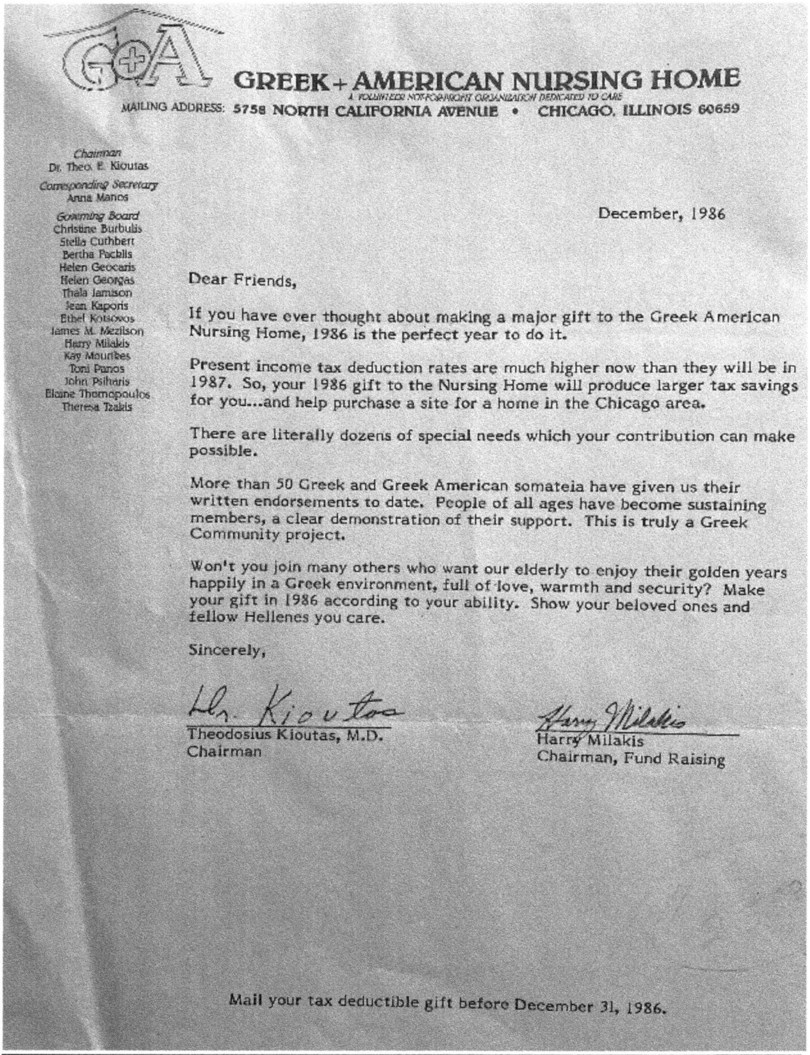

GREEK + AMERICAN NURSING HOME

A VOLUNTEER NOT-FOR-PROFIT ORGANIZATION DEDICATED TO CARE

MAILING ADDRESS: 5758 NORTH CALIFORNIA AVENUE • CHICAGO, ILLINOIS 60659

Chairman
Dr. Theo. E. Kioutas

Corresponding Secretary
Anna Manos

Governing Board
Christine Burbulis
Stella Cuthbert
Bertha Packlis
Helen Geocaris
Helen Georgas
Thala Jamison
Jean Kaporis
Ethel Kotsovos
James M. Mezilson
Harry Milakis
Kay Mouribes
Toni Panos
John Psiharis
Elaine Thomopoulos
Theresa Tzakis

December, 1986

Dear Friends,

If you have ever thought about making a major gift to the Greek American Nursing Home, 1986 is the perfect year to do it.

Present income tax deduction rates are much higher now than they will be in 1987. So, your 1986 gift to the Nursing Home will produce larger tax savings for you...and help purchase a site for a home in the Chicago area.

There are literally dozens of special needs which your contribution can make possible.

More than 50 Greek and Greek American somateia have given us their written endorsements to date. People of all ages have become sustaining members, a clear demonstration of their support. This is truly a Greek Community project.

Won't you join many others who want our elderly to enjoy their golden years happily in a Greek environment, full of love, warmth and security? Make your gift in 1986 according to your ability. Show your beloved ones and fellow Hellenes you care.

Sincerely,

Theodosius Kioutas, M.D.
Chairman

Harry Milakis
Chairman, Fund Raising

Mail your tax deductible gift before December 31, 1986.

An early fundraising appeal letter for the GANHC. December 1986. Elaine Thomopoulos collection.

American nursing home. The Articles of Incorporation were filed with the state on May 16, 1985, and the Certificate of Incorporation was issued on September 18, 1985. The registered agent was Dr. Kioutas, and the mailing address was 5758 N. California Ave., Chicago, IL 60659. Dr. Kioutas converted a patient exam room into an office. The GANHC received provisional approval of 501 (c) (3) tax exemption from the Internal Revenue Service in May 1986 and final approval in May 1991.

Elaine and I wrote the bylaws for the GANHC which were adopted unanimously. Elections were held. The initial GANHC board consisted of Christine Burbulis, Helen Geocaris, Helen Georges, Thalia Jameson, Jean Kaporis, Dr. Theodosis Kioutas, Anna Manos, Toni Panos, John Psiharis, and Elaine Thomopoulos. Dr. Kioutas continued as chair/president of the committee. Helen Georges was elected vice-chair, Toni Panos, secretary, and Anna Manos, treasurer. New board members included two representatives of Soteria: Theresa Tzakis and Bertha Facklis, longtime president of Soteria.

We introduced ourselves to the community through two community forums held at the Annunciation Cathedral. Several hundred people attended these meetings, which included presentations by Dr. Kioutas, Elaine Thomopoulos, Jim Mezilson, Bertha Facklis, and Christine Burbulis. Many in the audience represented organizations, churches, and fraternal societies. Most in attendance were supportive and some pledged financial support while others expressed encouragement but were non-committal at this early stage.

A report in the April 10, 1986, *Greek Star* described one of these assemblies:

> At a recent General Assembly Meeting held at Annunciation Cathedral, Greek-American Nursing Home Committee officers and members took a firm position toward achieving certain goals and objectives in establishing a much-needed geriatric center. The nursing home will exist to serve the Greek-American elderly and disabled of the Chicagoland area.
>
> Dr. Theodosis Kioutas, chairman of the Committee, spoke of the urgent community-wide need for the nursing home, graphically drawing upon his many personal experiences with elderly patients.
>
> In his presentation, he described the need for a 100-bed facility which would provide skilled, intermediate, and extended care for patients whose families are unable to care for them at home, and for elderly patients who have no families. The nursing home facility will be located in a centrally located area.
>
> Stella Cuthbert, moderator and legal counsel, presented a brief history of the Nursing Home Committee since its establishment, its legal status, goals, objectives, and safeguards.
>
> Psychologist Dr. Elaine Thomopoulos reported on the social service component concerning Greek nursing home residents at the Hellenic Nursing Home which is in operation in Boston, Massachusetts. She indicated that the establishment and continued operation of the facility is due largely to the efforts and support – through fundraising events and other means – of the various community-based organizations which provide its greatest support. Many Greek-Americans in the Metropolitan Boston community volunteer their services to the facility on a weekly basis in order to care for their Greek elderly with love and devotion.

> As President of the Sotiria Society which is not affiliated with the Greek-American Nursing Home Committee, Bertha Faklis, revealed the long-term commitment of her organization to the nursing home dream which is now coming to fruition.
>
> Realty specialist Christine Burbulis spoke to the GANHC search for a suitable property or an existing facility that would be acceptable to the community.
>
> Additional information was provided to the General Assembly by Mr. Harry Milakis of the nursing home movement in his presentation of a 16-point questionnaire. Issues that were covered included short – and long-term fundraising goals and suggestions concerning individual and organizational support for the project by Greek community and cultural organizations, fraternal and professional societies, churches, educational institutions, businesses, corporations, friends, other interested individuals and the community at large.
>
> Community leaders such as John L. Marks of the United Hellenic American Congress (UHAC) and William Vranas of the Assumption Church offered valuable input to the meeting.
>
> Dr. Kioutas informed the assembly that necessary funds will be forthcoming. Construction will begin upon approval of the GANHC certificate of need required by the State of Illinois and raising $1.5 million.

An article entitled "Greek American Nursing Home Receives Support" appeared in the June 27, 1986, edition of the *Greek Press* announcing Sotiria's support of the project:

> After thirty-five years of dedicating their efforts to establish a nursing home in the Chicago area, the Sotiria Society recently endorsed and pledged their support to the Greek-American Nursing Home Committee at a meeting with the GANHC.
>
> Representing the Sotiria Society were Bertha Faklis, president; Kay Mourikes, secretary; Theresa Tzakis, treasurer; and Sotiria attorney Thomas Yagnisis.
>
> Also present at the meeting was Dr. Theodosis Kioutas, president of the Greek-American Nursing Home Committee, who spoke to the group about the Committee's objectives and mission, and Harry Milakis, volunteer fundraising advisor.
>
> Kay Mourikes reported that many of the original members of the Sotiria Society were especially gratified to learn that their decades-long quest to establish a Greek American nursing home was a step closer to reality.

> 'The Sotiria Society is proud to be associated with this worthy endeavor and encourages the entire community to give their assistance for the completion of a nursing home to serve our community,' added Theresa Tzakis, society treasurer.

A 1986 year-end update included an update detailing the GANHC's accomplishments in 1986 and through July 1987:

> Obtained tax exempt status from the IRS (501c3).
>
> Received our Charter from the State of Illinois as a non-profit organization.
>
> Conducted two community meetings at the Annunciation Cathedral to announce our intentions and seek support.
>
> Searched relentlessly for a piece of property on which to build.
>
> Received approximately 100 letters of endorsement from church parish councils, Philoptochos organizations, women's groups and ethnic societies.
>
> Established a sustaining membership.
>
> Was unanimously voted by the 13th District Daughters of Penelope to adopt the GANH as their project.

The efforts of the real estate committee were also detailed. The city property referred to below is the Dunning location, near Montrose and Oak Park Avenues. The second site mentioned was Foster and Pulaski. The Japanese American Service Committee purchased the land to build their nursing home.

> The real estate committee has been looking for either an existing nursing home or a property on which to build a 100-bed facility. There are no operating nursing homes for sale. This conclusion was reached after an extensive search through real estate agents and nursing home associations.
>
> We have located two pieces of property. One site was in the process of negotiations and was purchased by another ethnic group for a nursing home. The other is owned by the City of Chicago and designated for other use. To date, all our efforts and those of our friends have not been successful, however, we are not giving up.

In referring to next steps, the report listed the following plans:

> Our organization, together with other supporting organizations, plans to submit our written endorsements directly to the Mayor [sic] and request his assistance in securing the aforementioned site.
>
> Consideration is being given to alternate sites in Chicago as well as the North and North West Suburbs [sic].

THE GROUND■BREAKER!

GREEK+AMERICAN NURSING HOME

A VOLUNTEER NOT-FOR-PROFIT ORGANIZATION DEDICATED TO CARE

ST. VALENTINE'S DAY BRUNCH HELD IN HONOR OF DR. JOHN NICHOLSON

On February 14th, 1988 the Greek-American Nursing Home Committee will host a St. Valentine's Day brunch honoring Dr. John Nicholson, a staunch supporter and major benefactor of the GANHC. The Brunch will be held at the Thirteen Colonies Restaurant and promises to be an informative and enjoyable afternoon for all.

THE NEED FOR A GREEK-AMERICAN NURSING HOME

America is graying rapidly. There are approximately 20 milllion people aged 70 years or older in the United States. Those over 85, the fastest growing percentage of the population are predicted to go from 2.9 million in 1985 to 5.2 million by the year 2000. At present, approximately 1.5 million elderly Americans are in Nursing Homes and that number is expected to rise to 2.5 million by the year 2000.

These statistics are as much of a concern to the younger generations as to the elderly because it is the younger generation which often has the responsibility of deciding where our elderly will live. For Greek-Americans this can be a particularly painful decision. In the traditional Greek family, great importance is placed on keeping the family together. The elderly remain at home throughout their entire lives, retaining their roles as elders and decision makers for the family. Nursing home care is not even considered except in rare cases where extraordinary medical care is required.

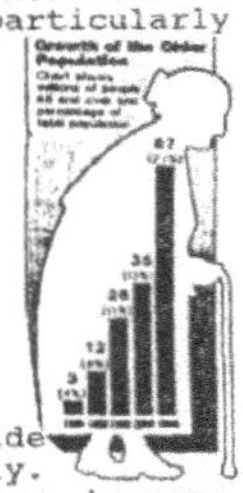

Regretfully, the demands of modern living make this a difficult task to accomplish. Safety and economic concerns may make it impractical to leave our elderly at home. In many homes the house is left empty all day because both spouses work. In-home nursing care is often too expensive and does not provide therapuetic equipment that could benefit the elderly.

The need then for a Greek-American Nursing Home becomes apparent It is the reasonable alternative which allows the ill elderly the opportunity to carry on as much as possible the life they would have had at home, along with the advantage of around the-clock medical attention, provided in an enviroment full of love and respect. A Greek-American Nursing Home can help accomplish the task of carrying-on our tradition of courage, faith, loyalty and love to the people who worked so hard on our behalf. The lecacy left to us by our elders demands at least this from us

WHAT TYPE OF NURSING HOME IS ENVISIONED?

Our goal is to have a nursing facility for the aged as well as young disabled individuals. Under consideration are also such features as an adult day care center for persons whose families are unable to care for them during the day or who seek companionship and activity, as well as respite care for short term care.

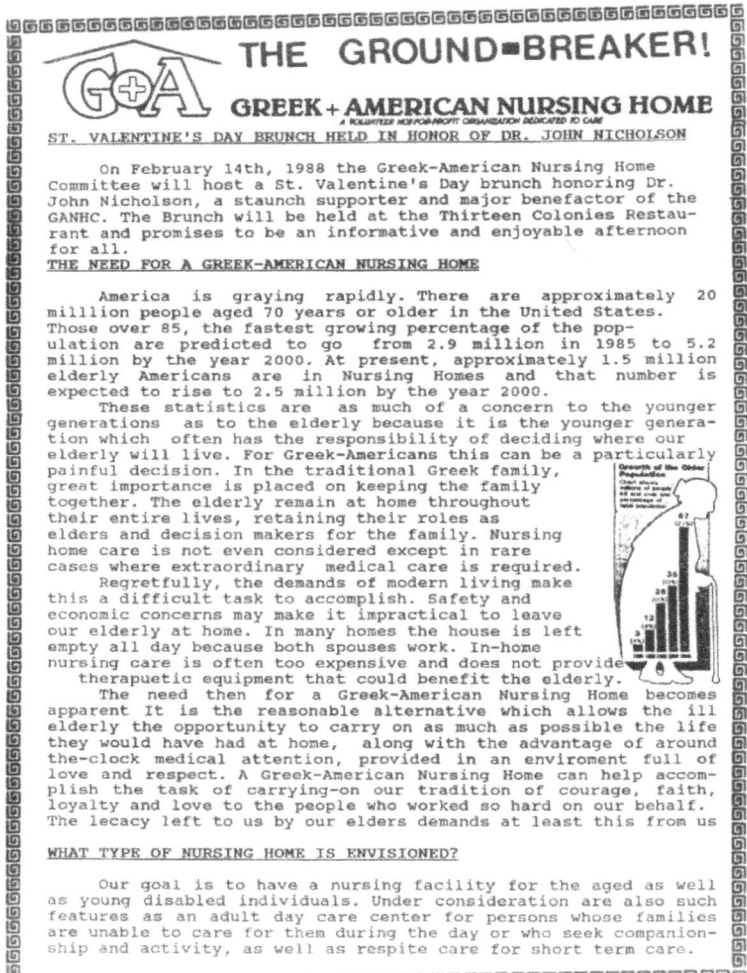

The GANHC *Ground-Breaker* newsletter. Circa 1988. Elaine Thomopoulos collection.

The enrichment of our recently established building fund. All funds collected are earmarked only for this purpose. All funds collected are refundable if we do not succeed.

A fundraiser will be held on Friday, November 20.

Quest for Land

The agenda for the October 27, 1987, GANHC board meeting detailed updates on properties that were under consideration including Glenview, Harms and Central (Emilee Alexandrou), Lincoln and Touhy Avenues (Thalia Jameson), Halsted and Van Buren, Holiday Inn property, and the McDade property.

G+A
GREEK-AMERICAN NURSING HOME COMMITTEE
DINNER DANCE
Hosted By Bill Kakavas and Family
Friday, May 6, 1988
13 COLONIES BANQUETS
8301 W. Belmont Ave. * River Grove Illinois
Cocktails: 6:30 p.m.
Dinner 7:30 p.m.
Donation:
$50.00 per person
TAX DEDUCTIBLE
№ 233
#12

GANHC Dinner Dance ticket. Lincoln, Nebraska Mayor Helen Boosalis, formerly director of the Nebraska Department on Aging, was the keynote speaker. May 6, 1988. John Psiharis collection.

One location considered early on was Martha Washington Hospital. The hospital which was established in 1867 closed in August 1991 after 124 years in operation. In its later years, it specialized in drug and alcohol abuse inpatient and outpatient treatment. The hospital campus was on the northeast corner of Irving Park Road and Western Avenue. We considered repurposing the existing structure as well as building a new facility. A retirement community was envisioned for the area by several neighborhood organizations, so our project fit into their overall plan. Despite the initial positive reaction, it soon became apparent to us that the local political apparatus, led by Edward Kelly, the area's powerful ward committeeman, had pre-determined the future of this property, and we were not part of it. In retrospect, it was a good thing this didn't work out. We were a new organization, and at this early stage, we did not yet have the knowledge, expertise, and most importantly the community support to take on a project of this magnitude. Although it seemed like an ideal location, we had not yet introduced ourselves to the community nor garnered credibility and trust. In short, this opportunity was ideal in many ways, but we weren't ready yet.

Another location briefly considered was a shuttered hospital located near the corner of Howard Street and Western Avenue on the Chicago-Evanston border. It had some pluses including the location, but we learned that hospital and nursing home codes were not the same, and to bring this aging building into compliance or demolish and rebuild it would be too expensive, so we passed.

I recall joining other GANHC board members in touring an elementary school in Wilmette on a Saturday afternoon. I believe Christine Burbulis, Dr. Kioutas, and Art Salk, at the time our pro-bono architectural advisor were there. There may have been others. Fairview North School in

Wilmette was on 4.8 acres with a school building and playground on the premises. It was right off the Edens Expressway and scheduled to be put up for auction on April 10, 1988, with a minimum bid of $950,000. The conclusion was that it would be too costly given that the school building would need to be demolished to build.

Also considered was land in the Dunning complex on Oak Park Avenue near Montrose Avenue. The nursing home would have been part of a redevelopment plan for the Chicago Read Mental Health Center property. At the time we looked at this, discussions were in their early stages and would have taken years to come to fruition, if at all.

At some point, the committee became aware of a parcel of land that seemed appropriate for this project. The land was on the south side of Foster Avenue, just east of Pulaski Road. It was next to the North Branch of the Chicago River and around the corner from a CTA Pulaski bus turnaround. Although the parcel was smaller than some had envisioned, it was workable, and its location, convenient to Chicago's north side and not far from the 90/94 expressways, made it appealing.

After a comprehensive review by architects who volunteered their services including Elias Pappageorge, it was determined that the parcel was in a floodplain given its proximity to the river. Based on this information, we decided to look for something else. I had shared information about this parcel of land with Rev. Nambu. Eventually, the Japanese American Service Committee purchased the land and began construction of their nursing home. Unfortunately, due to cost overruns and construction problems (parts of the building were not constructed to code), the nursing home experienced severe financial pressures that led JASC to sell the home within a couple of years of its opening. Today, it is a privately owned, for-profit nursing home called Harmony House. The area continues to experience periodic flooding when the river overflows.

Continuing the Search

In her October 8, 1989, *Greek Press* column, "View from the Pew," Kay Valone wrote an impassioned plea in support of the GANHC entitled, "Will the 'Real' Benefactors Come Forward." It read in part:

> In the early 50s, I recall the late Father George Mastrantonis making heroic efforts to mobilize the Orthodox Community to build a Home for Elderly Greeks in Chicago. You will remember the G.O.W.F. (Greek Orthodox Welfare Foundation) which then Bishop of Chicago, the Rt. Rev. Ezekiel of Nazianzus organized. The Archdiocese soon took over and changed the G.O.W.F to the G.A.W.F or the Greek Archdiocese Welfare Foundation. Somehow the momentum was lost. In time, we had a series of

purchases and sales of property until we finally ended up with Hollywood House.

Yet, strictly speaking, we do not have a home for the aged Greeks that is conducive to the lifestyle of the immigrants who had come over from Greece in the early 20th century, such as my mother and father. (My father was born in 1881 and my mother in 1896). Most of these early immigrants have died now and after nearly four decades, the so-called second wealthiest ethnic group in Illinois, the Greeks, have no institutions to speak of in the state, except for thirty-three churches we have built, and the three day-schools: Koreas, Socrates, and Plato.

This is in spite of the fact that Greek Americans have done well financially and have their properties, condos, elaborate businesses, etcetera, but most of them do not really care for their ethnic pride as much as their individual egos. They have forgotten those who need to be taken care of, and who need to be in a good and caring environment in their old age. Our elderly for the most part are lonely and feel unneeded or ignored unless they live in a happy extended family situation. For some reason, the Diocese has not followed through with its responsibility, and the laity has lost faith in the parishes to accomplish this dream in our lifetime.

The Greeks of Chicago who have made tidy fortunes seem to be uninterested in establishing a home for the elderly. Instead, they are giving the great bulk of their fortunes or charity to universities like Northwestern, Loyola, and DePaul, and to hospitals that are Roman Catholic and Protestant. Are none of our so-called “elite” concerned to do something for the Greek community? Yet they yearn for the adulation and admiration of Greeks. We have no “Zappa Brothers” in Chicago. (They built the famous Zappeion Building in Athens for the populace). Where are our truly great benefactors? One sees them at black-tie affairs hitting themselves on the back (their own) and brandishing their fur and gold jewelry. They have become an ingrown group that flaunts its riches as though that were a sign of accomplishment in itself. There are some exceptions, and I know of some who have quietly helped others. However, I know of the persons of modest means who have helped proportionately more. (Remember the widow’s mite?).

Then there are the laymen who often run the parish councils and who very often use the Church as a means of propelling themselves into the limelight. And of course, the clergy and Diocese go along with this, they will claim, out of necessity. In the meantime, we have alienated those who have talent and resources and who can help in other ways to build up the community.

Instead, heroic groups such as that under the leadership of Dr. Theodosis Kioutas, the Greek-American Community Services, the Hellenic Foundation, etc., are trying to raise money the slow and tedious way, by tens and twenties. It will take forever to do this if ever it is to be done. (I do not in any way minimize their great efforts!).

I CHALLENGE the Diocese, the UHAC (United Hellenic American Congress), the "topica somatea" (Greek federations and organizations), and the 'nouveau-riche' to step forward and do something to get a home for the seniors built. I CHALLENGE Bishop Iakovos of Chicago, the President of UHAC, Mr. Andrew Athens, the Chicago A.H.E.P.A, and those from Tripolis to Megalopolis, and from Icarus to Crete, to step forward and unite to commit themselves to building the Greek American Home for the Aged, including the sick, the orphaned, and the handicapped. Let us take care of our own.

I OFFER my full-time services to this end, free of charge since I plan an early retirement from teaching by January 1990. I OFFER the services of PHOS, INC, to these groups, if they want. I am determined to devote the rest of my life, the Good Lord willing, to God, the Church, and the welfare of our people. If allowed, I pledge to do all possible to build such a home and to give the Greek-American Community my all in honesty with integrity. PHOS has a large contingent of volunteers who will help in this effort night and day until it is done. But the money must come from YOU, ALL OF YOU. Not just the middle class but the wealthy as well. Now it remains for the real BENEFACTORS OF OUR GREEK COMMUNITY to come forward and to be counted in this enterprise. Here and now is when we will see if there is a genuine concern or just lip service. Everyone who contributes his or her time, talents, or treasure will be made known to the community at large. We could restructure PHOS so that our focus will be on the Orthodox here at home, their welfare, and their Christian growth. If we unite and work with a common purpose and in love, God will see this good work through. If you are called by the Greek Orthodox *"aisthema"* (feeling and sentiment) to help in this effort, let us know. We will be glad to discuss with you mutual visions for our people (with anyone and everyone). Remember, the downfall of the ancient Greeks was their jealousy and their fierce independence "egomania" (the latter may be good for some things but fails us whenever there is something that can be done only through cooperation). Today we need to show the world the Glory that is and shall be Greece through the efforts of us Greek-Americans throughout the U.S.A.

> I anxiously await your letters, support, encouragement, and above all, your commitment. An 'evolving' list of benefactors next week.

Unfortunately, it took some time for several of the "community leaders" Kay referred to in her article to support the effort, and a few never helped or at best gave lip service about the project, including some who were UHAC or Hellenic Foundation board members and supporters.

As I wrote in *Working to Preserve Our Heritage: The Incredible Legacy of Greek-American Community Services*:

> At this time, many considered to be the Greek 'establishment' in Chicago, were not supportive of GACS or the GANHC, although some became supportive as time went on. This was apparent in our dealings with the United Hellenic American Congress (UHAC), which claimed to be an umbrella organization for the Greek community. Founded and led by Andrew Athens, UHAC distinguished itself in lobbying for issues impacting Greece, Cyprus, and/or the Greek American diaspora. UHAC supported the Hellenic Museum and Cultural Center, and the Hellenic Foundation, and helped launch International Orthodox Christian Charities (IOCC), of which Andrew Athens was a founding member. After UHAC purchased the *Greek Star*, the newspaper also functioned as their house organ, highlighting UHAC activities and priorities.
>
> After a period of minimal communication with UHAC and the Hellenic Foundation, Andrew Athens, with little notice, invited the leadership of both GACS and GANHC to meet with UHAC executive committee members in a hastily arranged meeting held on July 3, 1992, at the UHAC office on Michigan Avenue. GACS was represented by Evangeline Mistaras (GACS president), Elaine, and me. The GANHC was represented by Dr. Kioutas and Helen Georges. Dr. Kioutas, Elaine, and I wore two hats during this meeting representing both GACS and the GANHC. In addition to Andrew Athens, UHAC participants included Bill Vranas, Frank Kamberos, and Helen Alexander, executive secretary of UHAC. George Collias, board president, and Cynthia Yannias represented the Hellenic Foundation. His Grace Bishop Iakovos was also in attendance. There may have been others as well.
>
> Once pleasantries were exchanged, Evangeline, Elaine, and I spoke about GACS while Dr. Kioutas and Helen discussed the nursing home. Cynthia and George then spoke on behalf of the Hellenic Foundation. They felt that the nursing home project should not move forward and argued there was little need for a Greek American nursing home and that it wouldn't be financially viable. They felt that Hollywood House was sufficient for the community. In terms of GACS, Cynthia felt that GACS was

taking money away from the Hellenic Foundation since they were also seeking community support. She felt there was a finite amount of money within the Greek community and that GACS and GANHC support was in effect reducing the amount of the pie available to them. The bishop was not enthusiastic about GACS and suggested that the GANHC consider a wing in a nursing home instead. He felt that a project of this magnitude would take years to achieve, if ever.

We in turn expressed our view that GACS attracted new dollars and grants to the community in support of services and programs that did not currently exist. Our community was enriched by these services. We did not see this as a competitive environment but one that should encourage cooperation and collaboration.

Evangeline articulated what was referred to within GACS as the "Mistaras Doctrine." This vision of Chicago's Greek community included a troika of services to the elderly. The Hellenic Foundation would provide housing for independent seniors and homemaker services; GACS would offer mid-range services to the elderly through the adult day care center and the GANHC would offer intermediate and skilled nursing care as well as rehabilitation assistance. She viewed these three co-existing organizations to be the community's safety net for its elders.

The end result was that no meaningful UHAC or Hellenic Foundation support or cooperation was forthcoming for GACS or GANHC as a result of this meeting. Worth noting is that we did not acquiesce. We conveyed that our organizations would go on with or without the support of UHAC, the Hellenic Foundation, or the church. The tone of the meeting reflected the fragmented state of Chicago's Greek community and a lack of unity, even though UHAC boasted that its role was to serve as an umbrella organization.

We were surprised but not surprised by the outcome of the meeting. Over coffee at a nearby downtown diner after the meeting, we discussed what had just happened. The overall feeling was that the individual churches would be supportive of the nursing home and that the bishop would come along eventually since he would not publicly want to be seen as an obstruction when the churches under his jurisdiction were supportive. The bishop's main focus was creating a Diocesan Retreat Center near Kenosha, Wisconsin. He was raising and had requested the churches within the Diocese to support this effort. With or without the support of UHAC and the Hellenic Foundation, we resolved to move forward.

Also in 1990, an unexpected development occurred. The Abington of Glenview, an upper-end nursing home in Glenview, established a "Soteria" Greek wing within their facility. They marketed to the Greek community and promised an exclusive wing for Greek residents that would offer food, activities, and religious services.

A May 12, 1990, article in the *Greek Press* newspaper entitled "Health Care Center Makes Wing Available to Greek Community," announced Abington's Greek wing:

> One wing has been set aside for persons from the Greek community requiring healthcare either on a permanent basis or for recovery from strokes or accidents. This section has been named 'SOTERIA' and will be the only wing, at the present time, with a Greek name. Other wings will be made available as required. The remainder of the wings at 'The Abington' have been given English names in keeping with the "Abington" theme.
>
> Mrs. Barbara Lyons, the Administrator, has taken great pains to assure that her staff will be very capable, and at the same time, caring to help make the patient's stay comfortable.
>
> His Grace Bishop Iakovos has given his blessing to this endeavor to bring some of our Greek people together under one roof.

On November 17, an *Agiasmos* service for the Soteria wing was officiated by Bishop Iakovos. The Soteria organization donated an icon painted by iconographer Melpo M. DeFotis, which was hung in the wing. A Greek lunch followed, prepared by the Abington staff, and a sweet table was provided by members of Soteria.

At this point, Bishop Iakovos proclaimed that the wing would adequately meet the needs of the *omogenia* and that a nursing home wasn't needed. Soteria volunteers visited Greek residents, but in the end, little came of this, and the project fizzled out. To me, it was telling that at the time the bishop supported a wing in a for-profit nursing home over a community-wide effort to establish our facility.

Once the Foster and Pulaski location fell through, the Greek-American Nursing Home Committee resumed the search for a suitable location.

During a GANHC Board of Directors meeting on June 26, 1991, the board reviewed the following properties that were under consideration: North Park Village, Rosehill Cemetery, Martha Washington Hospital, and a location on Milwaukee Avenue in Niles.

The Rosehill land was about three acres in size with frontage on Western Avenue at Bryn Mawr. It was surrounded by the cemetery on three sides. For this reason alone, I was opposed to this location from the beginning. I didn't like the idea of nursing home residents seeing a cemetery whenever

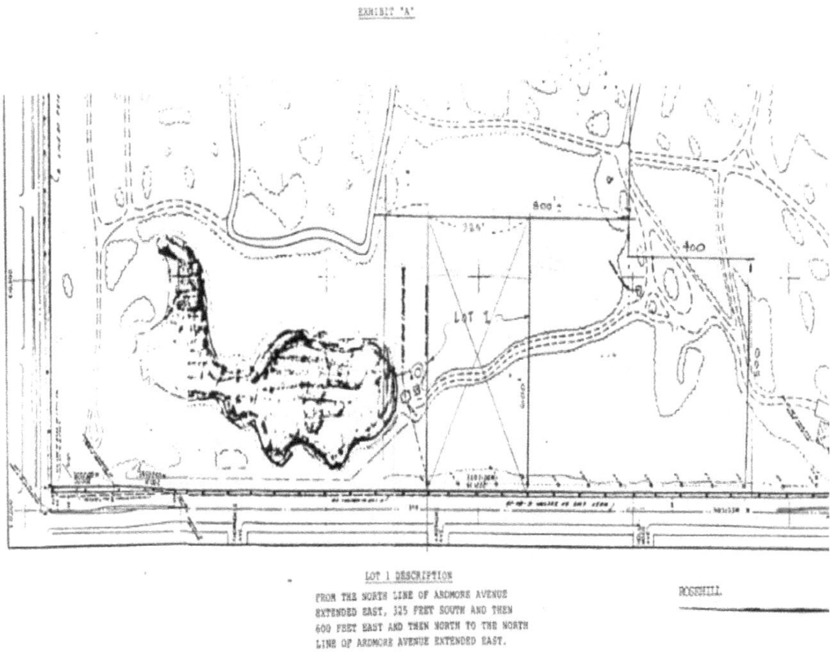

A plat of survey of the Rosehill Cemetery land indicating the proposed location of the nursing home. Circa 1991. National Hellenic Museum – James Mezilson collection.

they looked outside. A few others felt the same way. Nonetheless, the majority prevailed and the committee voted to express interest in pursuing this, and a deposit of $5,000 in earnest money was paid.

As the committee began to formulate plans for the site, a legal dispute of some sort between the Pritzker and Crown families involving the cemetery began to simmer. The Pritzker family owned the Hyatt Hotel chain and the Crown family-owned stakes in many businesses. Both were influential and wealthy families in Chicago and on the world stage. Given that the wealth of each of these families was in the hundreds of millions of dollars, we feared this dispute could take years to settle. Soon thereafter, the committee decided not to pursue this property, and the earnest money was returned.

By far the most promising location up to that point was a parcel of land within a development to be called North Park Village. It was about four acres in size and located near Bryn Mawr and Pulaski Roads. The land once housed Chicago's Tuberculosis Sanitarium. The property was adjacent to the North Park Nature Preserve and was convenient to several modes of transportation. It included a building that was a former nurses' residence. The city of Chicago owned the land and was preparing to put it out for bid.

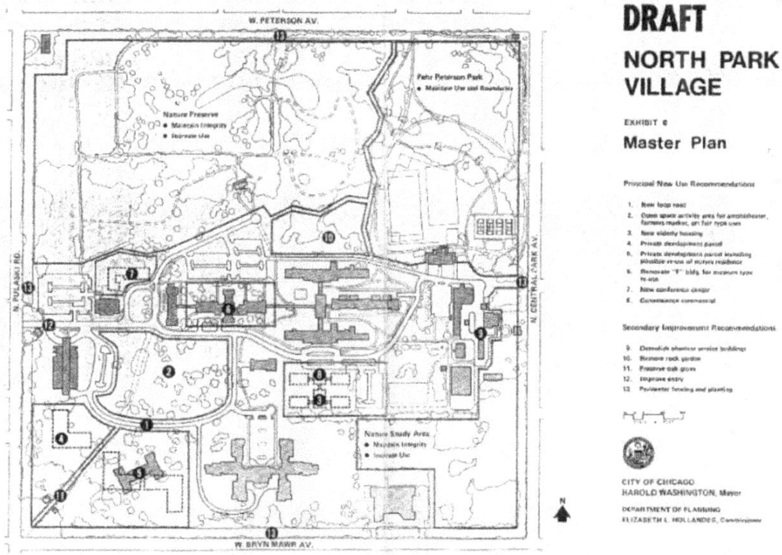

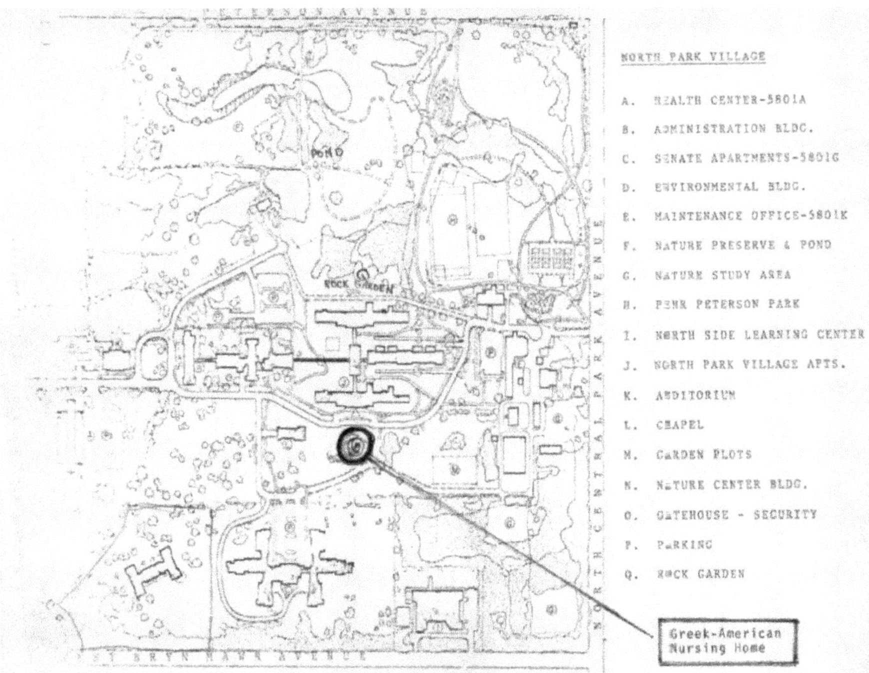

A diagram of the North Park Village property. **Top**: The highlighted "H" shaped building in the lower left corner was the original property GANHC bid on. **Bottom**: The circled location was the contaminated site the city offered as an alternate location. Circa 1993. National Hellenic Museum – James Mezilson collection.

(L-R): Alderman Roman Pucinski, Mayor Richard M. Daley, and John Psiharis during a Holiday Reception hosted by the mayor. I was discussing the nursing home with the mayor, and he invited the alderman to join the conversation when this picture was taken. Date unknown. John Psiharis collection.

The committee became excited about this site. We approached some within the Greek community who had influence with the powers that be to advocate for approval of this parcel of land for the nursing home. In August 1986, Angelo Geocaris, an influential advisor to newly elected mayor Harold Washington, wrote letters to the mayor and Paul Karras, commissioner of Public Works in support of the project.

To demonstrate widespread community support, the GANHC reached out to Greek churches, organizations, elected officials, and community leaders, for letters of support for the project. Eventually, the project garnered the support of Alderman Anthony Laurino (39th Ward), in whose ward the property was located, and Alderman Patrick Levar, of the adjacent 45th Ward, and a friend of Jim Kozonis.

In the summer of 1987, Mayor Harold Washington gave his support to the project. At a September reception for the Community Development Advisory Committee, a committee he had appointed me to, held in the Mayor's Office, I spoke to Mayor Washington about the project and expressed our gratitude to him for his support of the nursing home. He replied that he was happy the Greek community would take part in this development project and that he was for it. Two months later, on November 25, Mayor Washington died of a heart attack, and Alderman Eugene Sawyer was subsequently elected by the City Council to serve as interim mayor until a special election could be held. Sawyer affirmed his support for the project in the coming months but lost his re-election bid to Richard M. Daley.

GANHC Executive Board members review blueprints for the North Park Village property during a 1993 meeting at GACS. Pictured (L-R): John Rassogianis, Toni Panos, John Psiharis, Elaine Thomopoulos, Dr. Theodosis Kioutas, Thalia Jameson, Christine Burbulis, and James Mezilson. John Psiharis collection.

Richard M. Daley was elected to complete Mayor Washington's term of office in March 1989. Among Daley's key supporters were Nick Romas, owner of Mayors Row Restaurant; Jim Verros, owner of the Marquette Inn restaurants; and Jim Kozonis, a commercial property developer.

Since Romas, Verros, and Kozonis had donated and raised large sums of money for his campaigns; they had the mayor's ear. All three soon joined the board to help us advocate for the property. Mayor Daley eventually came out in support of the project. Considering these developments, the committee stepped up our work relative to the site. An architect's rendering was created, attorneys and consultants were hired, and fundraising around this location intensified. Several Greek organizations pledged a portion of the proceeds from their dinner dances to aid the cause while the GANHC organized a cocktail reception at an exclusive country club to raise more money.

After this parcel of land was finally put out for bid by the city, the committee submitted its application and plans to the Chicago Department of Planning. We initially offered $240,000 for the property. At some point, the offer may have been raised to $280,000. Two community hearings were held with presenters from the nursing home joining representatives of a Montessori school and Pontarelli Builders who were to build townhomes on portions of the land. I recall Arthur Salk (the architect) and Dr. Kioutas spoke. The nursing home received positive support from the meeting as did the school. Although the road was a bit rocky for the residential development that would occupy most of the land, the entire development plan for North Park Village was approved.

Many letters were written to the mayor and other elected officials in support of the project. They came from organizations, elected officials, and others who were influential. One such letter, written by Gerald W. Mungerson, president of Illinois Masonic Medical Center, and dated April 20, 1992:

> Dear Mayor Daley:
>
> I am pleased to write this letter of support for the Greek American Nursing Home Committee organization, which I understand is in the process of attempting to acquire land in the North Park Village Community. It is the intention of the Greek American Nursing Home Committee to continue its mission by developing a high-quality, not-for-profit nursing home on approximately four acres of land in the development area. Although this facility would meet the special needs of Chicago's Greek American citizens, it would be open to anyone who meets the criteria for admission.
>
> Illinois Masonic Medical Center has a long-standing relationship with the Greek-American Community Services organization. Over the past four years, we have financially supported their efforts to develop and implement a specialized adult day care program for Chicago's Greek elderly. It is important to note that although this program was particularly sensitive to the needs of Greek seniors, the program was and is used by people from a variety of ethnic backgrounds. Some four years [sic] after its inception, the adult day care program is providing services to many Chicago citizens and is a model for quality adult day care services.
>
> I am also very familiar with the Chairman of the Greek-American Nursing Home Committee, Dr. Theodosis Kioutas. Dr. Kioutas has been an active member of Illinois Masonic Medical Center's medical staff for over twenty years and is highly respected by his colleagues and administration alike. In addition to specializing in geriatrics, he is also a member of the faculty in the Department of Internal Medicine. He is sincere in his effort to develop the first nursing home facility for Chicago's Greek American community and has worked all his professional life in meeting both the medical and social needs of the Greek American community.
>
> Illinois Masonic Medical Center is supportive of this project, and we are ready to continue our work with the Greek American community.

After several years of effort and thousands of dollars spent, the GANHC received word from the city's Department of Planning that there had been a change. Pontarelli Builders, a large contributor to Mayor Daley, Alderman Laurino, and Alderman Levar, was given most of the parcel originally designated for the nursing home to build additional condos and townhomes.

The nursing home was offered an alternate parcel that was slightly smaller than the first. Soil samples that were conducted by the committee revealed underground fuel tanks from the 1920s and 1930s had leaked into the soil. The soil would have to be removed and replaced following hazardous materials protocols and there still was no guarantee that the area would be free of this environmental hazard because of seepage concerns. It was not a place where one in good conscience would build a nursing home.

In addition to being taken off guard by this new development, those who were political supporters of the mayor were disappointed and upset that despite all the support the mayor and the aldermen received from Greek Americans, and the many tax dollars they paid into the city, in the end, meant little. The developer with political clout and deeper pockets won out. Most of us felt betrayed and offended by the mayor's offer of a contaminated piece of land as an alternate site for a nursing home.

On January 6, 1994, the GANHC revised the initial bid of March 3, 1992, submitted to Benjamin Reyes, Chicago commissioner of General Services, for the acquisition of the site currently occupied by the main power plant and other small structures. The letter stated that an environmental report for the property indicates "extremely poor environmental conditions." The report concluded that it would cost more than $500,000 to clean up the site to an environmentally acceptable standard. Upon receipt of a report from an environmental engineer that even with the money being spent, there were no guarantees the nursing home wouldn't experience seepage. The GANHC revised its bid to $1 for the property. Soon thereafter, we withdrew our bid and went back to the drawing board.

An interesting side note is that federal investigators charged Alderman Anthony Laurino with ghost payrolling in 1995, a year after he had stepped down from the city council and installed his daughter Margaret as his successor. Since his health was failing, he avoided a court trial, but several family members were found guilty including his wife, another daughter, son-in-law, and stepdaughter.

An editorial in the February 7, 1999, edition of the *Greek Press* entitled, "Mayor Daley Continuously Disrespects Greek-American Community," articulated the feelings of many Chicago area Greeks and read in part:

> During the past few years, Chicago Mayor Richard Daley has taken extensive action that has damaged the Greek-American Community. The most appalling action was when Mayor Daley's administration lied to the Greek-American Community about establishing a Greek-American nursing home in the city of

Chicago. After several years of deceit and the expenditure of substantial sums of money that was raised through the contributions of Greek-Americans, the Daley administration told the Greek-American Nursing Home Committee that it had to build a nursing home for Greek-American senior citizens near a toxic site. The community's preferred site was given to a Daley politically connected developer. After Daley's shun, our community moved its plan for a nursing home to Wheeling, Illinois.

A majority of Greek-Americans were not surprised at the conduct of Mayor Richard Daley. Mayor Daley's administration has never assisted the Greek-American community. The evidence is clear. The Greek community has over 200,000 citizens in the Chicagoland area and yet we never received a single dollar of city subsidies for the establishment of a Greek-American hospital, nursing home, orphanage, or cultural center.

Suburb Bound

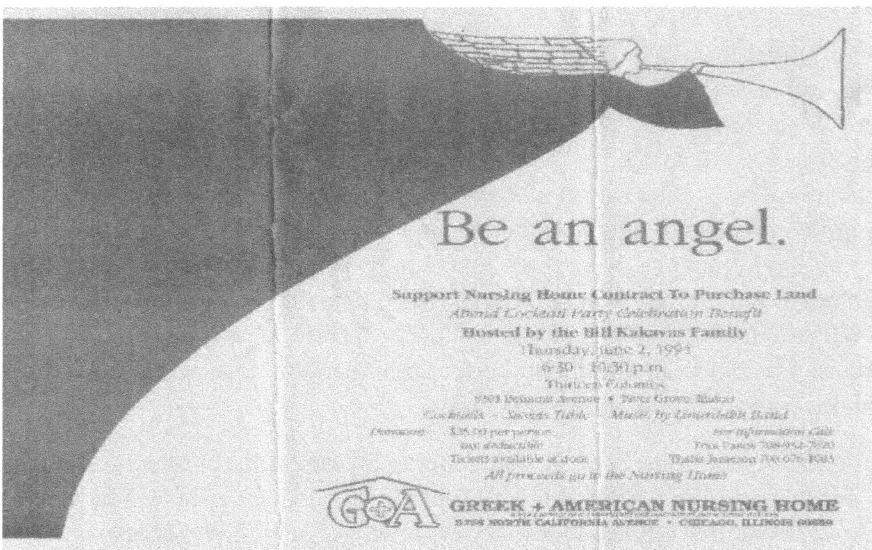

"Be an Angel" fundraising flyer. June 2, 1994. John Psiharis collection.

As the Greek-American Nursing Home Committee recalibrated from the North Park Village setback, board members were angry and discouraged by the way Mayor Daley and the city of Chicago treated the committee, and by extension the Greek community, concerning the North Park Village proposal. Most felt we should forget about the city and focus on the suburbs.

Christine Burbulis chaired the GANHC real estate committee, and through her position as an administrator with the U.S. Department of Housing and Urban Development (HUD) regional office, came across several properties that were deemed worthy of consideration by the committee. The committee briefly considered locations in Glenview, Oak Lawn, and Gurnee, Illinois before zeroing in on property located in Wheeling, Illinois.

The parcel at 199 First Street in Wheeling was located near the intersection of Milwaukee and Dundee Avenues and was blocks from downtown Wheeling and the Metra train station. It was easily accessible to both the Edens Expressway (I-94) and the Northwest Tollway (I-90). This proximity made it possible for those who lived in the city, the southern suburbs, and even Wisconsin or Indiana, to drive there with easy access.

The eight acres of land included two duck ponds. The property was surrounded by a park operated by the Wheeling Park District on one side, the Wheeling Senior Center on the other, and a couple of single-family homes to the north. A medical professional building was nearby, and a senior citizens' apartment building was about a block away. A nursing home would fit into these surroundings. Committee members visited the site and interest grew in this parcel. The asking price for the land was $425,000. It already had connections to water and sewer systems, which was a plus in that those costs could be avoided. The surroundings were serene, green, and inviting. The ponds added another dimension to the property.

It did not take long for the committee to embrace this location. Several special meetings were held and after a lengthy discussion, we unanimously voted to purchase the land and to put down the required earnest money to proceed with the purchase. The contract was signed in early April and GANHC announced the closing on April 20, 1994. $40,000 in earnest money was given and the balance of $385,000 was payable on November 30, 1994. We paid $215,000 from the treasury and obtained a mortgage from Columbia National Bank for the balance of $210,000. Dr. Kioutas and his wife Anna were co-signers and guaranteed the loan. The mortgage was paid off in full on April 5, 1996, with GANHC owning the property free and clear. In a special issue of the GANHC newsletter, "*The Ground Breaker,*" the following announcement was made:

> After years of trying to find a suitable site, we are pleased to announce that we have contracted to buy seven and one-half beautiful acres in the Wheeling area for the future Greek American nursing home. The land is free of any buildings and includes trees, vegetation, and two lovely ponds.
>
> A long time was spent pursuing the City of Chicago's premises for space in North Park Village. What was finally offered to us for sale was found to be environmentally unfit for development and our plans there were stopped.

> The Committee has retained an architectural firm, with expertise in nursing home development. The preliminary drawings and a rendering will be published shortly.
>
> Our committee is grateful to its loyal friends who have supported our goal during this long period. Special thanks to His Grace, Bishop Iakovos, the clergy, Greek social and ethnic organizations especially the Daughters of Penelope of the 13th District who have adopted our mission, and to the Greek-American Community Services who have provided us with space and resources for our meetings. The Bill Kakavas family deserves special recognition for hosting several successful fundraisers. They have supported us since our inception. The support of the entire Greek American community is now needed. We have finally embarked on a course of action that must be shared by all of us. The need for a nursing home is undeniable. Please become a sustaining member. Contribute to the building fund. Consider this project when remembering departed friends and relatives.

Around this time, GACS undertook a community survey to document the number of Greek patients in area nursing homes for the forthcoming zoning and CON process. Ethel Kotsovos coordinated the project with help from GACS volunteers. The survey was conducted in the spring of 1994 to identify patients who had been in a nursing home between 1992-1994.

Through letters and personal contacts, GACS reached out to physicians and hospitals, priests, and people who knew of nursing home patients. Publicity was also done in the Greek media. The results identified 310 people (unduplicated count) in 80 nursing homes in metropolitan Chicago. There were an additional 75 people identified who remained at home because of unwillingness to reside in a facility that did not offer "the type of service you intend to provide at the new facility" (i.e. Greek environment). Also cited in the report was the Hellenic House for the Aged in Toronto, Canada. It opened within the last year and had 78 beds devoted to nursing care. Within two months, it was filled. All were Greek, except three or four.

An article in the November 24, 1994, issue of the *Greek Star* reported on a November 13 luncheon benefiting the GANHC:

> 'On the Feast Day of St. Andrew, we will sign the papers for the property for sure,' pledged Dr. Theodosis Kioutas, President of the Greek-American Nursing Home Association to the 400 guests who had turned out at the $30 per person fund-raiser for the establishment of the Greek American Home. The affair was held at the Thirteen Colonies Banquet Hall and underwritten by Mr. and Mrs. Bill Kakavas. Ethel Kotsovos, a board member, spelled out the accomplishments of the association and its mission to the elderly.

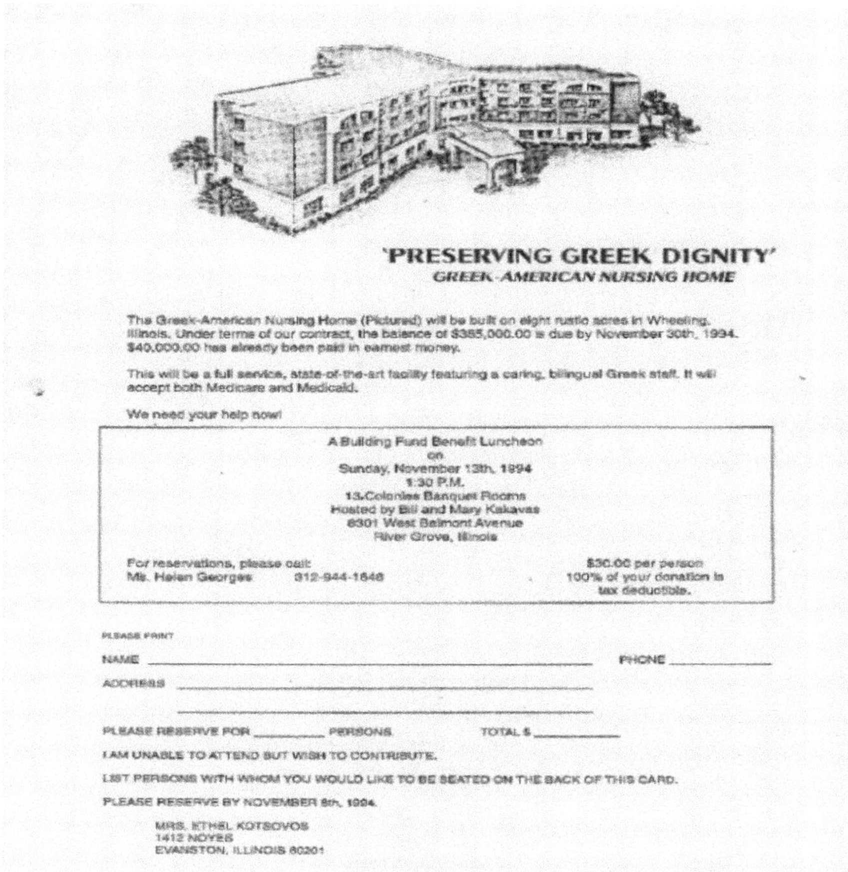

'PRESERVING GREEK DIGNITY'

GREEK-AMERICAN NURSING HOME

The Greek-American Nursing Home (Pictured) will be built on eight rustic acres in Wheeling, Illinois. Under terms of our contract, the balance of $385,000.00 is due by November 30th, 1994. $40,000.00 has already been paid in earnest money.

This will be a full service, state-of-the-art facility featuring a caring, bilingual Greek staff. It will accept both Medicare and Medicaid.

We need your help now!

A Building Fund Benefit Luncheon
on
Sunday, November 13th, 1994
1:30 P.M.
13 Colonies Banquet Rooms
Hosted by Bill and Mary Kakavas
8301 West Belmont Avenue
River Grove, Illinois

For reservations, please call:
Ms. Helen Georges 312-944-1648

$30.00 per person
100% of your donation is tax deductible.

PLEASE PRINT

NAME ______ PHONE ______

ADDRESS ______

______

PLEASE RESERVE FOR ______ PERSONS. TOTAL $ ______

I AM UNABLE TO ATTEND BUT WISH TO CONTRIBUTE.

LIST PERSONS WITH WHOM YOU WOULD LIKE TO BE SEATED ON THE BACK OF THIS CARD.

PLEASE RESERVE BY NOVEMBER 8th, 1994.

MRS. ETHEL KOTSOVOS
1412 NOYES
EVANSTON, ILLINOIS 60201

Flyer for GANHC Building Fund Benefit Luncheon. November 13, 1994. John Psiharis collection.

> Meanwhile, another fundraising mission was being held simultaneously at the St. Demetrios Community Center with Angeline Eliakopolos, President of the Philoptochos introducing psychologist Elaine Thomopoulos, GANHC co-founder John Psiharis, and GANHC publicity chairman John Rassogianis representing the Association. 'Three hundred Greek American elderly are *skorpizmenoi* in 80 nursing homes throughout this area,' they emphasized. 'And we are now ready to help them, thanks to you,' they added."

Architectural renderings and a plat of survey were needed to move forward with Wheeling's approval process. GANHC engaged Shayman Salk, a firm with expertise in nursing homes and health care facilities that had been helping us with site selection on a pro bono basis.

An essay by John Papson, entitled "Why a Greek Nursing Home…," appeared adjacent to the fundraiser article in the November 24, 1994, *Greek Star*, and is another example of the growing community sentiment for this project.

The Greek immigrants who arrived here at the beginning of this century came from a culture steeped in reverence for the elderly. Their forebears were traditionally valued for their years and the ultimate contribution they made to society was not by doing but simply by being. In turn, the immigrants set about establishing a broad and comprehensive Greek identity in this country, one that would ensure the same respect and regard in their later years their antecedents enjoyed.

The age of the immigrant is now almost past. The second, third, and fourth generations have become more or less Americanized. It is inevitable that there would be a clash of value systems. It is also inevitable that a lot of guilt and anxiety would be the result of that clash. Part of the value system the immigrants brought with them was the importance of a tightly knit nuclear family. As parents aged, they were afforded the hospitality of their children's homes and, while safety and economics were valid reasons for such an arrangement, other intangible values of mutual benefit were also perpetuated. The presence of elders was seen as a sign of respect and consideration. Grandchildren had role models and learned firsthand at the grandparent's knee. Meddling was never a consideration. The role of the elderly was to participate as active functioning members of the family. From such an arrangement all generations benefitted through security, advice, support, and unity.

Because the most essential part of Greek life is the family, greater importance has always been given to the family (extended as well as nuclear) than to the community or even society. The degree of importance increases with the decrease in size of the group. This stems from the traditional basic philosophy of the tightly knit Greek family that 'looks after its own.'

Now we come to the question of why a Greek nursing home. Given the conditions and mores of our American culture, there is a basis for conflict between two value systems, one of which calls on the family to care for its own and the other which espouses nursing home care. However, when a traditional Greek family is confronted with the realities of contemporary American life one can see that the real crisis is how to live that American life and still remain as loyal as possible to the value system brought here by the elderly generation from Greece. Each succeeding generation will find it harder and harder to balance that value system given the difficulties of dealing with elderly parents in a mobile active society.

The rationale then, for a Greek nursing home becomes apparent. It is a natural consequence of the value system transplanted to this country from Greece. It is an affirmation of the love and respect traditionally reserved for the elderly as well as an opportunity to develop a model for caring and living that allows

> the ill elderly the opportunity to carry on as far as possible the life, they would have had living in the community among family and friends.
>
> The ethnic nursing home allows us to fulfill our role as faithful children. We share a precious cultural and religious heritage as Greek Americans and Orthodox Christians which our parents and grandparents brought with them to this country so few years ago. That first generation is fast leaving us. Their love, dedication, and sacrifices have left us a wonderful legacy. The response of the second and third generations to their present need can be no less successful than their pioneering efforts on our behalf.
>
> Those of us who are very much the product of America, and yet are somehow mysteriously and wonderfully linked to that immigrant culture and faith, must learn to deal with the need for nursing home care and help provide an environment sensitive and responsive to that generation not only because the care is needed, but because our love for the elderly demands it of us, who live in a society whose way of life in great part looks to solutions foreign to their value system.
>
> We are instructed to honor our Father and Mother and, given the problems of our society, that is sometimes a difficult task to accomplish because of the circumstances such as the need for nursing home care. A Greek nursing home can help us accomplish that task. It is, ultimately, a matter of courage, faith, and love, and a willingness to honor the legacy we have inherited.

Next, the GANHC needed to apply for a zoning variance from the Village of Wheeling. This resulted in a hearing before the Plan Commission. Although there were some questions from commissioners, there were no indications of any opposition. Our plan received approval from the Commission and was forwarded to the Village Board of Trustees for final review and approval. We would need to submit building plans for approval before construction could begin. A carwash business that was considered during the same meeting did not receive approval.

To clear up confusion and misinformation about the nursing home project GANHC provided an update to the community entitled, "Greek-American Nursing Home Questions and Answers," which addressed these matters. Capitalization is per the original document and was used at the time for emphasis. This was a response to those who referred to the Hellenic Foundation's unsuccessful past efforts to establish a nursing home as a reason why the GANHC would not succeed. Many were upset that instead of a nursing home, the Hellenic Foundation purchased Hollywood House, a retirement home, and had subsequently lost faith that this goal would ever be realized. There was some confusion and hesitancy in the community because of this, and it was felt that we needed to formally clarify these matters.

> THIS ORGANIZATION IS WORKING TOWARD THE ESTABLISHMENT OF A NURSING HOME, WITHIN THE MEANING OF FEDERAL AND STATE REGULATIONS, CONCERNING NURSING HOMES WHICH ARE VERY STRICT AND PRECISE, REQUIRING ABSOLUTE COMPLIANCE.
>
> As such. the organization is not to be confused with other organizations which serve the Greek community in other capacities. It is not connected with the "GEROKOMION EFFORT" which started 40 or 50 years ago and resulted in the establishment of HOLLYWOOD HOUSE, as part of the activities of the Hellenic Foundation. The Greek-American Nursing Home Committee is aware of the fine work done by the Hellenic Foundation, appreciates its cooperation and assistance thus far, and hopes that such cooperation and assistance will continue in the future but not as a continuation of the old effort, respectfully suggesting that whatever questions exist regarding the "GEROKOMION" be properly addressed to the Hellenic Foundation.
>
> Also, THE GREEK-AMERICAN NURSING HOME COMMITTEE IS NOT CONNECTED WITH THE MONASTERY OF RACINE, WI. Again, we state that the Greek-American Nursing Home Committee will be in absolute need of the sustenance and support provided by our Greek Orthodox faith. Accordingly, we plan to have a chapel at the Nursing Home with regular church services for the residents. However, a nursing home, to be licensed to operate, needs to comply with very strict regulations and has to be BUILT and OPERATED accordingly. Also, this Monastery, a fine expression of religious sentiment, is not connected with the effort by this committee to build and operate a nursing home. We solicit their prayers, visits, and whatever help they may be able to provide.

A November 1994 letter to the GANHC from George Capulos, a retired educator and guidance counselor, and an early supporter of the Hellenic Foundation's efforts, entitled, "A New Beginning," was also distributed within the community. It was a follow-up to a March 26, 1986, letter Capulos had sent to Christine Burbulis in which he was critical of past efforts and skeptical that the GANHC would be successful:

> About forty years ago when we were all a little younger, I was invited to attend a meeting at a friend's house on the south side of Chicago to hear about an exciting idea that was being

proposed for the Greek Orthodox Community of Chicago. A group of individuals had become inspired by the concept of erecting a Home for the Aged. The author of this proposal was Rev. George Mastrantonis who outlined his thoughts about the project that evening. The seeds from this meeting eventually germinated into what became the Greek Orthodox Welfare Foundation.

It was an exciting time for all of us who became directly involved and also for those who could offer only their moral support. We had attracted many enthusiastic and talented individuals who were willing to give their time, money, and energy to something worthwhile for the Greek community.

Unfortunately, the promise and the dream of fulfilling the original and true objective of the Greek Archdiocese Welfare Foundation, namely, a nursing home for the aged, never materialized. The unity and professional manner with which the project started later began to deteriorate while the 'leadership' groped and fumbled to maintain direction and purpose.

On August 7, 1963. I received a response to my letter to Archbishop Iakovos stating that 'It is obvious that you write most sincerely about the great need for a Home for the Aged in the Chicago area. This matter is still very much alive, and we urge you to have a little more patience and forbearance, for we have reason to believe that it will be settled before too long.' This, however, did not happen.

One might ask, why the history at this time? Why bring up a story which in spite of a turn of events did result in a residential building for our elderly people as well as an agency providing social services to the Greek community, both admirable and worthwhile accomplishments? The answer is that this history could have a direct relationship to a similar project which has been currently launched and is now underway.

We are speaking of the Greek-American Nursing Home to be built in Wheeling, IL. To quote the announcement, 'This will be a full-service state-of-the-art facility with a caring bilingual Greek staff, it will accept both Medicare and Medicaid.'

Once again, the members of the Greek community are asked to support this endeavor. Once again, the rank and file is asked to lockstep and march to the anthem of solidarity and purpose. Once again, we reserve the right and privilege to collectively take care of our own and to foster our ethnic pride and compassion.

It is inexplicable why an ethnic community such as ours with so many promising and successful individuals composed of both entrepreneurs and professional people has found it so difficult to collectively muster up the will to accomplish a worthwhile goal.

> Could it be, as we are sometimes accused, that we have placed self-aggrandizement above that of the 'common good?'
>
> There are those who feel that a nursing home for the Greek community is no longer necessary. They say that for some it would be difficult to visit in its proposed location. They further say that it is too costly to maintain a home of this kind. They may be well-meaning with their expressions, but such negative attitudes tend to hinder and do not contribute to the promise and success of the project.
>
> Perhaps the approach to the fulfillment will become a reality this time. We have been given a second chance. Those responsible for taking the initiative are to be commended. Our Greek pride and our concern and care for our needy and elderly should override whatever differences might exist among us. This Greek-American Nursing Home should become a showcase of Christian charity for our loved ones. This time our efforts must not fail.

An article entitled "A Crown of Achievements for Kakavas's 13 Colonies Support of Nursing Home," written by John Rassogianis appeared in the June 1, 1995, issue of the *Greek Star*. It recognized Bill and Mary Kakavas for their wholehearted support of the nursing home project:

> It does not take long to conclude that Bill Kakavas is on a mission. As proprietor of 13 Colonies Banquet Room, his entrepreneurial energies and philanthropic spirit seem to have merged, as if reflecting two sides of a Greek *lira.*
>
> His passion for excellence in his business endeavors is also reflected in his deep desire for the realization of the Greek American Nursing Home goal. Those energies and ideals that he nourishes coincide with the genuine grace of commitment and accomplishment. Proud of his heritage, he was among the first individuals who realized that the nursing home vision was achievable.
>
> 'My mother was in a nursing home in Greece,' he said. 'She loved it. She didn't want to go back to the *horio,* she told me, 'All my friends are here.'
>
> 'I don't even remember when I started,' as he poured a cup of coffee with *paximadia*, referring to the nursing home project.
>
> '*To eho pari me pono.* A lot of people come here and say, 'Bill, we want to help. What do you want us to do?' But I don't have all the answers. We must get all the presidents of the organizations together.'

A fundraiser benefiting the GANHC at Thirteen Colonies Banquets. Date unknown. John Psiharis collection.

Alternating between her many duties in the banquet hall and the conversation in the office, Maria Kakavas interjected, 'We do a lot of work for handicapped children.'

Referring to a Christmas party sponsored by the Kakavas family, he also said, 'From that time every Christmas party was from me and my family.' He pointed to a trophy with the inscription, 'To a special family from your friends.'

Indeed, Kakavas has been serving the community well. Since he arrived from his hometown of Megalopolis and established the 13 Colonies Banquet Room in 1967, he has been donating his services including providing free breakfasts for *ta pedakia* at Plato and Socrates schools for many years at Christmas. 'Anything they want, hamburgers, French fries, pancakes.'

The Kakavas spirit has even reached out to the general community. He supported a party for an Assyrian church that was being established in Elgin and has given a party *'yia tous Italous'* to raise funds for the Italian earthquake.

Well-known in his local community as a sports booster who supported local sports programs, he was also given a special award by the Village of River Grove for providing food and refreshments to volunteers during the flooding of the Des Plaines River.

He is proud of his community of River Grove and proud of his affiliation with the United Hellenic American Voters of America.

Top: (L-R): Unknown, unknown, unknown, Mary Kakavas, and Dr. Theodosis Kioutas at the GANHC picnic. **Bottom:** (L-R): John Linardakis, Mike Annis, and Nick Gerakaris entertained picnic guests. June 25, 1995. Photos by John Rassogianis. John Psiharis collection.

> Espousing Hellenic-American values, he and his wife Maria, and children Peter, a cardiologist, and daughter Connie, are a family we can be proud of.

The committee hastily organized a community picnic on the grounds to celebrate the purchase of the land. The GANHC "First Annual Family Picnic and *Agiasmos*" was held on June 25, 1995, between the hours of 1:30 p.m. and 7:00 p.m. Bishop Iakovos conducted the traditional Blessing of the Waters ceremony at 3:30 p.m. The event featured barbecues, refreshments, and music from the Linardakis Brothers. More than 800 people attended the event including several elected officials. I recall Illinois Treasurer Judy Baar Topinka, State Senator and Zion Mayor Adeline Geo-Karis, Cook County Treasurer Maria Pappas, the village administrator of Wheeling, and Nicholas Zafiropoulos the consul general of Greece, but there were others as well.

Given the Wheeling location and the difficulty some might have in attending, GANHC chartered two buses to shuttle groups to and from the event. One route served Annunciation Cathedral, St. Andrews, and St. Demetrios. The second route covered Assumption, Holy Trinity, and St John's churches. GACS *Ya'Sou* vans also provided shuttle rides to and from its Pulaski center and the picnic.

Picnic sponsors included: Taylor Rental (Michael Armenakis), Thirteen Colonies Banquets (Bill and Mary Kakavas), Harlem Meat Co. (Pat Maurice), Fresh Produce (Dean Svigos), Delta Ice Cream (John Berbas), Master Caterers (Kostas Zografopoulos), Superior Coffee (Peter Economos), Coca Cola (Lou Paris), Kronos Central (Peter Bartsis), Gordon Foods (Steve Timmens), Chicago Sweet Connection, Cosmopolitan Linens (Dean Stavrakas), Hermes Distributors (Chris Tsilikas), Foreign and USA Truck Rental (George Stergiadis), National Bakeries (Tommy Lee), Portable John Inc., Chicagoland Meats, and Zorba's Pastries.

Final approval was needed from the Village Board of Trustees. When we arrived for the August 15 Trustees meeting that was considering the project, we were anxious but hopeful. Those attending included Dr. Kioutas, Helen Georges, Toni Panos, Theresa Tzakis, Elaine, John, and myself. Helen's partner, Strat Maheras, was the real estate attorney who represented the committee during the Plan Commission and Trustees hearings.

Strat was assisted by Anna Kioutas, Dr. Kioutas' wife and an attorney in her own right. After the Plan Commission's recommendations were presented and a few questions were asked, a vote was taken, and the project was unanimously approved. Unlike Chicago, Wheeling was interested in the construction jobs and the 300-plus permanent jobs the nursing home would have when in operation. They recognized the economic impact and sales taxes employees and visitors would generate by eating, drinking, and shopping in the area.

In September, the GANHC organized a community meeting at Annunciation Cathedral to provide an update on our activities. During this meeting, Dr. Kioutas described the Wheeling property, Helen Georges and Elaine Thomopoulos spoke about the types of patients the nursing home would serve, Christine Burbulis reported on the site selection process, and John Rassogianis discussed the need for volunteers. More than 100 people were in attendance and some made donations or pledges on the spot.

The committee's fundraising efforts kicked into high gear once the land was purchased. People were more supportive when they learned that we had acquired the land. It was a concrete accomplishment and increased confidence that the nursing home would become a reality. In 1994, we collected $304,863 in donations, including $58,840 in memorial donations, $11,000 from a cocktail party, and $35,106 raised during a luncheon event. We paid out $243,000 including $143,000 towards the property, $31,168 for architects, $7,500 for a lawyer, $6,066 for events, $3,178 in postage, and $3,500 for the accountant.

One ardent supporter of the GANHC was Mary Strouzas, a participant in the GACS Fabric Arts Program, who was featured in an article entitled "Supporter Boosts Greek-American Nursing Home Dream," written by John Rassogianis, which appeared in the December 28, 1995, *Greek Star*:

> If awards were passed out to people with a surplus of dedication to the vision of the Greek-American Nursing Home, Mary Strouzas would be a likely candidate for a special mention for her commitment proved itself as she braved her way through zero temperatures to St. Basil Church on a recent Sunday morning. Her self-imposed mission was to sell her homemade gifts during the coffee hour.
>
> 'I've spent $200 of my own money,' she emphasized pointing to her neatly arranged display.
>
> Items for sale included Christmas gift stockings stuffed with wine bottles donated by Bill and Mary Kakavas, lace-decorated candy cane ornaments, lace hearts, and fans, and off-white 12-inch spread-winged angels dressed in expensive gold-edged lace and gold beads tied in satin ribbons.
>
> Strouzas possesses a remarkable clarity of ideas concerning the direction of the nursing home goal. And she is no stranger to expressing them to anyone who may listen.
>
> 'This place is not only for the elderly,' she emphasized. 'Hospitals are now shoving their patients out. They are not ready to go home. Where can they go?'

GANHC board members with residents of Hollywood House at a GANHC fundraising event at Thirteen Colonies. (L-R): Dr. Theodosis Kioutas, Fannie Manos, unknown, Eugenia Seifer, Venetia Papamichos, John Psiharis, unknown, and Ethel Kotsovos. Date unknown. John Psiharis collection.

> 'And why don't we give it another name? How about Guardian Angel? We know it's a Greek-American Nursing Home.'
>
> 'This is my donation for the year,' she added with a tone of finality.
>
> Strouzas, the mother of a parish priest from New York, Rev. Dennis Strouzas, almost seems as if she has been touched by an angel.
>
> The truth of the matter is that she has been her own angel to the tune of a $20,000 pledge to the Wheeling nursing home.

Soteria transferred a portion of the funds they pledged to the committee. The Greek American Restaurant Association (GARA) donated some of the $100,000 that they had pledged. The Daughters of Penelope began to pay down their pledge and several fundraisers were held to support the nursing home. The Greek professional societies (the Hellenic Professional Society of Illinois, the Greek Women's University Club, the Hellenic Medical Society, and the Hellenic Bar Association) donated a portion of the proceeds from their annual joint Valentine's Day Dinner and Dance.

Even though much had been accomplished, way more needed to be done. The coming months were filled with meetings and events related to fundraising, architecture and design matters, licensing, and financing.

Full Speed Ahead

By this time, the GANHC had two annual events: a cocktail party and a dinner dance. Holiday appeals at Easter and Christmas were sent to a growing mailing list. There were also events hosted by other organizations in support of the GANHC. Several societies held events to raise money toward their pledges, as did several Daughters of Penelope chapters. Some of these events were dinner dances and fashion shows while others were smokers and higher ticket events.

Outreach to local churches and organizations intensified to keep the community informed of our progress. One such outreach was described in the April 27, 1995, issue of the *Greek Star* and entitled "All Roads Lead to Wheeling."

> 'All roads lead to Wheeling,' declared Ethel Kotsovos, social worker, while pointing to a large Chicagoland map set behind her at a recent presentation at Holy Apostles Church in Westchester. The topic dealt with the establishment of a Greek-American Nursing Home.
>
> 'Wheeling is not far from here. I know some of you who may want to visit your loved ones every day have concerns, but the care he or she would receive in a Greek environment would more than compensate for a daily visit,' she stressed.
>
> Also representing the nursing home was psychologist Elaine Thomopoulos, Ph.D. She also emphasized that distance was not a problem.
>
> The Wheeling facility will be the third Greek nursing home in North America. The second one is in Montreal, Quebec.

On May 26, 1995, the Greek Women's University Club, Hellenic Bar Association, Hellenic Medical Society, Hellenic Professional Society, Orthodox Singles, and KRIKOS – Midwest came together to host a fundraising dinner at Thirteen Colonies. Bill and Mary Kakavas covered the costs, so all proceeds benefited the GANHC. The well-attended event included remarks from the president of each of the organizations and the consul general of Greece. Dr. Kioutas provided an update to those who attended, and several generous donations were received.

The Hellenic Professional Societies Benefit planning committee: L-R: George Alexopoulos, president of KRIKOS; Barbara Javaras, president of GWUC; Frank Columbus, HPSI treasurer and chairman of the event; Elaine Barkoulies, president of HPSI; and Chris Kuvalas, president of Orthodox Singles. Circa 1995. Elaine Barkoulies Columbus collection.

GANHC established accounts at multiple banks to ensure that we remained under the Federal Deposit Insurance Corporation (FDIC) threshold of $250,000. In most cases, certificates of deposits with varying maturity dates were purchased so funds could be accessed as the project progressed. In addition to monetary donations, GANHC received shares of stock, including shares in AT&T, IBM, and other blue-chip companies. A donation of property and several bequests were also received.

For the first time, there was a rapid outflow of money to pay for the expenses that were being incurred. Tens of thousands of dollars were going out of our accounts each month. Be it for architect fees, project managers, construction costs, or fees to financial advisers, the outflow was significant.

Given the checkered history of past attempts to establish a Greek nursing home, the GANHC was always open and transparent with the community. Several strategies were employed to help get the word out and keep the community up to date.

Periodic GANHC arranged community meetings were held, and the public was invited to attend. The meetings were held in the Annunciation Greek Orthodox Cathedral Hall. Board members sat around a table facing the audience. Dr. Kioutas provided updates to the community on the status of our project, and then the floor was opened to questions or comments. About 100 people attended each of these meetings. Some in attendance wrote out checks or pledged support from their organizations during these meetings.

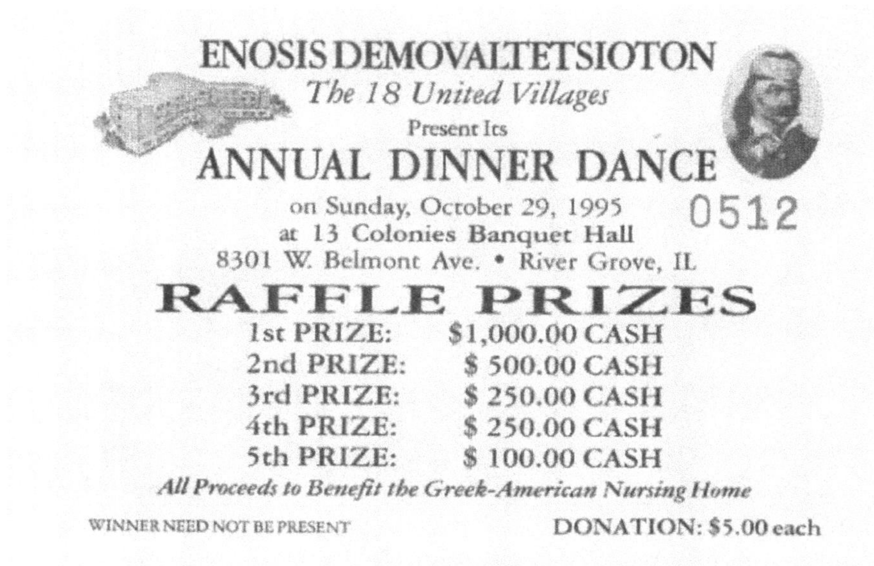

ENOSIS DEMOVALTETSIOTON
The 18 United Villages
Present Its
ANNUAL DINNER DANCE
on Sunday, October 29, 1995
at 13 Colonies Banquet Hall
8301 W. Belmont Ave. • River Grove, IL
0512
RAFFLE PRIZES
1st PRIZE: $1,000.00 CASH
2nd PRIZE: $ 500.00 CASH
3rd PRIZE: $ 250.00 CASH
4th PRIZE: $ 250.00 CASH
5th PRIZE: $ 100.00 CASH
All Proceeds to Benefit the Greek-American Nursing Home
WINNER NEED NOT BE PRESENT
DONATION: $5.00 each

Enosis Demovaltetsioton dinner raffle ticket. October 29, 1995. John Psiharis collection.

Weekly advertising appeared in the Greek American print media including a question-and-answer column that addressed common concerns or questions we encountered. John Rassogianis prepared and submitted these ads to the *Greek Star, Greek Press, Hellenic Community News,* and others. We published the audited financial statement to maintain transparency. At other times, we provided updates so the community could be informed of our progress. Publicity about events also kept GANHC in the news.

This period was one of continued perseverance and detailed planning at the GANHC. The vision was coming to life but as always, the devil was in the details. There were many meetings, at times even weekly, to address the many facets of bringing a project of this magnitude to fruition. Most of these meetings were held at GACS.

In typical Greek fashion, there were pre-meeting dinners at any of several area restaurants including Little Mike's, Buffalo Bill's, the Alps, Mr. Steer, and the Harris Restaurant. Each was a Greek-owned restaurant that in some way supported GACS and the GANHC, so this had the benefit of supporting them in return. Other meetings were held at the Elysion (it later became the Hilltop) or Sauganash restaurants, and we ate either during or before the meeting. Since these meetings could go on for several hours, it was important to eat before the meeting as you never knew when we would finish. Ample coffee was served to keep us juiced. After the longer meetings, it took me a while to wind down given all the coffee we drank as the conversation flowed! In time, I began to limit my coffee intake to two cups to help with this. There were days that I did not get home until midnight!

Gus Flessor, president of the American Hellenic Society of Berwyn (right) presents proceeds from the society's dinner dance to Dr. Theodosis Kioutas and Father George Massouras. Assumption Greek Orthodox Church. Jan. 21, 1996. Photo by John Rassogianis. John Rassogianis collection.

At each level of achievement by the GANHC, new donations were unlocked. The closer we got to our goal, the more the community gained confidence that this endeavor would happen. Numerous fundraisers were held during this time that were either directly organized by the GANHC or events done by other organizations for our benefit. A number of these events were held at Thirteen Colonies Banquet Rooms in River Grove, Illinois. Owners Bill and Mary Kakavas supported these events by donating the hall and food costs associated with GANHC events, so the results were all profit. Greek bands usually volunteered their services, and expenses were often underwritten by donors.

On March 2, 1996, the "Grand Ball to Benefit the Greek-American Nursing Home," was held at Ambassador West with the tagline "United in Purpose for the Greek-American Nursing Home." The event was a joint effort hosted by the community's professional associations: Hellenic Medical Society of Chicago (Chadwick C. Prodromos, President); Hellenic Professional Society of Illinois (Hara Anast, President); Hellenic American Dental Society (Dennis Costis, D.D.S., President); Greek Women's University Club (Barbara Javaras, President); Chicago Fine Arts Society (Don Dadas, President) and the Hellenic Bar Association (Leon Vainikos, President). Jimmy Damon was the headliner singing "Ode to Liberty" and "America the Beautiful." Music and dancing by the Al Sofia Orchestra and "OPA" Orchestra. The event raised $13,000 for the GANHC. On March 3rd, the 13th District of AHEPA hosted a fundraiser that resulted in $12,915.

"Hellenic Societies Unite in Support of Greek-American Nursing Home," an article promoting the event appeared in the February 25, 1996, *Greek Press* newspaper.

> A Greek American Nursing Home for elderly persons of Hellenic descent has long been a dream of civically minded Chicago area Hellenes. Such an undertaking, however, involves raising millions of dollars, obtaining a certificate of need from the appropriate agencies, and other daunting tasks. After several false starts, it appears that the current effort spearheaded by Ted Kioutas, MD., may finally be able to get the job done. Land has been purchased in Wheeling in a beautiful pastoral setting. A prominent firm specializing in Nursing Home Construction has developed plans for a high-quality facility befitting the important purpose for which it is intended.
>
> In other cities, such as St. Louis, such a facility has been successfully realized and serves to provide a pleasant environment for elderly Greek Americans and also as a community resource for the entire regional Hellenic American Community. Chicago should expect no less.
>
> The critical task at present is to raise the remaining funds necessary to be allowed to apply for a certificate of need. Toward this end, The Hellenic Medical Society has devoted its annual major social function to the purpose of raising funds for the Greek American Nursing Home. They have also united with The Hellenic Bar Association, The Hellenic American Dental Society, The Hellenic Professional Society of Illinois, The Greek Women's University Club, and the Chicago Fine Arts Society to increase the scope and fundraising potential of the event.
>
> The result of this union will be a Gala Grand Ball in support of the Greek American Nursing Home to be held on March 2 in the Guild Hall of the elegant Ambassador West Hotel. Music will be provided by the Al Sophia and Opa orchestras for the black-tie optional event. There will also be outstanding prizes such as a weekend in Las Vegas, an Amber Fox Coat, airline tickets, and fantasy weekends at the Abbey resort in Lake Geneva, the Ritz Carlton, and others.
>
> The event is the idea of Hellenic Medical Society President Chadwick Prodromos, MD., a Chicagoland Orthopedic Surgeon. He felt it important to demonstrate the support of the Greek American Medical Community for the Nursing Home and successfully solicited the participation of the other above-named societies. He and his lovely wife, Marilyn, a dentist, are serving as co-chairmen of the event and they report that so far, the response has been quite enthusiastic. Persons interested in attending the event (or buying prize tickets or purchasing space in the ad book), who have not received invitations from the

various societies are welcome and should call 708-699-6810 for more information. It is gratifying to see that Hellenes can unite and work together for a truly worthwhile cause.

An editorial in the April 14, 1996, edition of the *Greek Press* entitled "State Treasurer Judy Baar Topinka Proves Her Friendship" focused on the GANHC:

> For many years, the Greek-American community has tried to establish a Greek Nursing Home in the Chicagoland area. Community leaders Dr. Theo Kioutas, Eleni Bousis, and Loukas Pergantas, among many others, have attempted to effectuate that lifelong dream of our community by building a Greek-American Nursing Home. During the past several years, our community hoped that the Greek-American Nursing Home would be built in the city of Chicago. Our community's hopes were tied to Mayor Richard Daley's commitment that he would support the building of the Greek-American Nursing Home in the city of Chicago. Three locations were presented to Mayor Daley and his administration. The three locations were near downtown Greektown, near the intersection of Montrose and Oak Park Avenue, and near the intersection of Pulaski and Peterson. Many meetings were held with numerous City of Chicago commissioners and representatives. Many promises were made to the Greek-American community. Based on those promises, the Greek-American community expended a great deal of time and money. The money was expended on architectural drawings and plans. After all the meetings and incurred costs, the city of Chicago informed the Greek-American community that it had to build the Greek-American Nursing Home near a toxic site while the preferred site was given to a politically connected developer, Pontarelli Development! Feeling betrayed, our community leaders decided to move the Greek-American Nursing Home to the suburbs.
>
> Recently, the Greek-American Nursing Home Committee bought eight acres of undeveloped property in Wheeling, Illinois. The site is located near the intersection of Dundee and Milwaukee. At that site, plans have been drawn to build the Greek-American Nursing Home.
>
> The Greek-American Nursing Home Committee is actively raising funds for the project. Many individuals have made pledges toward this noble project. A majority of the Greek-American organizations in the state are committed to supporting the project.
>
> On March 24, 1996, the largest Greek-American organization in the state of Illinois, the Pan-Arcadian Federation of America, held a joint fundraiser with Illinois State Treasurer Judy Barr Topinka. All of the proceeds from that fundraiser were used as a

contribution toward the Greek-American Nursing Home. Pan Arcadian Federation of America District Governor George Palivos said, 'I urge all Greek Americans to support the establishment of a Greek-American Nursing Home in the state of Illinois. I call upon all Arcadians and all fellow Greek-Americans to support this noble cause.'

During the March 24, 1996, fundraiser, Illinois State Treasurer Judy Baar Topinka made a wonderful announcement. She announced that she will use the power of her office as Illinois Treasurer to help finance the establishment of the Greek-American Nursing Home. This will be done through a program called 'Link Deposits.' Through that program, the State Treasurer's office will contact numerous banks and coordinate financing for the Greek-American Nursing Home. This will be done by having the state deposit a large sum of money into specific banks. Those banks will thereafter be required to finance the Greek-American Nursing Home.

By announcing that her office will help with the funding of the Greek-American Nursing Home, Illinois State Treasurer Judy Baar Topinka has rendered a tremendous service to our community. Oftentimes, philanthropic programs in our community are not effectuated because we cannot procure funding. By putting the power of state government behind the funding, Illinois State Treasurer Judy Baar Topinka has eliminated that problem for the Greek-American Nursing Home.

The wonderful gesture of Illinois State Treasurer Judy Baar Topinka does not surprise community leaders who have followed her long and illustrious career. Treasurer Topinka has always been a friend of the Greek-American community. Her mentor in politics is the incomparable Illinois State Senator Adeline Geo-Karis.

Political observers say that State Treasurer Topinka is a rising star in Illinois State politics. Her gesture of friendship to our community will never be forgotten. Our community will always remember her wonderful gesture of friendship and loyalty.

Neither Elaine nor I recall this linked deposit program coming into play. Financing was completed through the sale of tax-exempt municipal bonds issued by the Village of Wheeling and guaranteed by H.U.D. It was, however, an example of how some political leaders took notice of our efforts and offered support.

In May, the GANHC received pledges from Annunciation Cathedral and Philoptochos Society ($25,000), Esther Christopher ($25,000), and St. Demetrios Philoptochos ($10,000), and the Pan Arcadian Federation announced their plans to hold a fundraiser later in the year. In October

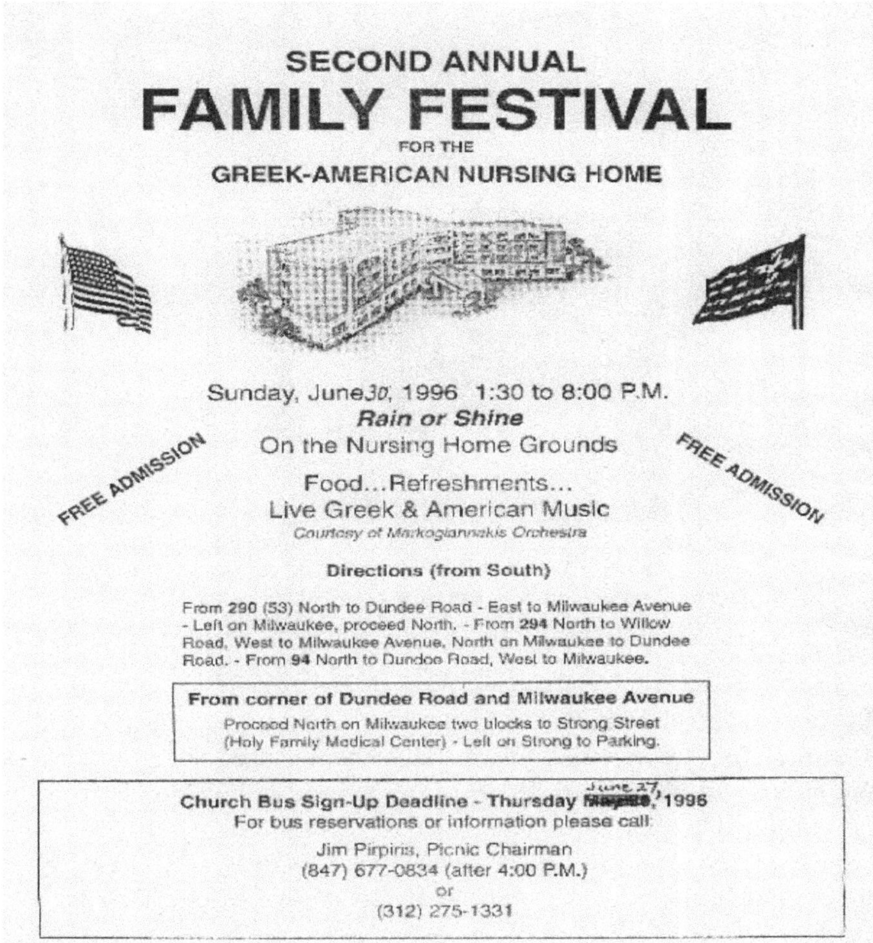

SECOND ANNUAL
FAMILY FESTIVAL
FOR THE
GREEK-AMERICAN NURSING HOME
Sunday, June 30, 1996 1:30 to 8:00 P.M.
Rain or Shine
On the Nursing Home Grounds
FREE ADMISSION
FREE ADMISSION
Food...Refreshments...
Live Greek & American Music
Courtesy of Markogiannakis Orchestra
Directions (from South)
From 290 (53) North to Dundee Road - East to Milwaukee Avenue - Left on Milwaukee, proceed North. - From 294 North to Willow Road, West to Milwaukee Avenue, North on Milwaukee to Dundee Road. - From 94 North to Dundee Road, West to Milwaukee.
From corner of Dundee Road and Milwaukee Avenue
Proceed North on Milwaukee two blocks to Strong Street (Holy Family Medical Center) - Left on Strong to Parking.
Church Bus Sign-Up Deadline - Thursday June 27, 1996
For bus reservations or information please call:
Jim Pirpiris, Picnic Chairman
(847) 677-0834 (after 4:00 P.M.)
or
(312) 275-1331

GANHC Family Festival flyer. June 30, 1996. Elaine Thomopoulos collection.

students from the Protypon School donated $400 they raised for the project, and the American Hellenic Society of Berwyn dedicated the proceeds from their annual dinner to GANHC.

Minutes from a June 13, 1996, board meeting held at GACS reported that the GANHC held $5,581.79 in the checking account and $35,748.18 in the savings account. CDs were not included in this total. Ethel Kotsovos resigned from the GANHC board in June to become GANHC office manager, and the necessity to put up signs saying, "no trespassing or swimming," because neighborhood kids are playing in the ponds, was discussed. Christine Burbulis is talking with the Regas family about a fundraiser that will be held at the Regas mansion soon.

From left, John H. Secaras, treasurer of Greek American Nursing Home Committee, Theresa Tzakis, board member, and James K. Marousis representing the George M. Eisenberg Foundation.

The *Greek Star*. August 12, 1999. Elaine Thomopoulos collection.

In August, we selected Pat Sweitzer as consultant to guide us through the Certificate of Need process, and in November engaged Honey Skinner as our attorney for this matter. Honey was a partner in the Sidley and Austin law firm and specialized in representing healthcare facilities before state regulators and commissions. Her husband Sam was U.S. secretary of transportation and White House chief of staff under President George H.W. Bush.

Much of late 1996 and most of 1997 was devoted to the lengthy process of applying for a Certificate of Need (CON). The CON was essentially a license to operate a nursing home granted by the Illinois Health Care Facilities Board. A case needed to be made that we would not simply shift residents from other nursing homes to ours and that there was a genuine need for this facility.

As a not-for-profit ethnic facility, we did not encounter as much scrutiny as some for-profit projects did during this process. In part, the state did not want to say no to the Greek community, but it was still a difficult and time-consuming process. Surveys about the numbers of Greeks who were in nursing homes or who were likely to become residents within the next few years were done. Letters of support from organizations and elected officials were collected.

John Regas, who had recently joined the GANHC board, offered to host a fundraiser in his historic home on Astor Street. One aim of the $500 per ticket event was to invite guests to join advisory committees to help guide and support us as we moved forward. An article in the November 21, 1996, issue of the *Greek Star*, written by John Rassogianis stated:

> One of the primary events of this season will be the Dec. 7 social at the David Adler-designed John Regas residence on Astor Street in Chicago.
>
> Guests attending the former Joseph Ryerson home, during the Saturday evening odyssey, will be treated to a glimpse into the continental and American cultural past at a cocktail buffet, thanks to Mr. Regas, who is hosting the event.
>
> The raison d'etre of the occasion will be to raise funds for the Greek-American Nursing Home project.
>
> The historic structure, once having fallen to disrepair, is the result of a large-scale reconstruction effort of the Adler dream, embraced and enhanced by the alchemy of the hand of professional interior decorator Regas. It now evokes the sweeping majesty of a reborn Louis XVI Directoire style and the elegance of an 18th Century French chateau.
>
> All of the rooms of the six-bedroom structure, ranging from the marbled entry foyer with its Sevres vase or the tapestried reception room set the tone for a French Impressionist painter's delight.
>
> For example, the warmth of pastels and walnut or cherry wood pervades throughout, rising up in the main salon with its 16-foot-high ceiling, gilded carved moldings, and mirrors, or complimenting the dramatic spiral staircase leading up several floors of the mansion.
>
> The dining room which is in an oval form resonates the elegance of the décor and furnishings with original murals, a marble fireplace, and Russian antiques.
>
> The Dec. 7 committee members helping Mr. Regas plan this extraordinary event are Eleni Bousis, Christine Burbulis, Joan Coletta, Maria Gebhard, Nicholas Kinnas, Anna Kioutas, Frances Kuchuris, Maria Lampros, Louis Malevitis, Anna Manos, James Mezilson, Maria Mitchell, Fran Nichols, Frances Papas, Timothea Papas, Arthur Peponis, John Rassogianis, Peter Regas, George Sikokis, and Gail Tokarz.
>
> 'No more than 200 tickets will be sold,' said Mr. Regas. 'We don't want to go beyond a certain comfort level,' he added.

Event committee meeting at the Regas residence: L-R: Seated: Anna Manos, unknown, Frances Kuchuris. Standing: John Rassogianis, Maria Gebhard, Christine Burbulis, unknown, unknown, unknown, and John Regas. Circa 1996. John Rassogianis collection.

GANHC Benefit program. Circa 1996. John Psiharis collection.

Initially planned for a different day, the event was hastily rescheduled to December 7, when it became apparent that several key invitees were not able to attend on the original day due to conflicting events related to the holidays. It was important that invitees attended in person to discuss their participation on the advisory committee, rather than just send in a donation.

From left, Christine Burbulis, Anna Kioutas, Dr. Mary Dochios Kamberos, Rev. George Massouras, Maria Gebhard, Dr. Theodosis Kioutas

Photo taken at the Regas Residence fundraiser, December 7, 1996. The *Greek Star*. December 12, 1996. Elaine Thomopoulos collection.

The cocktail reception at the historic John Regas residence on Astor Street raised $83,540. An article that appeared in the February 23, 1997, edition of the *Greek Press* described the event:

> One hundred and twenty-five guests sipped champagne and enjoyed sumptuous continental cuisine as they were invited to roam the beautifully restored mansion with Louis XVI Directoire style. The residence contains a five-story spiral staircase. It is the centerpiece of the structure which also boasts 16-feet ceilings.

In a February 1 report to the 13th District of the Daughters of Penelope, Toni Panos, GANHC recording secretary and liaison to the Daughters, wrote that the 1995-1996 year was "spectacular." "There were 14 fundraisers in this period that resulted in $147,000 being raised. This includes $400 raised by the children of Prototypon Hellenic School, 13th District Order of AHEPA and Daughters of Penelope, churches, professional and social organizations as well as the $80,000 fundraiser given by the Regas family." Toni further reports that GANHC has $322,642 in savings from prior donations and events, $4,088 in the operating checking account, and that we now own the property free and clear at $425,000. She also asked for help in identifying 184 Greek American individuals who entered a nursing home or hospital extended-stay facility in 1996. "We have already identified over 300 Greek Americans in nursing homes between 1992 and 1994. This includes, for example, a patient who

In Loving Memory of Our Departed Members across the years, 1952-1998.
The Hellenic Women's Philanthropic Association

Soteria

"Dedicated to an Aging Society"

Bertha Facklis, President
Mary Shopoff, Vice President
Stella Petrakis, Corresponding Secretary
Anna T. Crowley, Recording Secretary
Theresa Tzakis, Treasurer
Helen Flessar, Asst. Treasurer

We congratulate the Greek-American Nursing Committee and we are proud to support it.

A gold page message from Soteria in *the Greek-American Nursing Home Commemorative Album - 1998 Benefit Dinner Dance*. September 27, 1998. John Psiharis collection.

broke their hip and was placed in a rehabilitation center for therapy. The information to be obtained is the initials of the patient, Zip code or home address, and name and address of the nursing home."

Also in February, Soteria announced they would release their pledge when the GANHC reached $1 million in donations and the Certificate of Need was granted. In a February 23, 1997, article in the *Greek Press* newspaper, Soteria stated:

> 'We have carefully followed Dr. Kioutas' organization's development. Their perseverance has impressed us. Against all negative and discouraging circumstances, they have remained true to their task in the same way that we have persevered against many disappointments in the past.
>
> These disappointments have made us stronger and more determined. We, the Soteria members, have decided that we will now join our financial and moral support to their dedication and expertise to achieve our original dream of a facility for our disabled and elderly. We now pledge our treasury of $270,000 to the Greek-American Nursing Home Committee. The dream is now within our grasp.'
>
> In accepting the declaration from Soteria President Bertha Facklis, Treasurer Theresa Tzakis, Secretary Stella Petrakis, and members of their board, Dr. Kioutas remarked: 'We have many Greek elderly in nursing homes, at least 300 in 80 nursing homes now. They want to be in their own home. Look at what Soteria has done. We are clearly overjoyed with the announcement.' Dr. Kioutas continued, 'The Greek-American Nursing Home Committee is grateful to the ladies of Soteria who with great vision and sacrifice throughout many, many years have brought us very close to our objective. Just think. Their dues were originally $1 per year. Can you imagine that? This is what people who are dedicated can do'.

Notable 1997 fundraising highlights include a donation of $120,000 by Angelyn Boolookas in memory of her parents, Harry G. and Gianoula Boolookas, and a donation of $100,000 from Lou Mitchell. In March, the 13th District of AHEPA hosted the "*Yiayia* and *Pappou*" dinner dance honoring His Grace Bishop Iakovos, Governor James Edgar, Illinois State Senator Adeline Geo-Karis, and Andrew Athens, and a Hellenic Ladies Society of Constantinople banquet benefitting GANHC. Through the efforts of Dr. Angelo Creticos, GANHC received a $100,000 grant from the Washington Square Health Foundation. GANHC held a Poinsettia Ball dinner dance at Bristol Courts Banquets in Mount Prospect. There were 392 guests, and $49,687 was raised. That evening, a donation of $15,000 was presented by Mary Betinis in memory of her husband. Total donations collected that evening were $28,500.

The Lou Mitchell donation was announced in an article entitled, "Lou Mitchell Backs Greek-American Nursing Home Project with Major Donation," which appeared in the May 29, 1997, edition of the *Greek Star* and was written by John Rassogianis:

> Louis Mitchell continues to captivate the imagination of the doers and givers of the community by *parathiyma,* for example,

he recently donated $25,000 of a $100,000 pledge to the Greek-American Nursing Home Committee.

'I want it to succeed. We need one badly,' Mitchell said in a recent meeting. 'There is absolutely no reason why we cannot build a nursing home,' he emphasized.

A cultivated and colorful icon of Chicago's landscape from the world-famous Lou Mitchell's restaurant to the various Greek schools, churches, and societies where he extended his philanthropic imprimatur, Mitchell continues to understand the heart of Chicago's Greek-American community and the cultural and religious heritage it cherishes.

This gentleman of grand zest, who has joined the ranks of individuals and organizations supporting the Greek-American Nursing Home, has ideas and plans for everybody and everything, according to a friend. He relishes sharing his ideas to promote Hellas and his other pet projects with his fellow doers, never wavering from a profound moral sense of what is right and what is wrong.

'We must be mindful of the unsung heroes of our community,' he said, adding that 'they should decorate a lot of magnificent individuals. So many have not been acknowledged.'

Mitchell, an archon of the Ecumenical Patriarchate of Constantinople with the honorific Byzantine title of 'Depoutatos – Deputy' or 'Summoner,' is a member of the Order of St. Andrew the Apostle.

According to fellow archon Dr. Andrew T. Kopan, professor emeritus at DePaul University, 'Mitchell best typifies the values of the Greek-American community. Committed to Hellenism and Orthodoxy, he is without doubt one of the best exponents of our cultural/religious life as so amply reflected in his generosity and support of worthy endeavors in our community.'

Customers of yesteryear remember Mitchell for his trademark habit of doling out Milk Duds to his guests. 'I am the happiest man alive,' he reflected.

His experience as an archetype entrepreneur later led him to participate as a speaker with Kopan during a distinguished lecturer series of programs in conjunction with the *O Cosmos* exhibit at the Chicago Historical Society.

Mitchell is steeped in knowledge, especially the classics, gleaned from a lifelong habit of prodigious reading. The broad scope of his varied interests is evidenced by his bookshelf. He is now reading a literary work by Italian author Alessandro Manzone [sic].

> Mitchell's cultural roots are deep. Last winter, during coffee hour at Plato Academy Hall, he spent a few pensive moments identifying and pointing our notables pictured on the wall of the *O Cosmos* exhibit that depicted the personal and public lives of Greeks throughout the early decades of the century.
>
> Mitchell continues to respond to the right drumbeat – that of love of family, friends, and country. He resides in River Forest with his three sisters, Demetra, Pauline, and Virginia. The Greek-American Nursing Home Committee individually and collectively extends to him its most *thermo efharisto*.

With full ownership of the land, GANHC began the process of applying for property tax exemption from Cook County. In addition to removing the property from the tax rolls for future years, we were due a refund of taxes that had been paid during the closing. Although we were qualified, it was a lengthy process. Maria Pappas, as treasurer of Cook County, along with her first deputy, Peter Karahalios, sped up the process so that the money was refunded within a relatively brief time.

By June 1997, the GANHC had raised $1,103,857 and had pledges of $210,775. Full ownership of the property added $425,000 to the balance sheet. A condition of receiving approval for the state CON was that there be at least $2 million committed to the project.

In October, the Society of Paleohorion Kynourias, one of the oldest Greek village organizations in Chicago, held its 95th-anniversary dinner at Monty's in Bensenville, IL. An article in the February 19, 1998, edition of the *Greek Star* entitled "Society Paleohorion Kynourias Gathers to Celebrate its 95th Anniversary," read in part:

> The society donated the proceeds of $4,000 to the Greek-American Nursing Home, represented by Helen Georges, who accepted the check from President Regina Greven Bartzis and Treasurer Ted Symon at the society's annual Vasilopita recently held at Niko's Restaurant. The donation was in keeping with past contributions made to the Greek-American Nursing Home by the society as well as contributions to the complete restoration of the 900-year-old monastery, Agio Taxiarhi, near the village of Paleohori in Greece, to the U.S. war efforts, to the restoration of Ellis Island, and various charities of the Chicagoland community. President Bartzis expresses the hope that the club will continue into the 21st century and celebrate its 100th anniversary.

A listing of organizations that had donated to GANHC between 1987 and 1997 included:

A Greek dance troupe performs during a GANHC fundraiser, possibly at 13 Colonies Banquets. Date unknown. Photo by John Rassogianis. John Rassogianis collection.

AHEPA-13th District; AHEPA-Chapter #46; AHEPA-Chapter #423; AHEPA-#390; AHEPA-Chapter #388; AHEPA-Chapter #380; AHEPA-Chapter #202; American Hellenic Society of Berwyn; Annunciation Cathedral Philoptochos; Association of Aetos; The Biel Foundation; Brotherhood of Lidorikioton, Chicago; Brotherhood of the Village Paleohorioan-Kynurias; Brotherhood of Sterea Hellas Roumeli; Caphallonan Brotherhood; Chicago Chapter- Cardiology Institute of Northern Greece; Cretan Ladies Association "Amalthia;" Dara Association of America; Daughters of Epiros; Daughters of Mani; Daughters of Penelope; Past District Governors Club; Daughters of Penelope-Chapter #274; Daughters of Penelope-Chapter #121; Daughters of Roumeli; Dr. John Nicholson Trust; Enosis Demovaltetsioton; Elefteria Society; Enosis Tripoliton; Federation of Sterea Hellas – USA & Canada District of Illinois; Gortynian Society-Chapter 19; Pan-Arcadian Federation of America; Greek-American Community Services; Greek Women's University Club; Hellenic Bar Association; Hellenic Ladies Society of Constantinople; Hellenic Lodge #1084; Hellenic Medical Society of Illinois; Hellenic Philatelic Society; Hellenic Professional Society of Illinois; Hellenic Sisterhood of Tripolis; Holy Apostles Philoptochos; Holy Cross Philoptochos, Peoria; KRIKOS; Ladies Hellenic Society "Agia Paraskevi;" Ladies Philoptochos Society of Hegewisch; Lane Tech High School Hellenic Society; Macedonian Society of Chicago; Megalopolis Society of Chicago; Midwest District-Pan-Arcadian Federation of America; Nafpaktiaki Fraternity of

Chicago; National Bank of Greece; Organization Attikis & Piraeus Perikles; Pan Laconian Federation; Parnon Philanthropic Society; Patriotic Society of Distomitans; Philanthropic Society Scopion Neos Skopos-Elpis; Philoptochos Society Athena-St. George, St. Paul, Minnesota; Pontian Society of Chicago "The Seniteas;" Prodromian Civic Club; Protypon Hellenic Society; Society Hrisafiton of Chicago; Society Mytilene-Theophrastos; Socrates Greek-American School (Holy Trinity Church); "Soteria" Hellenic Women's Philanthropic Association, Inc.; Sparta Society of Chicago; St. Andrew Society of Patras; St. Andrew Philoptochos; St. Demetrios Philoptochos, Chicago; St. Demetrios, Chicago, Senior Citizens Club; St. Demetrios Philoptochos, Hammond, Indiana; St. George Philoptochos, Chicago; St. George Philoptochos, Schererville, Indiana; St. Haralambos Philoptochos; St. Helen Women's Philoptochos; St. John the Baptist Philoptochos; St. Nectarios Church; St. Nectarios Philoptochos; Sts. Peter & Paul Young Adult League; Syndesmos Stereoelladiton - "Athanasios Diakos;" Three Hierarchs Ladies Philoptochos – All Saints Church; True Hellenic Guardian-Chapter #720; United Hellenic American Congress; Washington Square Health Foundation; Women's Club of Sts. Peter & Paul; Women's Tageatic League; Young Adult League of St. Andrews.

Common Threads

(This section is reprinted from *Working to Preserve Our Heritage: The Incredible Legacy of Greek-American Community Services*. The picture of Efthimios Vlahos is different than the photo of him in the first book and the GANHC executive committee photo was added).

Since its earliest days, Greek-American Community Services cooperated with many organizations within Chicago's Greek community. Some of these relationships grew into steadfast alliances while others, regardless of efforts made, never came to fruition, or if they did, were minimal in impact.

The closest relationship GACS had by far was with the Greek-American Nursing Home Committee. GACS had been the parent organization, and after separating, we continued as sister organizations. Some board members served on both boards. There was an effort by a few on the nursing home committee to distance the committee from GACS. Although this created some tension early on, the ties between the two organizations were strong and remained so throughout the existence of GACS.

GANHC Executive Committee members at a fundraiser, (L-R): Elaine Thomopoulos, John Rassogianis, Eugenia Seifer, Helen Georges, Dr. Theodosis Kioutas, Christine Burbulis, Toni Panos, John Psiharis, and Ethel Kotsovos. Date unknown. John Psiharis collection.

Beyond founding the GANHC and nurturing it through its first few years of operation, GACS and the GANHC worked together in many ways. Over the years, GACS board members who were also on the board of the nursing home committee included: Emily Alexandrou, Eleni Bousis (advisory board of GACS), Christine Burbulis, Helen Geocaris, Thalia Jameson, Bill Kakavas, Mary Kakavas, Jean Kaporis, Dr. Theodosis Kioutas, Anna Manos, Toni Panos, Dr. Nicholas Papanos, John Psiharis, John Rassogianis, and Elaine Thomopoulos. Elaine served as second vice president of the GANHC for a number of these years and I was assistant treasurer for a period. GACS was the regular meeting place for many nursing home board and committee meetings.

Dr. Theodosis Kioutas was intimately involved with both organizations from the first meeting in 1982 onward and is a major part of the story of both GACS and the GANHC.

Ethel Kotsovos, GACS social worker, at first volunteered and later was paid, to run the Greek-American Nursing Home Committee office located within Dr. Kioutas' medical office suite on California Avenue near Lincoln Avenue. Before becoming a staff member, Ethel was a GANHC board member.

John Rassogianis, a GACS board member and then Cultural & Arts Program director, was a board member of the nursing home committee and its publicity chairman. In this capacity, he generated countless press releases of all levels of detail, from coming event notifications to two-page photo spreads, and everything in between. He also coordinated other publicity activities to help inform and update the Greek community about our progress. Additionally, John represented the GANHC on the board of the Coalition of Limited English Speaking Elderly (CLESE).

Maria Toledo (Villalobos) became the secretary/administrative assistant for both organizations. Initially working for GACS, in later years she divided her time between the GACS and GANHC offices.

The GACS *Ya'Sou* vans were used to transport residents from Hollywood House to GANHC fundraisers and to shuttle supporters between the GACS center and GANHC events in Wheeling.

Over the coming years, the nursing home committee gained the support of several influential and wealthy members of the community who also were benefactors of GACS. These included GACS Advisory Board members Irene Antoniou, Eleni Bousis, Aphrodite Demeur, Demetrios Kozonis, Loukas Pergantas, and Chris Tomaras. Dr. John D. Nicholson bequeathed money to both organizations.

A 1990 GACS Cultural and Arts Program touched on the need for a Greek nursing home in a lecture entitled, "The Scalabrini Order: Leadership in the Italian American Community," by Dominic Candeloro, Ph, D., and "The Failure of the Greek-American Community to Build a Hospital," by George Christakes, Ph, D, held at both the GACS Adult Day Care Center at Alvernia Place and the Italian Cultural Center in Stone Park. The Scalabrini Order, over many years, was able to establish the Villa Scalabrini Nursing Home in Villa Park, Illinois, while there was a failed attempt within Chicago's Greek community, to establish a hospital in the 1920s and 1930s. The lively discussion periods following each of the well-attended lectures evoked the need for a Greek nursing home. Although the mood was hopeful, the discussions amplified skepticism about whether this goal would ever be achieved. The lectures were part of the "Ethnic Identities and American Values: Leadership Development in Illinois," series sponsored by GACS and funded by the Illinois Humanities Council.

GACS submitted a written testimony to the Illinois Health Facilities Board in support of the nursing home project. Once the home opened, GACS referred potential residents and employees to the home.

A 1994 study to document the need for a Greek nursing home was conducted by GACS for the GANHC. Coordinated by Ethel, the results were submitted to the city as part of the bid for the North Park Village parcel. It found that there were 340 Greek elderly nursing home residents scattered throughout eighty-five facilities and that another 400 were

A GACS nursing home visit with Efthimios Vlahos. Seated: Efthimios Vlahos. Standing (L-R): John Rassogianis, Margaret Nikolopoulos, and Toni Panos. Circa 2001. John Rassogianis collection.

expected to need adult day care or nursing home care within the next three years.

The study further reported data from the 1990 census compiled by Northeastern Illinois University. There were approximately 240,000 Greek Americans in the Chicago metropolitan area. Of those, 21 percent or 50,400 were over age 60, and 23 percent, or 11,592 were non-English speaking.

One of these individuals was Efthimios Vlahos. Mr. Vlahos was a GACS adult daycare client for a couple of years. In his nineties, Efthimios was alert but physically frail and actively participated in center programming. A favorite activity for him was to teach Greek to Ricardo Rodriguez, a non-Greek volunteer who eventually became a GACS board member. Efthimios prepared weekly lessons and engaged in conversational Greek with Ricky. He also joined in with fabric arts participants during their Wednesday classes. Efthimios was an ardent supporter of the nursing home project and had hoped to be the first resident of the new facility. He frequently inquired about the latest progress and any news on the project. Efthimios and his family attended several GANHC fundraisers, and he was profiled in the *Groundbreaker*, the GANHC newsletter.

For some of us, Efthimios exemplified the need for a nursing home. He was the face who personified the many whom the nursing home hoped to serve once it opened. We were eagerly expecting him to become the first resident, but it was not meant to be. Unfortunately, his health had declined, and he was admitted into an area nursing home. He passed away in February 2002 at the age of 95, just weeks before GANHC admitted its first residents in early March. GACS and GANHC members, and several of his friends from the center, visited him at the nursing home and attended his wake.

A profile of Efthimios in the Fall 2001 issue of *the Greek-American Nursing Home Committee Newsletter*, read in part:

> Efthimios Vlahos is 95 years old and has anxiously been waiting for the Greek American Rehabilitation and Nursing Centre to open. He would like to be the first resident.
>
> Mr. Vlahos is very social, loves the companionship of friends, and looks forward to having a conversation with anyone around him who is pleasant, but he cannot. He would like to have a Greek meal regularly, but he cannot. Mr. Vlahos has been in a very fine nursing care facility for several years. All his physical needs are met. He longs for "parea" (companionship). His English is limited, and he has no one to speak with in his native tongue most of the time. He can't wait to be transferred to our nursing home.
>
> After the death of his wife Maria, Mr. Vlahos followed his sons, George, Elias, and Constantine to America in 1969. He had passed some very hard times in his village of Kalavrita. First the Italians, then the Germans, and lastly the "Antartes" (the leftists in the civil war). His homes were burned twice because he was anti-Communist. He served as a soldier twice.
>
> Mr. Vlahos and his sons are donors and their Society Kalavriton made a generous donation to the nursing home project. Now, all he wants is to be in a dignified, orthodox, and Hellenic environment. He is on our waiting list.

Another example of the need for the nursing home project was Mrs. Stella C. Coroneos. Profiled as "Someone You Should Know," in the Spring 2000 issue of the *Greek-American Nursing Home Committee Newsletter*:

> Mrs. Coroneos has been a resident at Alshore Nursing Home in Chicago for seven years. She is 98 years old. Her life involved many changes and family tragedies.
>
> She was born in Smyrna, Turkey, however, she and her family were forced to escape to Greece. She married in Greece and came to the United States with her husband in the 1930s. They had one son who passed away while at university when he was only 21 years old. She has been a widow for over 30 years.
>
> Mrs. Coroneos began working after she lost her husband. While in Greece, she was one of the recipients of training in needlework

at the "Vasiliki Pronia" (Queen's Charity). She was very talented and was able to support herself and save some of her earnings.

In 1993 she fell and broke her hip. She became unable to care for her daily needs, and her doctor recommended she be placed in a nursing home. She states that she misses the friendships that she had, someone to speak with in Greek, and especially to worship in her church and celebrate religious holidays. When the plan to build a nursing care facility to meet the needs of Greek-Americans became known to her, tears came to her eyes, and she said, 'I am sure to find friends there.'

Mrs. Coroneos is visited by a distant relative of her late husband. She has no one else.

Seal of Approval

Throughout 1997, work continued on the Certificate of Need process. During a special October GANHC Board meeting at Costa's Restaurant, the completed documents were signed, and the CON application was submitted. Responses to questions and requests for further information from the IHCFB were answered in the ensuing weeks.

A November 5, 1997, letter from Illinois Treasurer Judy Baar Topinka was sent to the Illinois Health Facilities Planning Board in support of the Certificate of Need application. In her letter, Topinka wrote:

> As you are aware, the Greek community is rich in tradition and culture. Many of these Greek American citizens live in Cook County and counties contiguous to Cook, representing 81,147 people according to the 1990 census. Yet, there is not one Greek American Nursing Home that addresses the needs of our aging Greek American population. The only facility in the United States to date is in Boston, Massachusetts. In Canada, Toronto has one Greek American Nursing Home and that facility was fully occupied within the first year that it opened. I truly believe that it would be in everyone's best interest that a nursing home serving our Greek-American community come to fruition, and hope you share my feelings.

These efforts culminated with the November 21 meeting of the Illinois Health Facilities Planning Board where the Certificate of Need application was to be considered. The night before the meeting Dr. Kioutas, Father George Massouras, and several board members, gathered to pray at Assumption Church before Dr. Kioutas and Father Massouras left on their 130-mile trip to Champaign for the meeting. We all breathed a deep sigh of relief the following day when the CON was unanimously approved.

Although the fact that the home was geared toward the Greek community contributed to the swift approval from state agencies, things soon changed, and ethnic-focused facilities could no longer be exclusive. Up to this point, ethnic projects were considered unique since they catered primarily to underserved populations and would not be in direct competition with other area nursing homes. This change was explained during a June 14, 2004, board meeting and summarized in the minutes taken by Assistant Secretary Christina Spiratos. "John Secaras expressed concern about such statements as 'preference is given to Greeks.' He reminded the Board that although we were initially given authority to build our facility by the State of Illinois based on our ethnicity, (and our community's need for a nursing home), the Federal courts subsequently struck down that state law as unconstitutional, and as a result we are prohibited from giving preference to any one ethnicity and from discriminating against anyone based on sex, age, race, religion, etc."

Another major focus was financing for the project. Financing a project of this scope is not easy or cheap. It required a lot of knowledge and experience with these sorts of things. That is something the board lacked. With the help of professionals from the community, we were able to explore options and perform the due diligence necessary for a project of this magnitude.

Neither Elaine nor I recall who these professionals were, but I remember Faye Pantazelos who briefly was also a GACS Board member and worked as a senior vice president at the Bank of Ravenswood (since bought out by J.P Morgan Chase Bank) being involved. Faye went on to start New Century Bank.

After months of effort, a plan to finance the construction took shape. The experts arranged for Cambridge Realty Capital, Ltd. of Illinois to underwrite the sale of about $13 million in tax-exempt bonds sold through the Village of Wheeling. This bond sale would finance the building's construction and start-up.

A Preliminary Sources and Uses Statement provided the following details:

<u>SOURCES</u>

Bonds	$11,275,000
Owner Cash	1,931,495
Prepaid Land	403,750
Prepaid Architect	350,168
Prepaid Other Fees	55,967
Prepaid HUD Examination Fee	33,750
Prepaid Appraisal	8,000
TOTAL SOURCES	<u>$14,058,493</u>

<u>USES</u>

Construction	$9,945,810

Architect	427,655
Owner's Other Fees	108,000
Interest (14 + 2@ 8.75%, @50%- outstanding)	657,708
Taxes During Construction	20,000
Insurance During Construction	13,000
Title	5,000
Audit	10,000
Major Movable	882,227
HUD Mortgage Insurance Premium	112,500
HUD Application Fee	33,750
HUD Inspection Fee	56,250
Land	403,750
Initial Operating Deficit	1,085,000
Working Capital	225,000
Minor Movable	62,480
TOTAL USES	$14,058,130

Once the CON was granted and financing was finalized, we appeared at a village council meeting in Wheeling to obtain the final approvals necessary to build. Anna Kioutas, Dr. Kioutas, Elaine Thomopoulos, Helen Georges, John Rassogianis, Toni Panos, Theresa Tzakis, and I attended. Others may have also attended. Anna Kioutas and Strat Maheras, Helen Georges' partner and a real estate attorney, represented the GANHC. The architects were also there. The zoning change passed unanimously with minimal discussion. Cited as one of the key reasons there was no opposition were the expected 300 plus jobs the project would create and the spillover effect that would benefit area residents and businesses.

With the CON in hand, the necessary zoning approvals granted, and financing in place, it was on to the next phase of this amazing roller coaster ride.... Pre-construction.

Breaking Ground

Although our backgrounds were diverse and we were each successful in our chosen fields, it is safe to say that building a nursing home is something most people have not done before, and we were certainly in that camp. While we had the vision and passion for this project, we lacked the expertise and skillset to competently deal with the many facets of such an undertaking. We worked to establish a team of experienced professionals to guide us through this process.

The GANHC Board grew to include an impressive array of individuals. Among the newer members were two representatives of the Greek American Restaurant Association. GARA pledged $100,000 to the Home, Tom Diamond, owner of the Fountain Blue Restaurant in Des Plaines, and Tom Pappas, owner of Market Square Restaurant in Wheeling. Bertha Facklis, the president of Soteria, was not able to continue serving on the board and was replaced by Tina Spiratos, who was an attorney by profession. Jim Christie, the owner of Bon-Ton Foods, a supplier of poultry to Chicago area restaurants and supermarkets, became a new member. Bishop Iakovos appointed Rev. George Massouras of Assumption Church as his representative to the GANHC. Father George was an early supporter of the project. Faye Pantazelos, a banking executive, briefly joined the board. John Secaras, a retired regional solicitor for the U.S. Department of Labor Chicago (Midwest Region), became treasurer and later fundraising chairman.

The bishop was not an enthusiastic supporter in the early days but grew to embrace the effort as we progressed. The bishop attended several GANHC functions, but to some of us, his initial support seemed low-key or lukewarm at best. Once the land was purchased, and the viability of the project was apparent, the bishop embraced the effort as it became clear the project would succeed. At this point, he accepted our invitation to be honorary chairman of the committee and became a vocal supporter of the cause.

A sign of the bishop's evolving position in support of GANHC was heard in his remarks during an October 1994, $500 per person fundraiser in the elegant Tudor Grand Ballroom of the Michigan Shores Club in Wilmette. An October 14, 1994, press release entitled "Successful Greek-American Nursing Home Fundraiser Held at Michigan Shores Club in Wilmette" included the following description of the event:

> One hundred selected leaders of Chicagoland's Greek community turned out to dine and listen to Greek favorites emanating from the piano of maestro Vasili Gaitanos at the Michigan Shores Club in Wilmette. The overriding reason for being at the $500 per person fundraiser, however, was to raise monies for the Greek-American Nursing Home.
>
> The elegance of the banquet, held in the Tudor Grand Ballroom of the club, was validated by the unity of purpose of the event itself. It was matched with the inspiring words of His Grace, Bishop Iakovos, the Reverend George Massouras, and a report on the facility by architect Arthur Salk.
>
> 'We are the church, the people of the church,' stated Father Massouras in response to a query posed by a guest. 'The secret is not to give up. Once you have a dream, you must constantly work on it,' he stated, acknowledging the efforts of Dr. Theodosis Kioutas, President of the Greek-American Nursing Home Association who with his wife, Anna, underwrote the event.
>
> His Grace stated 'EINE SPOUTHEO TO ERGO.' He continued, 'Our old people are in a foreign environment. They cry. It's not

their home.' Referring to previous attempts to establish a nursing home, he added: 'We had considered a wing...but this is better. People are in need. All of us may need this care when the time comes. We must participate to raise the money for the nursing home. We will be in our own home, with family, friends, and priests. We must raise the money. It is a priority. We embrace it. Referring to an old Greek saying he said 'FASOULI ME FASOULI. YEMIZEI TO SAKOULE.'

> Later in the evening, Arthur Salk presented the vision of the nursing home. 'If you don't go out to see it, you're missing something. It is just magnificent. Large trees, two ponds. The environment is perfect. To the west, the property is bordered by a lovely park owned by the village of Wheeling. Across the street is a senior center. Nearby there is a residential complex for the elderly.

On December 7, 1997, during their final luncheon, held at the Angus Restaurant, the Hellenic Women's Philanthropic Association "Soteria" finalized the transfer of their treasury to the GANHC. According to an article in the January 25, 1998, edition of the *Greek Press*, President Bertha Facklis reported:

> On December 7, 1986, the 'Soteria' organization pledged our treasury in its entirety to help establish a Greek Nursing Home (provided the state of Illinois gave consent) to honor our parents and grandparents.
>
> On November 21 (Esothia Panagia), the Greek American Nursing Home did obtain the much-needed 'Certificate of Need' from the state of Illinois, thus making it possible for our attorney, Tina Mourikes Spriratos, to present the resolution to transfer our funds to the Greek-American Nursing Home Committee which was approved unanimously by the membership.

The Poinsettia Ball, held in December 1997 at the Thirteen Colonies, was the final fundraising event of the year. Hosted by Bill and Mary Kakavas, who underwrote the costs, the event raised $49,687. There were 392 guests in attendance.

An article by John Rassogianis that appeared in the December 25, 1997, edition of the *Greek Star* described the success of the recent Poinsettia Ball:

> A magnificent display of affection poured out for the principals of a holiday benefit program; the Poinsettia Ball recently held on behalf of the Greek-American Nursing Home Committee.
>
> The festive evening was the culmination of a momentous fortnight of solid progress reported by Dr. Theodosis Kioutas, president of the committee, as he announced the formal approval by the state of Illinois for the establishment of a Greek American

Invitation to the GANHC Poinsettia Ball. December 7, 1997. Elaine Thomopoulos collection.

nursing home facility in Wheeling, IL. The acceptance by the state board, he said, was unanimous, moving the dream of establishing a nursing home one step closer to reality.

Costas Zografopoulos, who served as master of ceremonies, described the need for the project. Guest speaker and respected novelist and short story writer Harry Mark Petrakis thundered in graphic and dramatic detail a tale from his experience as a student at Koraes Elementary School. Guests attending the event were mesmerized by Petrakis' presentation.

'I urge you; I beg you. Go to your individual clubs and societies,' was the plea delivered by Tina Spiratos, representing a major donor, the Hellenic Women's Philanthropic Association Soteria, as she assisted Bertha Facklis, past president of that respected society, to the podium to receive her award of outstanding service to the community.

The Soteria Society gave over $300,000 to the project. 'This is the single most important project in decades that we must complete. May we never forget this. This nursing home will honor those who have come before us. This money was saved and never spent because they [the ladies of Soteria] stayed focused. They never gave up. Again, I urge you,' implored Spiratos, 'go to your individual clubs and societies. We want the

> names of all the organizations on our wall of life in the nursing home. Let's get the whole thing going.'
>
> Spiratos also represents Soteria on the Greek-American Nursing Home Committee board. Facklis had spearheaded the drive on behalf of the nursing home during her many years at the helm of the Soteria organization. The ladies of the society had begun their fundraising toward this goal over 50 years ago, many times under humble and difficult circumstances.
>
> The message was well-received, judging by the numerous donations and renewals or new pledges made by guests who were seated at tables, many of which were delineated along supportive organizational lines.
>
> The interior landscape of the Bristol Court banquet room, dotted by clusters of cream, red, and pink poinsettias at each table almost seemed to glow during special moments of conviviality, such as the singing of happy birthday greetings to Fr. George Massouras, a nursing home board member.
>
> Special recognition went to Bill and Mary Kakavas, co-chairs of the event, who left no stone unturned to make the Poinsettia Ball a most remarkable and inspiring evening for all.

Once the CON had been granted, the next order of business was to select the architect for the project. The initial renderings and advice had been done on a pro-bono basis by Shayman, Salk, Aaronson & Sussholz & Co. Architects. It had always been our intention to put the project out for bid to locate the best possible architect, with all things being equal, we preferred a Greek-owned architectural firm. A request for qualifications was put out. John Regas chaired this effort, and five firms presented their qualifications to the Architectural Committee.

Based on this due diligence and recommendations from the committee, the board narrowly affirmed the recommendation of the Architecture committee, and in early March, Jensen and Halsted, a firm led by a Greek American, was chosen project architect.

A special board meeting was held at Annunciation Cathedral on March 2, 1998. The minutes, taken by Toni Panos, give a sense of the due diligence taken to select an architect:

> The GANHC met at Annunciation Cathedral on Monday, March 2, 1998, at 7:30 p.m.
>
> The following committee members were present: Dr. Kioutas, Helen Georges, Eleni Bousis, Bill and Mary Kakavas, John Secaras, Tina Spiratos, Elaine Thomopoulos, John and Peter Regas, Anna Manos, John Psiharis, Demetri Kozonis, John Rassogianis, Eugenia Seifer, and Toni Panos.

The purpose of this special meeting was to vote on an architect and also make the final decision on a loan.

John Regas introduced a guest that evening, Mr. John Tatoolas, an attorney who deals with health care.

On Saturday, February 21, 1998, an interview session took place at 350 W. Ontario where five architectural firms presented their qualifications to our architecture committee: Mr. John Macsai from O'Donnell, Wickland, Pigozzi & Peterson, Mr. Ken Behles from Behles & Behles, Mr. Arthur Salk from Shayman, Salk, Arenson & Sussholz & Co., Demetri Criezis from Criezis Architects, Inc., and Ivan Tshilds, George Chapman, David Daslur from Jensen & Halstead.

Attending this interview session were several qualified people to judge the architect's presentation on qualifications and give us their recommendations. At the meeting some of our Board members were present.

Letters were sent from the following judges recommending their selection of an architect: Jay Bradarich, Landmark Construction Corp; James E. Tatooles; C.E. Nesbitt, Signature Development; Miltiades Bolaris; John Theodosakis, Sr., Landmark Construction; John Theodosakis, Jr., Landmark Construction. The rankings were distributed.

The vote was taken by secret ballot. Those Board members absent; Jim Pirpiris, Jean Kaporis, and Christine Burbulis were contacted by telephone to register their presence and were given particulars. Dr. Chad Prodromos and Fran Kuchuris were unavailable. There were 18 votes, 10 of which were for Jensen & Halstead and 8 votes for Shayman Salk.

MOTION: A motion was made by John Secaras that an architect be selected from three firms. Shayman, Salk, Jensen & Halstead and Behles & Behles. Whoever the majority votes for will be given the contract subject to a delay of a period of two weeks to check into the ability of that firm to fulfill the requirements of the Certificate of Need. This was unanimously agreed to by the members of the Board.

Peter Regas reported that he needed more time to contact additional experts in the Greek community regarding financing.

Dr. Kioutas stated that Tom Pappas from the Restaurant Association will be at the groundbreaking in May 1998 and will present a donation.

John Secaras reported on the forthcoming dinner dance to be held at the Fontainebleau on Sunday, September 27, 1998.

> There being no further business, the meeting adjourned at 10:30 p.m. Our next Board meeting is scheduled for Monday, March 16, 1998.

At the March 16, 1998, board meeting, we were advised of an unintentional error that had been made. As the committee worked through this process, we were unaware that the CON was considered inviolate and that the details and plans submitted in the application, as well as testimony from our representatives, could not be altered. Selecting a different architect or materially deviating from the CON would be cause for revocation of the Certificate and possible financial fines for any willful misstatements. After a lengthy and sometimes heated discussion, the board approved the selection of SSAS as the project architect.

As he convened the meeting, Dr. Kioutas read from a letter that was also passed out to board members:

> In preparation for our scheduled meeting today, March 16, 1998, I would like to alert you to a critically important issue that must be addressed.
>
> It has been brought to my attention that I inadvertently allowed deliberations on a subject, which apparently should not be open to deliberations.
>
> The Certificate of Need obtained by this Organization, based on the application submitted and the statements made by myself and the other Board members present at the hearing of November 21, 1997, is specific as to site design, architectural plans, cost (finance), methods of operation and mission. Although our mission has not changed, through my error in allowing deliberation by the committee, there have been substantial changes from our original plans recommended by the committee.
>
> At our previous meeting, we designated an architect different from the one who has done all the architectural work up to now and proposed changes in our original design, subject to a review of the designated architect's record of previous health care projects completed in this state. It is now apparent that we cannot vary the design. I have also been informed that the firm designated has no record of work done in the healthcare field for the past five years, a critical factor due to radical regulatory changes during this time.
>
> I have learned that the application submitted to obtain the Certificate of Need is considered inviolate by the Health Facilities Planning Board. Just as a building permit granted is based on the plans submitted, the Certificate of Need may be withdrawn if the facts represented in the application are changed. In addition, the Board may impose fines in the hundreds of

> thousands of dollars if they suspect deliberate misrepresentations.
>
> As the Chairman of this organization and someone who has devoted 13 years to this project, I do not want to see our efforts wasted. We must recognize the limitations of our application and proceed with the plan in strict compliance with the design as presented to the IHFP Board. This issue has to be resolved quickly if we are to proceed with the groundbreaking this spring.
>
> I have called Mrs. Pat Sweitzer, who is our consultant for the Certificate of Need application, to enlighten us as to our limitations and responsibilities and she has graciously accepted and is here.
>
> I am also attaching to my remarks a photocopy of the American Institute of Architects sample of agreement which clearly shows the danger of trying to change the architect at this point.
>
> Before us, we have the Community, which has contributed over a million dollars to this project to date. If we jeopardize or lose our CON, we may be accused of collecting the money so that we can sit on a large pool of money and just invest it here and there. We cannot allow this to take place.
>
> We have the plans, we have the zoning, we have the CON and we have enough money to start.
>
> We bought the land with only part of the price at hand. The Community rallied when they saw we had the land. They will rally again when they see the ground broken and the building starting.
>
> After Pat explains the nature of our CON, which incidentally is an extremely valuable asset, we will consider starting to build, while we are seeking financing.
>
> I do not want anyone to accuse us of taking their hard-earned dollars and efforts and instead of providing our needy elders with a very urgently needed facility, we sit on their contributions and become investors. I am sure no one on this Committee is willing to take this risk.

This misstep ruffled some feathers and caused dissent amongst a few GANHC board members. John Regas and a couple of other members of the architects' committee were upset that we reversed course and didn't approve their recommendation. Further, some in the community were upset that we did not hire a Greek architect for the project. For most of us, the overriding concern was the big picture and doing whatever was necessary to build the home. On April 1, John Regas, Peter Regas, Christine Burbulis, and Frances Kuchuris resigned from the board in protest.

In her letter of resignation, dated April 1, 1998, and sent to board members, Christine wrote:

> I am disappointed!
>
> The completion of the Greek-American Nursing Home has occupied my dreams, my efforts, and my very thoughts for so many years. In spite of our many problems, I sincerely believed that the entire Greek community would eventually come together and cooperate to achieve this goal.
>
> But, now I see that even within our committee there is no spirit of cooperation and that a few will disregard the wishes, and even the vote, of the entire committee to pursue their own desires.
>
> I believe I owe a duty to every person who has contributed even one dollar to the Nursing Home to have our committee function in a climate of open dialogue, complete disclosure, and majority decision-making. Therefore, very regretfully, I submit my resignation.

This matter became public when a letter to the editor was sent to various media by John Regas. It was published in the March 7, 1998, issue of the *Greek Press*, the March 11, 1998, edition of the *Greek Star*, and in other media, criticizing the decision to engage SSAS. Entitled "Support Young Greek Americans," he wrote:

> I am writing to bring an important matter to your attention – as well as all readers of your newspaper – that involves an unfortunate but prevalent attitude in our community that is detrimental to its ultimate growth.
>
> Several years ago, I got involved with an organization whose goal was to open a Greek-American nursing home in Chicago – a place where our elders can live in dignity, with the special care required, as they approach the dawn of their lives.
>
> The committee worked fine together, and we raised tens of thousands of dollars for the proposed project. When the time came to award the architectural contract for the design of the building, a rift developed on the board over who would be awarded the job.
>
> I along with others on the board encouraged the board to select a young, Greek architect for the position. It sounded logical to me, that a Greek-American organization attempting to build a Greek-American nursing home should hire a Greek-American architect.
>
> Of course, if the other architects who bid for the job presented superior work at a lower cost, that would have been different. But this was not the case. Clearly, personal interests got involved, and board members who had a questionable (and dubious)

relationship with a non-Greek architect fought tooth and nail – even countering the board's decision – to give their man the job.

The ultimate result was the rescinding of the board's legal decision. I and others on the board who supported the young, Greek architect were accused of 'not having assimilated enough into American society.'

I, personally, was also slandered when one board member said I was being anti-Semitic for not supporting the Jewish architect over the Greek architect. The accusation was unfounded.

A similar, equally unfortunate situation recently occurred in Milwaukee, when a Greek Orthodox church hired a non-Greek architect to design the church's addition over the proposal of a Greek American.

How will the Greek-American community progress if we do not support our own, young professionals in situations like these? How do we expect young Greek-Americans to stay active in the Greek-American community if we, the leaders of the community, continue to close doors on them?

The GANHC response, via a letter to the editor from Dr. Kioutas, appeared in the March 21 issue of the *Greek Star* and in the *Greek Press* of that same week.

The Greek-American Nursing Home Committee (GANHC) takes exception to the March 7th Letter to the Editor from John Regas appearing in your paper. About ten years ago the Greek-American Nursing Home Committee researched to identify an architectural firm with experience in designing nursing homes and a good reputation. The name that was most frequently brought up among both the Greek-American and non-Greek building and financial circles was Shayman, Salk, Aaronson, Sussholz & Co. (SSAS). We engaged them and since that time this firm has assisted us enormously and has not charged for its principals' many services. To date, this architectural firm has designed and built 83 nursing homes.

In November 1997, our application to the State for a Certificate of Need (CON) along with the designs completed by SSAS was unanimously approved by the Illinois Health Facilities Planning Board (IHFPB). Shortly thereafter, Mr. Regas, then a Board member, advised that he and several others wanted a Greek-American architectural firm and that he was not satisfied with the State-approved plans.

After lengthy interviews and reviews, a fine architectural firm with a Greek principal was narrowly accepted, PROVIDING that the CON would not be jeopardized. An investigation to

> determine whether this would occur was to be completed within two weeks.
>
> Prior to the next meeting, the Greek-American architect withdrew.
>
> At the meeting, our CON consultant reported that the chairman of the IHFPB told her that we would not be reconsidered for a different CON, especially if the footprint of the building were to be changed. Our hard-won permit would be revoked. The board opted to continue with our initial architectural firm.
>
> At all times the GANHC has acted in the best interest of the community, the donors, and our primary mission to build this nursing home. We are one of the very few not-for-profit Greek-American organizations that have a yearly independent audit of our funds. Mr. Regas' statement that the board members had a 'personal interest' and 'dubious' relationship with a non-Greek architect is ludicrous. We had worked for ten years with this firm whose plans we liked and which met the budgetary restrictions of the State. We had accepted their generosity and loyalty. None of their nursing homes had licensure problems. All this, plus the experience of 83 nursing homes built, could not be matched by another of the candidates' credentials.
>
> To assuage Mr. Regas, please know that we have three firms with Greek-American principals working with us.
>
> Since Mr. Regas shared this dream and worked toward it, and we are very close to our goal, may we respectfully suggest that now is the time for the KALO LOGO.

Planning was well underway and notes from a May 5, 1998, meeting between representatives of the GANHC and SSAS illustrate the range of items that were being addressed:

> Discussed the apparent increase in the lake size. The lake shown on the most current (1994) Plat of Survey is larger than the previous Plat of Survey. The lake now encroaches on the proposed building footprint. The Village of Wheeling has indicated that there is no 'outfall' from the lake. Why is the lake getting bigger?
>
> Steve [Sussholz] suggested that rain runoff is probably filling the lakes. The lakes seem to interconnect with the lake on the adjacent property. A wetlands survey and a topographical survey need to be done for the site. A Civil Engineer also needs to be hired. SSAS was given the okay to hire a wetlands surveyor. If the wetlands had to be mitigated it could be done on site. The worst-case scenario would be to move the building out of the footprint of the lake and re-lay out the parking.

GAC asked if they could build an addition or add a floor to the building in the future. *No, the project was approved by Wheeling as it was submitted.*

GAC asked if the building would flood from the lakes. *No. The building cannot be located withing [sic] the 100-year flood plain. The 100-year flood plain will be determined and the first floor will be located a minimum of 18 inches above that point.*

All present reviewed the floor plans (the plans had been revised since the last meeting). The following are the comments from that review:

> All the spaces in the building are the same as the original design but have been reconfigured.
>
> GAC asked if the Mall and Lobby could be open to each other. *SSAS explained that they are separated for a number of reasons. One is the need to keep the administration and public areas separated from the resident areas.*
>
> The Mall was included in the design to reduce the institutional feel of the building. The Mall will be open with a high ceiling, benches, plants, etc.
>
> GAC said that the [sic] will bring as many residents as possible to the Chapel services and therefore the wall between the Chapel and the Activity Room should be a retractable partition in order to add more seats if necessary.
>
> The Chapel should have about three rows of fixed pews at the front and then stackable chairs behind the pews.
>
> GAC asked if stained glass can be added to the front of the Chapel. *SSAS will add back-lit stained glass to the front of the Chapel.*
>
> GAC said that the Conference Room needs to seat 30. *SSAS will review the possibility of relocating the Conference Room in order to enlarge it enough to seat 30.*
>
> GAC suggested that the Ice Cream Parlor be more open to the Mall. *SSAS will relocate the Ice Cream Parlor closer, and mor* [sic] *open, to the Mall.*

The conversion of one of the wings on a floor to an Alzheimer's unit was discussed. The southwest wing of the fourth floor will be utilized as an Alzheimer's unit. This will require a redesign of this wing of the floor in order to 'loop' the corridor, add a nurse 'sub' station, a dining room, and pairs of doors to separate this unit from the rest of the floor. These separation doors will have delayed egress magnet locks on them. Whatever plan changes are made to the fourth floor will have to be carried down through the building to the other floors in order to keep the mechanical systems and stair tower lined up. SSAS will also develop a wander garden for the alzheimer [sic] residents.

The northwest wing of the fourth floor will be utilized as a ventilation unit. This will require the addition of an outlet on critical power for the ventilators and an alarm to the Nurse Station.

GAC asked if skylights could be added to some of the fourth-floor areas. *Skylights could be added, however, they are not really necessary. There will be a lot of natural light in all spaces. Skylights can be expensive and of course, can also leak.*

All present discussed acoustical ceilings. GAC didn't necessarily think that acoustical ceilings are "residential" looking. *Drywall ceilings could be used throughout, however, they are very expensive and provide no acoustical qualities. We could use drywall ceilings in selected locations for aesthetics. Also, there is a wide variety of acoustical ceiling designs and styles to choose from that have more of a residential feel.*

GAC asked if there were single bedrooms in the facility. *Yes. The code requires that a minimum of 3% of the rooms be singles.*

GAC asked if the mechanical systems could be located on the roof in order to use the Mechanical Room space on the first floor. *They could. However, it would require the construction of a mechanical penthouse because most of the equipment requires protection from the elements. Building a penthouse would be expensive.*

GAC asked if the patient room sizes were adequate. *The C.O.N. limits the gross square footage of the building so the size of the rooms is limited. The rooms as currently designed are larger than the code requirements but are with the C.O.N. parameters.*

SSAS recommended that an interior designer be selected as soon as possible. SSAS will forward a couple of names to GAC.

SSAS recommended that a management company be selected as soon as possible. They could then help lay out the data and communications systems to fit their needs. SSAS will forward management company names to GAC.

GAC said the entry to the building must make an architectural statement.

GAC asked how best to incorporate donations and naming into the building. For example, if somebody wanted to donate money for a stained-glass window. Should money be given to the Contractor to purchase and install window? *SSAS recommends that in order to stay under the C.O N cap that these types of items be purchase [sic] by the G.A.C. and given to the Contractor to install.*

GAC said that there was somebody who would donate marble to the project if it could be incorporated, SSAS will review the possible use of marble in the project.

SSAS will create a schedule for the project.

SSAS recommended that a meeting be set up with H.U.D. to review the project. A set of preliminary drawings and an outline spec will be required.

SSAS estimates that the building will require a 14-month construction schedule and should start in the spring.

GAC asked if it would be possible to have the General Contractors request bids from Greek subcontractors. *This can be done.*

On May 17, 1998, the GANHC held a Ceremonial Groundbreaking Celebration on the property. Among those who took part were His Eminence Metropolitan Iakovos; Lee Zaras, governor of the Federation of Sterea Hellas (Roumeli); Gus Christofidis, AHEPA 13th District; Nicholas Zafiropoulos, consul general of Greece; Rita Mullins, mayor of Palatine; Senator Adeline Geo-Karis; Cook County Treasurer Maria Pappas; Chris

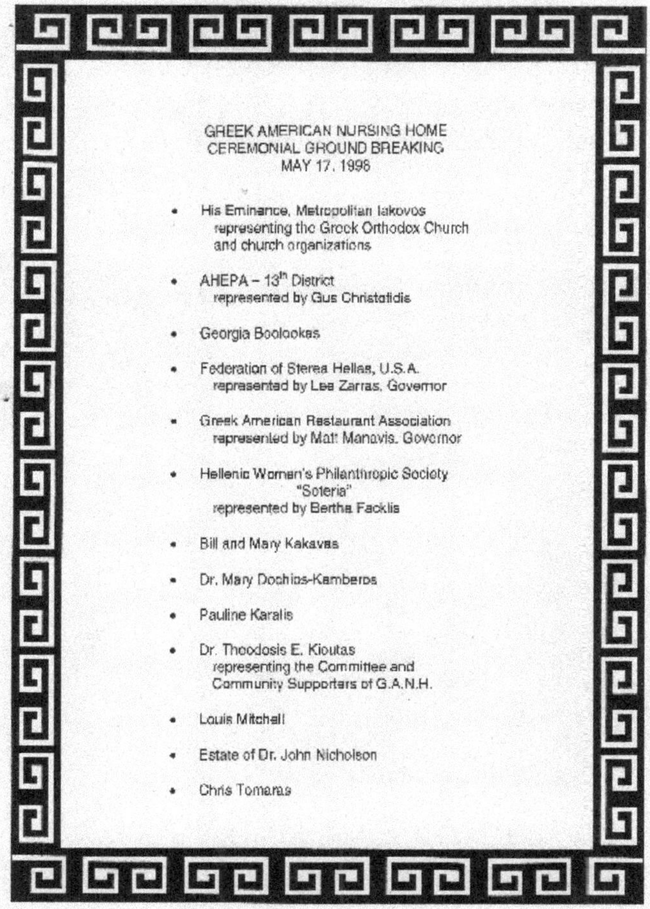

GREEK AMERICAN NURSING HOME
CEREMONIAL GROUND BREAKING
MAY 17, 1998

- His Eminence, Metropolitan Iakovos
  representing the Greek Orthodox Church
  and church organizations
- AHEPA – 13th District
  represented by Gus Christofidis
- Georgia Boolookas
- Federation of Sterea Hellas, U.S.A.
  represented by Lee Zarras, Governor
- Greek American Restaurant Association
  represented by Matt Manavis, Governor
- Hellenic Women's Philanthropic Society
  "Soteria"
  represented by Bertha Facklis
- Bill and Mary Kakavas
- Dr. Mary Dochios-Kamberos
- Pauline Karalis
- Dr. Theodosis E. Kioutas
  representing the Committee and
  Community Supporters of G.A.N.H.
- Louis Mitchell
- Estate of Dr. John Nicholson
- Chris Tomaras

Ceremonial Ground Breaking program. May 17, 1998. John Psiharis collection.

Tomaras, SAE president for North and South American; Matt Manavis, president of the Greek-American Restaurant Association; Tom Pappas, president of the GARA board; Bertha Facklis, president of the Hellenic Women's Philanthropic Association "Soteria;" Georgia Boolookas; Pauline Karalis; Dr. Mary Dochios Kamberos, and Louis Mitchell. Ceremonial shovels were given to those who had given $50,000 or more. Nearly 700 invitations were sent out and more than 250 attended. Food and entertainment added to the festive mood of the afternoon. Blueprints, renderings, and schematics of the soon-to-be-built building were on display.

Following the groundbreaking, GANHC hosted its annual meeting at the adjacent Holy Family Wheeling Professional Building. During the meeting, Dr. Kioutas reported on the status of the GANHC, and John Secaras provided a financial report and fundraising update. Approximately $186,000 was raised during the groundbreaking in cash and pledges. Notable donations included: the Association of Aetos, Messenia, $1,000;

THURSDAY, JUNE 25, 1998

94th Year **THE GREEK STAR**

Nursing home breaks ground in Wheeling

Pictured above, from left, are His Eminence Metropolitan Iakovos of Krinis, Palatine mayor Rita Mullins, Louis Atsaves of the 13th District of AHEPA and Anna and Dr. Theodosis Kioutas at the May 17 ground-breaking ceremonies for the Greek-American Nursing Home. Many local dignitaries and benefactors were among the more than 250 persons who gathered for the event. A 204-bed skilled care facility will be built on land located one block north of Dundee Road and one block west of Milwaukee Avenue on First Street in Wheeling, IL. The nursing home will be located across from the Wheeling Senior Citizens Center. See page 8 for complete coverage.

The Greek Star, June 25, 1998. John Psiharis collection.

Sparta Society, $2,000, and the Argolis Organization, $1,000. Chris Tomaras pledged $50,000 and Lou Mitchell $25,000.

An article written by John Rassogianis that appeared in the May 28, 1998, issue of the *Greek Star* entitled “Community Celebrates Ceremonial Groundbreaking of Greek-American Nursing Home in Wheeling,” described the historic day in this way:

> The many-decades-long, yet sure-footed sojourn of the Greek Community pursuing the narrow, uneven path to erect a Greek-American Nursing Home (GANHC), reached another landmark

Gust Christofidis of the AHEPA 13th District chats with His Eminence Metropolitan Iakovos as Chris Tomaras, SAE president of North and South America, looks on. Others preparing for the ceremonial ground breaking are Matt Manavis, Greek American Restaurant Association President, Bertha Facklis, president of Soteria, Georgia Boolookas and Pauline Karalis.

John Secaras, Pete Photopoulos, Consul General of Greece Nicholas Zafiropoulos, Jim Pirpiris, His Eminence Metropolitan Iakovos, Bill Kakavas, Jim Kotsovos, Toula Mourafetis, Dr. Theodosis E. Kioutas, and Chris Tomaras.

Supporters of the Greek-American Nursing Home include Bertha and George Capulos.

Anna Kioutas, Suzanne and Dr. Taso Hinaris.

Greek-American Nursing Home supporters include George Daylantis and Mary Secaras.

Pictures of the groundbreaking ceremony. *The Greek Star*, June 25, 1998. John Psiharis collection.

on Sunday, May 17. It happened during the historic groundbreaking ceremony held on the grounds of the eight-acre plot in Wheeling, IL.

Calling it a 'humanitarian milestone for the Greek and general community,' Dr. Theodosis Kioutas, president of the GANHC, and John Secaras, chairman of the fundraising committee, made opening remarks in an afternoon fraught with optimism and excitement.

His Eminence, Metropolitan Iakovos of Krinis, had just concluded the ancient religious Orthodox drama of the *agiasmos* as a cool breeze swept through the assembly, a hiatus in an otherwise unseasonably warm afternoon.

The Consul General of Greece, Nicholas Zafiropoulos, reminisced by recalling his first gala, a nursing home function, upon his arrival from Greece. Expressing his ongoing interest in the project in his remarks, he said, 'I feel that I too have grown with this project.'

Twelve leaders representing all aspects of the *omogenia* formed a long line. Facing the crowd, with their red-ribboned shovels glistening in the sunlight, they scooped up the earth. The symbolism of the parting of the ground brought home the reality of the project, to the delight and applause of all.

The leaders were His Eminence, Metropolitan Iakovos of Krinis, representing the church and its organizations; Zafiropoulos; Rita Mullen, mayor of Palatine, IL; Bertha Facklis, representing the Hellenic Women's Society 'Soteria;' Bill and Mary Kakavas; Gus Christofidis of the AHEPA 13th District; Georgia Boolookas; Lee Zarras, governor of the Federation of Sterea Hellas; Chris Tomaras, SAE president of North and South America Region; Matt Manavis, governor of the Greek-American Restaurant Association; Pauline Kafalis, and Dr. Theodosis Kioutas, representing the committee and community supporters of the GANHC.

A reception immediately followed across the street at the Holy Family Wheeling Professional Building. At the social, Chris Margetis captured the spirit of the event when she was overheard to remark to a friend, 'We all have to work together. There is no other way.' Margetis is the wife of Peter Margetis, 13th District lieutenant governor, Order of AHEPA.

During the hour-long general meeting, Secaras acknowledged the Kakavas family of the 13 Colonies Restaurant who were the individuals most responsible for their financial contributions as well as raising the tone and awareness of the project in the community.

Tomaras provided a dash of elegance in his remarks promising greater support in the future by accepting an invitation to join the fundraising committee of the advisory board.

The twin miracles of patience and dedication, and all the values the GANHC holds dear, closed their ranks again at sunset, having witnessed a day of triumph that pervaded a community and its faith in a committee that never lost sight of its ultimate pledge and accountability.

Next, we needed to finalize site plans and building designs. The designs took advantage of the water ponds and had the four-story building (with a basement) positioned to the side of it with a gated walkway included along its side. A plat of survey was finalized.

The interior layout included private and semi-private rooms that catered to all levels of care: skilled, intermediate, and sheltered. In addition to offices, reception areas, and physical therapy, the ground level would include a chapel, ice cream parlor, beauty shop, and a large activity area that could be subdivided for smaller groups to use. The basement housed utilities, laundry, kitchen, and housekeeping functions.

GANHC Executive Committee reviews blueprints for the nursing home during a meeting at Greek-American Community Services. Pictured (L-R): Seated: John Psiharis, Ethel Kotsovos, Dr. Theodosis Kioutas, Toni Panos, and Eugenia Seifer. Standing: George Alexandrou, Christine Burbulis, George Alexandrou, and John Rassogianis. Date unknown. John Psiharis collection.

Each of the three patient floors included patient rooms, activity space, a dining room, shower facilities, and nursing stations. In total, the facility would be licensed for 204 beds.

This was a busy time with many meetings dealing with a range of matters both large and small. In June we were made aware of problems with the pond and informed the property contained wetlands that required special attention. The Committee engaged the civil engineering firm of Pearson, Brown & Associates to help close the "channel" at the property.

The summary of a July board meeting held with SSAS at their office offers a glimpse of the various matters that were in play:

> Instructed SSAS to add the words "Greek-American" to all drawings. SSAS will obtain additional brick samples to provide a range of colors and textures to choose from. They suggest using smooth face stone at the base of the building and not the chiseled face to provide a more Mediterranean aesthetic to the building. SSAS suggests first-floor elevation a minimum of eighteen inches above the 100-year flood elevation. The lake area is being expanded to provide compensatory floodwater storage for the area of the site occupied by the new building. The lakes will also be used for stormwater detention. It was decided that a chain-link fence be installed around the lake to prevent residents from

> wandering into the water. A landscaping architect can help "beautify" the lake. A number of tweaks were made to the designs. Discussion on how to go about selecting a contractor and assuring that Greek contractors and subcontractors have the opportunity to bid on the work.

During an August 17 board meeting, the GANHC board formalized the mission to provide charity care to those in need with three motions that were unanimously approved. One formally confirmed the intentions of the board that the facility provides for charity cases and that our policy will be not to evict someone if unable to pay. A second motion required that two percent of all monies raised through fundraising be placed in a separate account for charity cases and the third authorized the opening of a separate account for charity purposes with an initial deposit of $750. At that point, we had spent $145,017 on construction expenses that fell within the $12.5 million cap outlined in the CON.

The board then turned its attention to the selection of a management company to manage pre-and-post-opening operations. The stakes were high, and we needed to get it right to receive federal and state approval and open the nursing home. Staff needed to be hired and trained, marketing and outreach initiated, administrative and financial systems established, and medical protocols developed. Decisions needed to be made about who our pharmaceutical, physical therapy, and food suppliers would be and much more.

Throughout the summer, a sub-committee met with a few management companies and recommended we hire Bethany Methodist Hospital's Management Division which had expertise in running several nursing homes and health care facilities. I recall being on this committee and attending several presentations by different companies. We were leaning toward hiring Bethany but deferred the decision until after the fall fundraiser since that decision required our full attention.

On September 27 GANHC hosted "The Autumn of My Years" dinner dance at the Fountain Blue in Des Plaines, IL. Bud Photopoulos was the master of ceremonies. The well-attended event raised $308,049 in donations and pledges. Dr. Mary Dochios Kamberos pledged $250,000 at the event, and others followed suit. Those in attendance were enthusiastic about the project, and the event helped to galvanize additional support in the coming months.

"The Autumn of My Years" invitation cover. September 27, 1998. Elaine Thomopoulos collection.

A message from Metropolitan Iakovos of Krinis for the dinner's Commemorative Album said in part:

> "How fitting it is that you have chosen these first days of autumn for such an event. Even as the days grow shorter, as the sunlight grows softer, as the leaves begin to change their colors, you gather to support those of our elders who are now facing the autumn of their lives. Like you, so many of those who will need this home will have spent much of their lives laboring for the needs of our Greek Orthodox Communities serving in Philoptochos Societies and on Parish Councils, chanting and baking, teaching and giving of their resources.
>
> How fitting it is, then, that we who are able-bodied should now strive to provide for the final years of their lives. How fitting it is that we should build a final earthly home for our infirm elders – a home where they can create community, a home where their mother tongue is spoken, a home where they can keep the traditions of our people with a degree of comfort and with all-important dignity."

A message from Wheeling Village President Greg Klatecki officially welcoming the Greek American Nursing Home to Wheeling was also published in the dinner album.

> As I look back in my life, I remember what my sister and I went through as our parents aged. I remember our parents appreciated being with people of similar backgrounds.
>
> As I look at what your group is trying to provide, I see an environment that people of Greek Ancestry will feel comfortable in. I applaud you for this.
>
> On behalf of the Village of Wheeling, I am pleased to officially welcome you to our community. I know you will become an important part of our family.

Additionally, a two-page spread entitled, "Background and Update," appeared in the 1998 commemorative album detailing the progress made to date:

> In the late 1940s and early 1950s, civic and philanthropic-minded individuals in the Chicago area envisioned a need for a Greek American nursing home. Two organizations were established to pursue, among other things, the raising of funds for the establishment of a Greek American nursing home. They were: The Hellenic Women's Philanthropic Association Soteria*(1) and the Greek Archdiocese Welfare Foundation. *(2). Though successful in other ways, these groups did not establish a nursing home facility.
>
> Early in the 1980s, statistics revealed that the country's senior population was exploding. The statistics showed that the number of people over 65 years of age has grown by 55% in a decade and that 1 out of every 5 Americans over 65 would require nursing home care at some point in his/her life. A grass root [sic] group, headed by Dr. Kioutas, confronted with these statistics determined that the Greek-American community still lacked a major service for seniors- a Greek-American Nursing Home. Thus, in 1985, the Greek-American Nursing Home Committee (an Illinois not-for-profit corporation and tax-exempt under section 501 (c) (3) of the Code) was formed. The five directors listed on the Articles of Organization are Dr. Theodosis E. Kioutas, Helen Georges, Ethel Kotsovos, Toni Panos, and James Mezilson.
>
> The Committee, starting only with an idea, planned the type of Greek-American Nursing Home it believed would be best for our community. It determined that the nursing home would, among other things, provide skilled care, accept Medicare and Medicaid residents, have an Orthodox Chapel, and serve food with a Greek/Mediterranean flavor. The home would be under the

direction of an experienced nursing home administrator. Professional staff, such as social workers, registered nurses, nurse's aides, occupational and physical therapists, doctors, and dietitians would be hired (some bilingual).

The Committee received the Metropolitan's blessing (then Bishop Iakovos) and began fundraising. It purchased slightly over 8 acres of land in Wheeling, Illinois. It is on this acreage that the nursing home will be built. It is bordered on one side by the Wheeling Senior Center and on the other by the Park District. It is located one block north of Dundee Road west of Milwaukee Avenue. The 8 acres cost $425,000.00 and are paid for and clear of any debt. Wheeling Township unanimously approved zoning of this land for the nursing home, subject to the submission of final drawings.

The footnotes at the bottom of the first page read:

(1) Funds collected by Soteria are in Certificates of Deposit. These sums, upon financing of the Greek-American Nursing Home, will be turned over to this current project.
(2) This foundation spearheaded by Reverand George Mastrantonis, who envisioned a nursing home facility, an orphanage, and social services for the Greek community, became the Hellenic Foundation, and the funds collected were used to help purchase Hollywood House and start Social Services for Greek-Americans.

The second page provided an update on recent activities.

<u>UPDATE SINCE JANUARY OF 1997</u>

These past 2 ½ years have been a period of tremendous progress. Foremost in accomplishments was the completion and filing of the application for a Certificate of Need. On November 21, 1997, the Illinois Health Facilities Planning Board unanimously granted the request for a Certificate of Need to proceed with the planning and construction of a Greek-American Nursing Home in Wheeling, Illinois.

The Committee was advised that it was most unusual for the Planning Board to grant a Certificate at a first hearing. The members of the Planning Board congratulated the Nursing Home Committee for its successful past work and fine presentation but counseled that this hard work must now continue. The Certificate of Need (Permit) requires that we comply with a timetable and complete all pre-construction activities prior to May 21, 1999. These pre-construction activities include: (1) completed and approved architectural drawings, (2) completion of financing, (3) a contract with a reputable construction firm approved by the State Board, and (4) an increase in our assets to approach 20% of the projected cost of the project which is $12,500,000.

> The architectural firm has been selected. It is Shayman, Salk, Arenson, Sussholz, and Co. whose offices are located in Northbrook, Illinois. As of this date, architectural drawings are almost 95% completed. The financial advisor has been selected – the firm of Cambridge Realty Capital Ltd. of Chicago, Illinois. Currently, the Committee is meeting with HUD to have the loan guaranteed by the said agency, and funding will be obtained soon afterward. The Committee has interviewed, to date, several management firms and will shortly make its selection. Solicitation will soon go out for bids by general and subcontractors.
>
> Currently, everything is on a fast track toward the realization of the community's dream to have a Nursing Home with a Greek and Orthodox atmosphere for the Greek community in the Chicagoland area.
>
> The Greek American community is asked to participate in fueling this effort through prayers, encouraging words, and financial support.
>
> In the past, local Greek Orthodox church communities have each built their own churches and community centers. However, the construction of a **NEW FACILITY** built from the ground up and supported by the **ENTIRE** Chicagoland Greek Community has yet to be achieved. The Greek-American Nursing Home will be the **FIRST** project in the Chicago area to be built and supported by all Hellenes and Philhellenes in the Chicago land area.
>
> To be the **FIRST** we need your help, and we need it now!

Throughout the remaining months of 1998, the GANHC dealt with a myriad of details that had to be decided. In addition to financing and fundraising, we needed to deal with construction and planning matters as they arose. In November, we formally selected Bethany Management Firm to manage the nursing home. We hired Design Trends International of Houston, Texas to provide interior design services. An aviary with birds was approved for the lobby and a 20-foot-long fish tank for the second floor. Decisions on mattress types, acoustics, acoustic wallpaper, lighting, tub rooms, overhead televisions, and the positioning of toilets in bathrooms to allow room for walkers were made. With these changes, there were 538 square feet per bed.

Although the board had previously adopted three motions expressing its intention that the GANHC provide charity care and that no one should be denied admission or discharged due to inability to pay, per legal advice, this was further enshrined by amending the bylaws. During a November 16, 1998, meeting at the Sauganash Restaurant, Article II (entitled Governing Policy) was unanimously amended to include the following statement: "In accordance with the charitable purposes of the corporation, the policy of the corporation will be that upon establishment of our nursing home facility, a provision will be made for charity cases. Further, it will be the policy of the corporation not to evict a resident of the nursing home facility if he/she becomes unable to pay."

Our first task in 1999 was to select a general contractor for the project. After having issued RFPs and reviewing several bidders, the board selected the applicant who we thought was the most qualified bidder from those who met the submission deadline of January 10, 1999. There were five qualified bids. We selected A.J. Maggio General Contractors. They had a good track record of past projects including several nursing homes and healthcare facilities and were also recommended by the architect. The final contract was for $9,895,000.

At the following meeting, after the decision had been made, Jim Kozonis offered, on behalf of his company, to do the job for between $ 200,000 and $400,000 less than the lowest bid received, because he would donate back his profit.

From the GANHC meeting minutes of February 15, 1999:

> A discussion followed, questioning the timeliness of this offer, whether this would be ethical, and whether there existed a conflict of interest since Mr. Kozonis was a board member and had obtained off his computer the amounts of the bids. Mr. Kozonis stated that no problem existed since we were still holding discussions with the low bidders to come within the amount budgeted, but if someone thought it was not proper, he would withdraw. Helen Georges stated that as far as she knew, some people would consider this unethical. John Secaras thought that since Mr. Kozonis was a member of the board a conflict of interest could exist. Elaine Thomopoulos asked Mr. Kozonis if he had not received the mailings sent out to the board members. Specifically, she referred to a letter dated September 8, 1998, sent to all board members regarding qualifications needed by the General Contractors to bid. Mr. Kozonis stated that since he was unable to attend our board meetings, he did not look at these letters nor respond. Mr. Secaras then stated that since we have always strived to have people with Greek roots work on this project and in as much as we were not able to determine timeliness etc. that this should be referred to the architect and if the architect believed that this would not be considered untimely, constitute a conflict of interest, etc. that then Mr. Kozonis should be given the plans to formulate his bid. This became the consensus of the board members, and it was decided that his request to bid would be relayed to the architect by the chairman of the committee.

Although appreciative of Jim's generosity, like most of the committee, I felt uncomfortable with the ethics of this. We were overseers of a multi-million-dollar project and custodians of hundreds of thousands of dollars entrusted to us by the community, and this didn't sit well with me. I was concerned that even the perception of insider dealing of any sort could derail all we had achieved, and it was clear to me that this was a conflict of interest. To allow a board member's company to bid after the bidding process had concluded with knowledge of the other bids seemed unethical, even if it saved us a significant sum of money. Although he had good intentions, I feared this would not be perceived favorably in the community at large. It would be seen as an insider deal and jeopardize the community trust that we worked so hard to build. Had Jim submitted a bid during the open bidding process as the others did, he would likely have been competitive, and our preference to hire Greek American contractors whenever possible would have been at play. We had always been honest, careful, transparent, and responsible custodians of the funds connected to this project, and I didn't want to stray from that path.

The tension was still apparent at the next board meeting when Jim stated his disagreement with the minutes of the prior meeting. The minutes of the March board meeting describe the discussion: "A lively discussion ensued with Dr. Kioutas reminding us that extending the bidding would cause a delay and jeopardize our Certificate of Need. The minutes continued: John Secaras and Theresa Tzakis reminded us that it was too late to make a change since a contractor had been selected. Jim submitted a letter to board members dated February 8, 1999, presenting his view of the events, and it was attached to the February 15 minutes as part of the record." Jim resigned shortly thereafter.

Beyond this internal dissent, GANHC experienced other challenges. For example, in October 1998, as we were in the process of submitting our application to HUD to guarantee the loan, they raised a concern about a conflict between State and Federal law. HUD maintained that the state's rule regarding the ethnic variance of our CON, i.e. that 85 percent of residents admitted to the GANHC must have a Greek connection, limits access, and is discriminatory per Title VIII. In November we were told that HUD and HHS will take time to resolve the ethnic variance issue and that we may need to find a Plan B.

Bricks & Mortar

While the HUD matter played out and 1999 began, our attention was, as usual, focused on money. Fundraising efforts continued but now there was also the matter of arranging the financing for the project. In February, HUD reported that it would meet with the Village of Wheeling to see if they could issue our bonds, and up to that point, their response had been positive.

One of the first activities of the new year was attending the liturgy of the Feast Day of St. John held on January 7 at St. John the Baptist Greek Orthodox Church in Des Plaines. After the liturgy, Philoptochos president Nikki Melachrinakis presented a check for $3,350 towards the society's $10,000 pledge. Parish council outreach member John Gatsis also presented a $700 check to the nursing home. The three Johns - John Rassogianis, John Secaras, and I attended, along with Dr. Kioutas and Sam Tzakis (and possibly others), who took photos of the presentation. Metropolitan Iakovos participated in the check presentation ceremony. In April, upon the dissolution of the Hellenic Workers Association, the organization donated $3,085.25 to the GANHC.

At this time, GANHC maintained accounts at Atlantic Bank (formerly National Bank of Greece), Cole Taylor Bank, and Broadway Bank. Certificates of Deposits were held at Edens Bank, First Chicago Bank, Cambridge Bank, Western Springs Bank, St. Paul Federal Bank, Liberty Federal Savings, and North Shore Community Bank. A donation of ATT stock by Dr. Dochios-Kamberos split and the GANHC now owned 183 shares valued at $10,867. In February, George Lekas and Gerry Garbis joined the board.

Fundraising efforts focused on the ample naming opportunities associated with the new facility. Every residential room, vestibule, office, common space, therapy room, and even the campus and building, were available for a price. More than one donor might have sponsored a room. When that was the case, all donors were included on the plaques displayed. A September 1999 listing included the following opportunities:

1.	Nursing Home Building	$3,000,000
2.	Pavilion Floors (3)	900,000 (ea. floor)
3.	Campus Grounds	500,000
4.	Floor Wings (9)	300,000 (ea.)
5.	Kitchen Equipment	250,000
6.	Chapel (1st floor)	100,000
7.	Lounge (1st floor)	100,000
8.	Ice Cream/Coffee Shop (1st floor)	100,000
9.	Front Elevators (2) ($37,500 ea.)	75,000
10.	Resident Outside Patio	50,000
11.	Alzheimer's Patio	50,000
12.	Private Dining Room (1st floor)	50,000
13.	Dining Rooms (2nd, 3rd & 4th floors)	50,000 (ea.)
14.	Kitchen (1st floor)	50,000
15.	Staff Lounge (1st floor)	40,000
16.	Activity Room	35,000
17.	Vestibule	30,000
18.	Laundry Equipment	28,000
19.	Occupational Therapy Room (1st floor)	25,000
20.	Conference Room (1st floor)	25,000

21. Physical Therapy Room (1st floor) 25,000
22. Beauty Parlor (1st floor) 25,000
23. Nurses Station (2nd, 3rd & 4th floors) 25,000 (ea.)
24. Lounges (2nd, 3rd & 4th floors) 25,000 (ea.)
25. Rear Elevator 25,000
26. Fountain #1 25,000
27. Fountain #2 25,000
28. Private Patient Rooms (6) 25,000
29. Semi-Private Patient Rooms (99) 20,000 (ea.)
30. Administrator's Office (1st floor) 25,000
31. Administration Office (2) 10,000 (ea.)
32. Whirlpool Tubs (6) 8,000 (ea.)
33. Director of Nursing Office (3) 5,000 (ea.)
34. Nourishment Stations (3) 5,000 (ea.)

On June 27, 1999, the GANHC published an open letter from Dr. Kioutas in the *Greek Star*, recognizing Bill and Mary Kakavas for their support of the project. The letter read: "Dear Bill and Mary, it is with much pleasure that I advise you that your gifts totaling $147,000 have played a major role in our success thus far. The chapel at the Greek-American Nursing Home will bear a plaque with whatever names or message you determine. Please let us know in writing what you prefer. As board members of the Greek-American Nursing Home Committee, you have worked endlessly toward the completion of this humanitarian project. I look forward to the time we can stand together in the chapel and read the inscription you selected."

Minutes from the June and July board meetings reflect the varied priorities being addressed at the time. In June, the U.S. Department of Housing and Urban Development (HUD) formally approved GANHC's application to guarantee the loan. Guest Bessie Pantazelos reported that the 13th District Daughters of Penelope released $15,000 of their pledge to GANHC. Tina Spiratos reported the transfer of $307,000 from Soteria on June 3rd. Father Massouras, Gerry Garbis, John Secaras, and Dr. Kioutas scheduled a meeting with Metropolitan Iakovos to update him on our progress. The Village of Wheeling asked GANHC to pay for the paving of a portion of the street that is close to the property.

During the July 26th meeting at Annunciation Cathedral, James K. Marousis, president of the George M. Eisenberg Foundation for Charities, presented a $50,000 donation from the Foundation. The second-floor dining room was named in honor of the Eisenberg Foundation. Checks were presented by AHEPA and the Daughters of Penelope. Updates on contracts with the management firm and Maggio were provided by Tina Spiratos and Gerry Garbis.

An article in the September 2, 1999, issue of the *Greek Star* reporting on the meeting of July 26th included the following summary:

> Daughters of Penelope 13th District Governor Chrysanthie Margetis and committee members recently met with Dr. Theodosis Kioutas, president of the Greek-American Nursing Home, and his officers and members to present them with the Daughters of Penelope's check for $15,000 – a pledge made at the 13th District convention.
>
> In addition to the 13th District Daughters of Penelope's contribution, the following chapters and members also made contributions: Past District Governor Bessie Pantazelos, representing Danae Chapter #121 donated $10,000. Pantazelos also donated a personal check of $1,000 in the name of her late husband, Thomas Pantazelos; Past President Dini Eliopoulos of Danaids Chapter #287 presented the chapter's check for $2,000, while past President Daisy Agres, of Homer Chapter #98, gave a personal check of $500.
>
> Other organizations that donated that evening included the George Eisenberg Foundation, which donated $50,000. Soteria donated $1,678.41, which completes its pledge, and the Greek Women's University Club donated $1,000.
>
> Members of AHEPA and the 13th District governor Peter Margetis, at the meeting, announced that AHEPA is planning a dinner dance to be held in the fall, and asked for everyone's support by attending the event.

By August, many naming opportunities had been reserved, paid for, or pledged: Chapel (paid), first-floor lounge (pledged), main lobby (paid), conference room (paid), physical therapy room (paid), six private patient rooms (paid), administrator and two administration offices (paid), three nourishment stations (paid), three directors of nursing offices (paid), private dining room (paid), occupational therapy room (paid), front elevators (paid), second-floor dining room (paid), activity room (pledged) and campus grounds (paid).

On August 17, 1999, the Illinois Health Facilities Planning Board obligated (approved) the project granting us until August 16, 2001, to complete the nursing home. Late in the month, GANHC was advised for the first time that HUD would not accept premium payments and required us to have a total of $3,631,186 in cash and payments made on preliminary construction costs before it would guarantee our loan for the sale of tax-exempt bonds or have $2,783,493 to obtain a taxable mortgage.

In October, an urgent appeal letter, signed by Dr. Kioutas, as chairman, and John Secaras, as treasurer and fund drive chairman, was sent to past donors and others who could help.

DEAR FAITHFUL SUPPORTERS:

WE PROMISED YOU WE WOULD START BUILDING IN LATE SPRING/SUMMER OF 1999. WE KNOW THAT WE OWE YOU AN EXPLANATION FOR WHY THE BUILDING OF OUR LONG-AWAITED NURSING HOME HAS NOT STARTED YET.

THE EXPLANATION IS:

1. Although our plans and contracts are completed and approved by the State of Illinois, HUD has not yet approved the guarantee of our mortgage.
2. A last-minute problem developed because the Chicago HUD Region refused to accept our financing proposal to include monies obtained as a premium from tax-exempt bonds as cash on hand. We understand that other HUD Region offices do accept this procedure but not here in Chicago.
3. The Chicago HUD Region accepts only cash and specific pre-paid building expenses toward the $3,631,186 minimum we are required to have on hand prior to its guaranteeing our loan.
4. On 9/20/99 our cash balance and approved pre-payments made on construction costs totaled **$2,782,720** leaving us a shortfall of **$848,466**. It is **URGENT** that we raise this amount as soon as possible.

We did not plan to ask you again for additional help during this phase of the project. Nonetheless, we must. **OUR GOAL IS SO NEAR.** Please make as generous a tax-deductible contribution as you are able and tell a friend about our **URGENT NEED** to begin to build. The State mandates that the building be ready by **August 16, 2001**.

This is a **GREEK-AMERICAN COMMUNITY AND ORTHODOX** project to care for and protect our fragile, ill, and disabled members. We will build it and it will be a jewel among us and for us.

Please call the GANHC office (773) 561-8865 if you wish a copy of the Naming Opportunities available to honor family and other loved ones. Enclosed are two pledge cards, one to complete with your gift and one to give to a friend.

HUD's new requirement set off a frenzy of fundraising activities to bring in additional dollars. In September $285,270 in donations were received. Cash balance and payments made on preliminary construction costs totaled $1,938,099 leaving a shortfall of $845,394 for the sale of taxable securities. By October 21, the amount needed decreased to $573,538, and by November 6 the shortfall had been reduced to $373,538. By Thanksgiving, the balance needed was $335,858 at which point HUD began to process our loan. By Christmas, the remaining amount needed had fallen to $142,451.

On December 27, 1999, GANHC raised $82,000 from 146 callers during a four-hour-long Radiothon hosted by Sotiris Rekoumis.

In light of these developments, Dr. Mary Dochios-Kamberos made additional donations bringing the total of her support to over $500,000 at that point. An appreciation of her generosity, written by John Rassogianis, appeared in community media, including the November 18, 1999, *Greek Star*.

> Dr. Mary Dochios Kamberos' parents set an example of Christian love and community which defined her character from an early age. Her father, Chris Dochios, originally a seaman from the Greek village of Litohoro near Salonika, and her mother, Helen, from Kandela, Greece, kept their Idaho farm home open to those in need of a meal or a place to stay, especially during the depression years. Soon the Campus of the Greek-American Nursing Home will be named the "***Chris and Helen Dochios Campus***" in their honor.
>
> Although modest in means, Chris and Helen Dochios sent four daughters to college. In addition to Dr. Dochios Kamberos, a pediatrician, her sisters' professions included an attorney, a teacher, and a teacher/businesswoman. Dr. Dochios Kamberos attended the University of Idaho and Hahnemann Medical School in Philadelphia. The early years were very difficult. She was a pioneer woman medical student and physician overcoming discrimination because of her gender. She was determined to be the best for her patients. She broke ground for other women physicians in what was previously a man's domain.
>
> Dr. Dochios Kamberos is a board-certified pediatrician. She was the Chief Medical Officer for the Cook County Temporary Juvenile Center (formally the Audi Home) for 32 years. She was also an attending physician in pediatrics at St. Bernard and Christ Hospitals until her retirement from private practice in July 1999. She was married and lived happily for over 25 years with Constantine Kamberos, an actuary, until his death. She continues to live in their home in Beverly and has a Gold Coast apartment.
>
> In addition to the recent very generous gifts to the Greek-American Nursing Home Committee, Dr. Dochios Kamberos contributes to other Greek organizations. She awards scholarships to inner-city children to attend private parochial schools, assists college students, sponsors special education students with various needs, contributes to her parish, St. Nicholas Greek Orthodox Church in Oak Lawn, and routinely and generously assists the Pacific Garden Mission during special holidays.
>
> When asked what motivated her philanthropy, she stated her parents' examples as well as those people in the community who

had faith in her ability and helped her. 'You have to give back,' she said.

Dr. Mary Dochios Kamberos is an altruist, who dignifies her profession, her heritage, and her Greek Orthodox faith. The Greek-American Nursing Home Committee is most appreciative of Dr. Mary Dochios Kamberos' continued support. ***Axia***

In the first months of the new millennium, attention was focused on finalizing the financing of the project and dealing with the logistics of a tax-exempt bond offering as well as a continued focus on fundraising.

An update and appeal letter sent to board members by Dr. Kioutas on March 8, 2000, reported on where things stood at this point:

GOOD NEWS

On February 28th, HUD issued a decision to guarantee our loan of $11,275,000.00. This occurred after we raised the sum of $2,783,493.00. This amount was the minimum we needed in order to meet HUD's requirement to permit us to obtain a conventional mortgage. Closing with HUD will occur on or about April 14 and construction on our nursing home will begin shortly thereafter. (The authority to purchase and fabricate the needed steel for the project has already been given by us to our general contractor).

WINDOW OF OPPORTUNITY

HUD will permit us to sell tax-exempt bonds at a premium if we raise, prior to closing, an additional sum of $219,308.00. As of today, we have raised all but $100,000.00 of that amount. We must advise our financial consultant within two weeks whether to proceed with the issuance of tax-exempt bonds or to continue financing through a conventional mortgage. By raising the additional $100,000.00 we will be able to obtain our loan at 1 ½ % points less than the conventional mortgage. This translates into yearly savings of $169,000 on interest alone. And, because the bonds will be sold at a premium, an additional $500,000.00 to $600,000.00 will be generated to offset any initial operating losses. As you can see, the benefits to be reaped by the sale of tax-exempt bonds far exceed the additional funds we need to raise.

An article written by Dr. Kioutas entitled, "Sts. Peter and Paul Brunch Benefits Nursing Home Project," appeared in the April 13, 2000, *Greek Star*:

On behalf of the Greek-American Nursing Home Committee: What a beautiful and successful brunch the Sts. Peter and Paul Philoptochos recently presented on behalf of the Greek-American Nursing Home project. The great effort of your

> Philoptochos and parish was very evident. The church hall was filled and beautiful. The food delicious! It was easy to see that the heart of the organization is behind this considerable effort that we have been working toward for many years. The exact donation amount was $8,700.
>
> We are the [sic]beginning to see the light. We now do not anticipate any difficulty in securing HUD's approval.
>
> Our financial consultant has sent the application, and we should hear within 30 days. Our general contractor will begin to break ground as soon as weather permits.
>
> Thank you for your commitment to the nursing home project, your hard work, and your loving hearts.

The HUD paperwork was signed on May 3, 2000. HUD approved $11,400,000 to construct and open the home. Efforts to raise funds to meet tax-exempt bond requirements continued. At this point, $106,000 was still needed to meet the minimum. Tax-exempt bonds would reduce the interest rate by approximately 1.50 percent annually resulting in an estimated savings of $169,000 per year and generating up to $600,000 to offset operating losses during the initial lease-up period. Nuveen purchased all the bonds, which offered an interest rate of 7.9 percent, for inclusion in their portfolios of different funds. American National Bank held the funds for this transaction.

During this time, GARA donated an additional $106,000 to GANHC and we were notified that $100,000 would be coming from the Lou Mitchell Estate. In March, the St. Demetrios of Waukegan Philoptochos Society hosted a *Makaronada* Luncheon after Divine Liturgy. Father John Sardis gave a moving address about the importance of this project. Theresa Tzakis provided an update on our progress to those in attendance. The luncheon raised $5,000.

One example of the various community events being held to benefit the GANHC during this time was the Millennium New Year Luncheon sponsored by The Hellenic Sisterhood of Tripolis held on February 12, 2000, at the Fountain Blue Banquet Hall. Tickets were $25 each. In a January 5, 2000, letter to the committee, Alexandra Kallas, president of the organization, wrote:

> On behalf of the Hellenic Sisterhood of Tripolis, it gives me great pleasure to inform you of our Millennium New Year Luncheon. As a philanthropic women's organization with a 73-year history in Chicago, we often have events that will specifically support a local Greek group or one in our hometown of Tripolis, Greece. Although we have supported you yearly with various donations totaling over $6,000, we would like to present the profits from our luncheon this year for the Building Fund. We realize how difficult it is to raise money and hope

Greek-American Nursing Home Committee

Congratulations Chicagoland Greek Americans
Our Nursing Home is No Longer
a Dream

The Streets Are In!
The Land Is Cleared!

Celebrate Father's Day With Us

A Picnic with Great Food & Music
On the Site of the Nursing Home
In Wheeling

Sunday, June 18th

1:00 to 5:00 p.m.

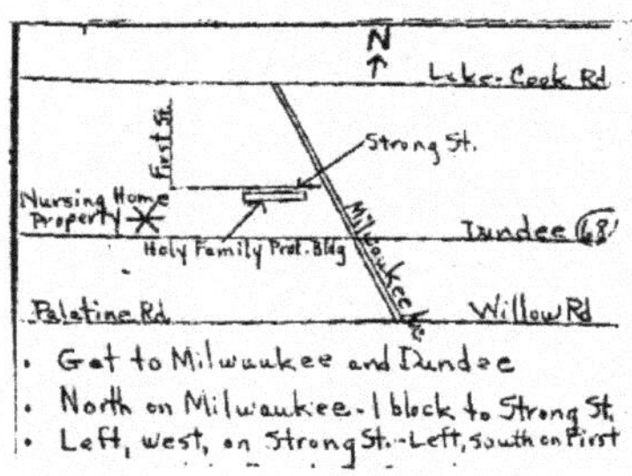

Plenty of Parking is Available

GANHC Father's Day Picnic flyer. June 18, 2000. John Psiharis collection.

> that our gift will benefit this drive. Although we don't have a solid amount yet, we are aspiring to a minimum amount of $2,000, and depending on attendance and generosity, it may even reach $3,000 for the Fund.

A.J. Maggio began their first day of work on the 7th of May. During a special dinner meeting at Costa's Restaurant to celebrate the HUD closing and the beginning of construction, the board approved payment of $60,000 to Mr. Maggio for fees related to obtaining various permits from the Village of Wheeling. The company that was digging at the property pulled out and a new excavator needed to be found. Risk hazard and flood insurance were approved, and the need for a project manager was discussed.

On June 18, GANHC hosted a Father's Day Picnic and festivities on the nursing home grounds. Despite the rain and occasional thunderstorms, the event was a success with hundreds in attendance. Co-chairs of the event were Jim Pirpiris and Gerry Garbis.

GANHC Treasurer John Secaras served as emcee and recognized significant donors including AHEPA, the Daughters of Penelope,

Philoptochos societies, "*topika somateia,*" and other fraternal and religious groups. John singled out the Hellenic Women's Philanthropic Society "Soteria," Dr. Mary Dochios Kamberos, and the Greek-American Restaurant Association (GARA) for their major support of the project and recognized Bill and Mary Kakavas for their significant contributions and fundraising prowess.

Event supporters included Jim and Rita Christie (Bon Ton Foods) for chickens and trimmings; Tom Pappas of Market Square Restaurant who loaned his executive chef, cooking and cleaning staff, and gave us access to his kitchens; Eleni and Demetri Bousis for cheeses, olives, tomatoes, and cucumbers; Paul Vadevoulis family; LeFrancais Bakery for Danish rolls, bagels, and croissants; McDonald's for napkins; Gordon Food Co. for assorted cookies; Frank Kuchuris (East Balt Commissary) buns and rolls; Chris Mendones (Cardinal Liquors) pop; Fritzy Konstantelos, ten cases of beer, and Sam Koutsoulis (Sam's Meats) locanico and hot dogs.

The rest of the year was spent focusing on a myriad of details, and of course, fundraising. This can be seen in several board meeting minutes:

> A July 24 meeting at the Greek Islands restaurant. The discussion included a report on the nursing home design. A color chart was passed around to board members. A neutral color was selected for the elevators with white on the outside. The walls will be a distinct color on each floor. The first floor will have a homey atmosphere. No decision on color has been reached yet, but there will be Greek flavor throughout. Dr. Kioutas met with neighbors at the property. They were pleased with the nursing home project, and the meeting went well. Discussion on a fall fundraiser. Concrete pouring had begun. Estimated completion in June 2001.
>
> An August 28 meeting at GACS. Construction progress and updates were discussed along with plans for a fall fundraiser. The steel structure was being fabricated, and the timetable was for one wing of the building to be erected every month. Underground plumbing for "B" Wing completed and "A" Wing" to be finished by the end of the week. Steel for "A" will be onsite on September 1. The roof is scheduled to be installed in December. We were informed that the late Mr. and Mrs. P. Ladas left the GANHC a bequest of about $100,000.
>
> An October 23 meeting at Annunciation Cathedral. The Board discussed an update from Diversified Management, and the project managers, and outlined our process forward. The Village of Wheeling will grant a certificate of occupancy when the project is complete. The papers are then sent to the state. One month for the state to review. Second month for them to visit and inspect. We should be able to open 90 days after the inspection. We need $2 million to open (we have $1.4 million to date). When we open the doors, we need $600,000, and the year after opening $1 million will be needed. We need to train Greek-speaking CNAs. GACS should explore creating a program for this. Approved the purchase of three washers

Toni Panos and John Rassogianis visit to check on construction progress. Circa 2001. John Rassogianis collection.

($5,800 each) and four dryers at $3,700 each for the laundry room. We need to approve the purchase of physical therapy whirlpool tubs. Dr. Kioutas reports that the whole facility is licensed for skilled care, but these beds can also be used for intermediate care.

Fundraising continued at a frenzied pace. Notable in this period were:

- April: Sts. Peter and Paul Philoptochos Society holds a brunch after church services to benefit the GANHC and $8,700 is raised.
- September 24: The American Hellenic Society of Berwyn hosts its 40th Anniversary Dinner Dance at the Skylite West, with the proceeds benefiting GANHC. Tickets are $35 each and music by Stevie "B" D.J.
- October 15: Order of AHEPA, Chicago Chapter #46 of District 13 "75th Anniversary Celebration Dinner Dance Honoring Dr. Theodosis Kioutas" at Avalon Elegant Banquets, with proceeds to benefit GANHC.
- November 4: The Hellenic Society of Constantinople hosts its annual dinner dance at Crystal Palace Banquets, 2648 Dempster Ave, Des Plaines, IL. Donation is $60 per person and the proceeds benefit GANHC.
- November 5: Gortinia Society has a fundraising dinner dance at Crystal Palace with proceeds to benefit GANHC.
- November 11: The Greek-American Restaurant Association holds a fundraiser in support of their $200,000 pledge to GANHC. The event is held at Crystal Palace Banquet Hall. Tickets are $40 per person.

- November 18: The Laconian Ladies and Misses Benevolent Society unanimously votes to donate $50,000 to the GANHC during a meeting at St. Demetrios Church.
- December 29: The Hellenic League holds its annual cotillion with a portion of the proceeds benefiting the GANHC. A donation of $50,000 from the proceeds of the Hellenic League's Crystal Ball and Debutante Cotillion 2000, held at the Chicago Hilton and Towers Hotel in Chicago was received.

A half-page essay written by Louis Atsaves entitled "A Dream Comes True! Community Succeeds in Building a Rehabilitation and Nursing Center," that appeared in the November 15, 2001, edition of the *Greek Star*, reflected on the significance of this monumental achievement. Louis was a leader within AHEPA. While the first part of this article is a poignant recollection of his grandmother and other older Greeks who could have benefitted from the nursing home and is included below, the second part of his article deals with the history of the nursing home effort, which is described in far more detail throughout this book, so it is not included here.

> **A Personal Reflection**
>
> I was walking to church one Saturday morning following my grandmother. The walk occurred nearly 40 years ago and was but a single city block if one took the shortcut through the Budlong School playground. I was pulling a little red wagon filled with homemade Greek pastries that she along with others had prepared during the week for a bake sale. She was part of an organization named "Soteria" which had dedicated itself since World War II to the construction of a "*gerokomio*" (nursing home) for elderly Greek Americans.
>
> My grandmother, Antonia, never saw the day when that dream would become a reality. She died following a very brief stay in a nursing home where she seemed to be the only person who spoke Greek. She was admitted to that nursing home when all other avenues of care for the elderly were exhausted, including home companions, nurses, and daily visits by a loving daughter, my aunt. Before being admitted to that nursing home, she would walk out of her home and walk, usually to Amundsen High School. The Chicago police found her on two occasions and would take her to St. Demetrios Church, where someone would identify her. The Chicago police often would find wandering elderly Greeks in the neighborhood and take them to the church.
>
> She would endlessly talk of events in Arna, Greece that had happened when she was a young child, vividly remembering small details of a day from her youth, for in her mind when she walked to Amundsen High School, she was going to school in the neighboring village. She would laugh and blush and protest

that she was far too young to have 15 grandchildren and 26 great-grandchildren. When speaking with her oldest grandson, she marveled that he had the same name as the man she married, and demanded to know his family history and why he claimed he was from Budlong Woods and not Kotsatina (Sparta), Greece.

She would insist that she just ate lunch, when she did not, and would stubbornly refuse to eat. My poor aunt, at that point in time, was exhausted and frazzled from the daily challenges posed by caring for her elderly mother, who could no longer care for herself. But in the end, *yiayia* Antonia would violently refuse to be put into a "*geronimo*," even after the years she spent trying to raise money for one.

During my teenage years, I often worked at my father's restaurant. I met two elderly Greek men then, one blinded in a mysterious circus accident, the second who claimed that he was 100 years old. 'Chris the blind man' lived by himself and rode the Halsted CTA bus to the corner of Fullerton and Lincoln avenues each day, where he would spend over an hour sitting at the restaurant counter with a roll and coffee, spiked with six spoons of sugar. It was the responsibility of the cashier to keep him company while working, along with reading aloud the occasional letter or postcard sent to him by an old circus friend. The teenaged cashier would soon notice that he would read the same series of crumpled letters out loud over and over again while being regaled with adventures and stories of when the circus was the king of entertainment in America. Several were postmarked years earlier.

Later Chris would board the Halsted bus and ride to Greek town where he would hang out in one of the restaurants and would later reappear at the counter in the evening for another cup of coffee. A lonely routine life replaced the earlier years of excitement.

'John' claimed to be 100 years old, and no one questioned him, as he looked his stated age. After drinking some free coffee at the counter, John would spend most of his day sitting on the windowsill in the front of the restaurant and watching customers coming in and out all day, especially the young pretty ladies. He had no relatives and lived in a one-room apartment half a block away on Fullerton, on the third floor, where there was no elevator. He and Chris the blind man would rarely speak to each other, and when words were exchanged, they were usually hostile.

Occasionally, an old circus friend would pick up Chris, and they would disappear for a day or two to visit a race track, John would then repeatedly ask what happened to Chris, then scowl when

Chris would later reappear. One day, John did not appear at the restaurant, and Chris was the first to notice.

Several days passed and the police finally agreed to check up on him. He was found in his bathroom, sprawled out on the floor, having passed away a few days earlier.

During all of our lifetimes, we all have run across and met such individuals. Many are part of our immediate families. We all have stories to tell about them.

I am now 46 years old. The Greek-American community of Chicago finally is opening a facility that would have cared for *Yiayia* Antonia, Chris the Blindman, and John. It's being called the Greek American Rehabilitation and Nursing Center located in Wheeling, IL. It will begin caring for its first patients just before my 47th birthday at the very start of next year.

One of our largest fundraising events was the November 26 "A Dream in Progress Celebration Dinner Dance" at the Crystal Palace Banquets. It featured a capacity turnout of 650 guests and raised more than $500,000. The emcee was NBC TV Chicago news anchor Allison Rosati. The menu featured: avgolemono soup, Crystal Palace salad, bon filet or broiled salmon, double baked potato, vegetables du jour, dinner rolls, wine, ice cream, assorted pastries, and fresh fruit. Tickets were $75 each.

Underwriting donors included: Dr. Mary Dochios Kamberos ($50,000) and the Lakonia Ladies Society ($50,000). Donating $2,500 or more were the American Hellenic Society of Berwyn, Mr. and Mrs. John Apostolou, Mrs. Anastasia Kakis (in memory of Stella Svourakis and Stanley Kakis), Mr. and Mrs. Paul Kalpake, Dr. and Mrs. Theodosis Kioutas, Mr. and Mrs. Steve Mash, and Mrs. Estelle P. Strempek. That evening, Senator Adeline Geo-Karis read a resolution of the Illinois State Senate congratulating the GANHC, and Pat Michalski, representing Illinois Governor George Ryan, extended congratulations to the gathered guests.

A full-page article (including photos) on the back page of the January 18, 2001, issue of the *Greek Star* prepared by John Rassogianis and Elaine Thomopoulos entitled "Greek American Nursing Home Crystal Palace Fundraiser in Excess of $500,000," described the energy and enthusiasm of the evening:

"A Dream in Progress" invitation. November 26, 2000. John Psiharis collection.

'Kosmos, kosmos, kosmos' was a refrain dramatically, almost prayerfully, intoned by Greek radio host John Kanellos in the not too, too far distant past. Yet these emphatically uttered words marvelously captured the emotion of the big Nov. 26 turnout for the Greek-American Nursing Home fundraiser gala. The theme was 'A Dream in Progress,' and the site was the Crystal Palace - and it was *kosmos, kosmos, kosmos* for the nearly 650 guests. Mrs. Stella Mash, chairperson, and her committee would certainly agree with these long-spoken words used to hype great events to a receptive *omogenia*.

The capacity turnout and the enthusiasm generated by Allison Rosati, NBC Channel 5 News Anchor, and mistress of ceremony, made the event one of the main attractions of the year. Addressing the guests, Rosati traced the beginnings and development of the nursing home dream, referring to it as 'just a thought, just an idea, just a possibility, now a reality,' where 'families will be caring for families.' She continued, 'Our numbers are strong, our hearts are big, our people are generous.'

Rosati's presence contributed to an occasion laced with a mix of the serious, the sumptuous, and the sensuous, each mood balancing the other, blending in with the musical tones provided by John Linardakis and his orchestra. Indeed, the melody of words and music that went on inside the Crystal Palace coincided with the magical spirit of the winter theme design by Dean Quintas. Elegant floral centerpieces highlighted crystal vases high on each table. Boughs of snow-tipped pinecones cascading from evergreen branches revealed tiny white orchids. Banquet tables were accented by elegantly draped chairs covered with white covers, carefully tied with oversized bows – all of which were donated by Senya and Paul Kalpake and Stella and Steve Mash.

Giant photographs of the Greek-American Nursing Home in various stages of construction, taken by Sam Tzakis, were displayed in the Crystal Palace lobby. Welcoming the guests were the board of directors: Gerry Garbis, Helen Georges, Bill and Mary Kakavas, George and Sophie Lekas, Toni Panos, Jim Pirpiris, John Psiharis, John Rassogianis, Eugenia Seifer, Tina Spiratos, Elaine Thomopoulos, and Theresa Tzakis. Kudos to George A. Lekas, chairperson of the publicity committee, for a great job.

The meticulous planning of Stella Mash's dinner dance committee was apparent throughout the evening. In her remarks, she expressed her gratitude and deep appreciation to her co-chairperson, Helen Georges, and to the outstanding work of her committee members. She continued by referring to the nursing home odyssey as, 'the first in the Midwest, the second in the nation.' In saluting Dr. Theodosis Kioutas, she said, 'This project never could have come to this point without you, the people, and the organizations who have supported and collaborated with us in approaching our goal. Dr. Kioutas' dream, his vision, is becoming a reality. Dr. Kioutas, we did it. You are the man of the year. Congratulations.'

Dr. Kioutas, in his brief remarks, during this emotional evening, reminded the guests of the fulfillment of a great task given to us, now being completed. 'Our generation is fulfilling the dream of past generations,' he said.

John Secaras, GANHC treasurer and fund-raising chairman, thanked Dr. Kioutas and the early members of the organization who started the project. He reported that construction had begun in May 2000. He advised that now, months later, the steel structure is up, floors have been poured, and the stone and brick are being laid. Secaras declared that the GANHC met all HUD requirements to guarantee the building loan at a favorable interest rate. He emphasized, however, that it was not without the help of the community and three special entities – Dr. Mary Dochios Kamberos (with current pledges and contributions far in excess of $800,000), the Women's Philanthropic Society SOTERIA ($330,000), and the Greek-American Restaurant Association (GARA) ($306,000).

Among the evening's surprises, Illinois State Senator Adeline Geo-Karis read a resolution by the Illinois State Senate commending Dr. Kioutas for his lifetime of excellent, responsible, and compassionate medical practice, as well as his civic and charitable good works. Pat Michalski, of the State of

> Illinois Ethnic Affairs Office, presented Dr. Kioutas with a book listing all state offices from Governor George Ryan for his outstanding accomplishments. Dr. Kioutas graciously expressed his appreciation but emphasized that the nursing home is a community effort. He thanked the board and the many individuals and organizations who have given their support so generously.
>
> Guests that evening were very generous in making contributions toward the needed start-up operation expenses. All were touched by the $50,000 donated by the Laconia Ladies Society and presented by Eugenia Stathakis, president, and Beulah Iatropoulos, vice president. In her stirring remarks, Iatropoulos said, 'The women that started this organization, our mothers and grandmothers, are long gone. They left us a treasury and a fine membership. We did not squander what they left us. We had to find a cause – the Greek American Nursing Home.'
>
> What a wonderful evening! What a great committee: Mary Dennis, Helen Flessas, Bill Kakavas, Harriet Karamidas, Ethel Kotsovos, Frances V. Pappas, Betty Quintas, Dean T. Quintas, John and Mary Secaras, Laverne Stellas, and Theresa Tzakis.

As we began 2001, about 35 percent of the construction had been completed, and $3,114,088 was expended towards the cap. By the end of February, construction was 52 percent complete. In April we began to get complaints from the contractor that too many visitors were coming on-site without authorization. When board members visited, it was with the knowledge of Mr. Maggio who was usually there to walk us through. These were members of the public and donors, and there was a concern about safety as well as construction delays. More fencing was put up. Although we spread the word in our publicity, it was difficult to stop something like this and the complaints continued for the duration of the project. We also authorized the purchase of a new generator for $39,710. In June we were informed that 35 additional parking spaces needed to be added at a cost between $65,000 and $75,000. Shut-off valves in each room at an additional cost of $10,513 were necessary.

"The Greek-American Nursing Home Will Soon Be a Reality," proclaimed an article in the February 2001 edition of *Mosaic*, the monthly newsletter of Holy Apostles Greek Orthodox Church. It read in part:

> For years, elderly Greek-Americans who were finding it increasingly difficult to live without assistance, have had few options. They could reside with relatives or take up residence in a senior housing facility.
>
> But that second option often led to alienation and loneliness because the Chicagoland Greek-American community had no

nursing home that catered exclusively to the elderly of Greek descent.

This shortfall is about to change thanks to the efforts of many in the community who saw a need and responded generously.

In May of last year, construction began on the Greek-American Nursing Home on eight bucolic acres in Wheeling. When completed around August of this year, the home will include a Greek Orthodox chapel, a menu that will routinely feature Greek dishes, employees who are bi-lingual in Greek and English, and a social calendar that will offer Greek cultural and social events in and outside the residence, among other amenities.

'The Greek-American Nursing Home was conceived as a means to provide for the medical, social and spiritual needs of the fragile and ill members of the Greek-American community,' the organizing committee states in its most recent newsletter. The focus will be to offer 'an environment which will support individual dignity, cultural heritage, access to religious worship and quality care – all essential to daily life.'

Many in the community have made generous donations of money, time, and effort to get the $12.5 million project underway. On November 26, 2000, the nursing home committee celebrated that effort and the rapid progress with a dinner dance featuring Allison Rosati, NBC Channel 5 News anchor. The celebration, at the Crystal Palace Banquets in Des Plaines, raised slightly more than $500,000 – funds that will be needed to meet operating expenses until 70 percent of the facility is filled.

Other generous donors included Dr. Mary Dochios Kamberos, who gave more than $550,000 to the effort. In addition, the Hellenic Women's Philanthropic Association, Inc. donated its entire treasury of $330,000. 'Soteria' had collected the money for the past 50 years for the purpose of establishing a home for the aged. Also, the Greek-American Restaurant Association made two contributions totaling $306,000.

That outpouring of support was the culmination of an effort that began 50 years ago, when 'Soteria' and the Greek Archdiocese Welfare Foundation were established to pursue, among other things, fundraising for the establishment of a Greek-American nursing home. Those organizations, while doing good work for a number of causes, were unable to establish a nursing home.

In the 1980s, statistics showed that the senior population was exploding. To serve the growing number of elderly Greek-Americans, Dr. Theodosis Kioutas and four others formed the board of directors of the Greek-American Nursing Home Committee, a non-profit organization in 1985. In 1994, the group purchased 8.5 acres in Wheeling for $425,000 as the site of the

The Greek-American Nursing Home under construction, spring 2001. John Psiharis collection.

nursing home. The land is bordered by the Wheeling Senior Center and the Wheeling Park District.

After that, events moved rapidly. Within a year, Wheeling officials approved zoning for the building. In 1997, the Illinois Health Facilities Planning Board authorized planning and construction to begin.

The architectural firm of SAS Architects & Planners of Northbrook was selected in 1998. Bulldozers began clearing the land on May 25, 2000, and the committee held a picnic on June 18 on the site to celebrate the start of construction. Spirits are running high as construction progresses, but support is still needed.

In 2001, GANHC amended the bylaws to increase the size of the board from 25 to 28 and provided for honorary board members. Bishop Iakovos became the Honorary Chairman. Also, during this period, we were gratified to receive a donation of a Baldwin Piano from Bill and Mary Kakavas.

Fundraising was in overdrive. There were several events held for our benefit and we were organizing our fundraisers as well. GANHC was in the process of selling $165,000 in stock donated by Dr. Kamberos as well as other stock that had been donated by James Christie, A. Anthony, and Dennis Karalis. $100,000 from the Ladas estate was also in process.

In June, First Health Care was selected as the new management company. We had initially hired Bethany Methodist but for some reason, it did not work out. Neither Elaine nor I remember why there was a change in the

The *Greek-American Nursing Home Committee Newsletter.* Circa 2001. Elaine Thomopoulos collection.

management company, but we do remember that Arthur Salk, the architect, recommended First Health Care.

At the time, it was felt that given the major decisions, many moving pieces, and our collective inexperience, it was best to hire nursing home professionals to run the home for the first few years to ensure we got off to a good start. Everything that we achieved was in jeopardy if we failed to operate according to a myriad of codes, policies, and practices governing every facet of a nursing home.

Among the challenges were fully staffing the facility from scratch, creating human resources, training, and accounting systems, establishing medical procedures, and selecting purveyors for food, medical supplies, therapy providers, and pharmaceuticals. We needed to purchase washers, dryers, refrigeration, china, pots, pans, and bed linens to name just a few of the many matters we dealt with. We also continued to focus on fundraising. Having a management company would ensure that the facility opened on schedule and in compliance with all standards and allow us to get our footing. After the three-year contract ended, GANHC would take over the operations of the facility.

A June 22, 2001, written update provided to board members by the management company detailed areas being worked on: "Hiring the executive director, obtaining opening day list of equipment and supplies, obtaining three bids when appropriate for purchases, determining facility name, visiting two Boston area Greek facilities, HUD (management agreement and payment protocols for purchases), development of purchase order systems, meeting with Pat Sweitzer, cash flow projection, determination of key staff (Greek), building delivery date, preliminary rates from IDPA, setting up ongoing meetings with executive liaison committee, meeting with individual responsible for fund raising efforts, marketing (demographics, competitive pricing structure, advertising, data base with family listings and major communities, church listings, senior or elder clubs, summer events, list of parish members, market research on Greek papers and magazines, contact with other Greek homes in North America to obtain various information, developing environmental plan for facility, and identifying referral sources - including hospital and senior placement centers), and preparing of job descriptions for facility."

A review of meeting minutes and notes from the second half of 2001 illustrates some of the matters that were discussed and decided:

- July 9: A fundraising dinner dance is planned at Crystal Palace on the Sunday after Thanksgiving. The board narrows the possibilities for the name of the facility to three: Hippocrates Home - a Greek-American Nursing & Rehabilitation Center, (Reverse); Greek-American Nursing & Rehabilitation Center - Hippocrates Home or Greek-American Nursing & Rehabilitation Center. First Health Care recommended Susan M. Barbian as administrator.
- July 20: GANHC and First Health Care Associates Liaison Committee at FHC offices. Agenda items include building status; operating projections; supply bids; medical director and physician team; name and logo; security systems, Wanderguard, parking lot, and pond aerator; staff hiring, and Frank Macknick, marketing consultant. Susan Barbian, the executive director, will begin on August 6.

- July 23: GANHC Board meeting at St. Demetrios Church. Discussion includes additional construction expenses of $62,000 for the extra parking spaces, $28,358 for fire lane replacement due to an undercut, and $20,402 for additional security cameras. Bids for resident safety systems were reviewed. Dr. Kioutas, John Secaras, and First Health Care to speak to American National Bank about obtaining a line of credit.
- August 24: GANHC Executive Board meeting. Agenda items include answering services versus answering machines, occupancy timeline, advertising for key staff including the Director of Nursing (DON), bumper guards in the parking lot, exterior signs, and copy machine quotes.
- August 25th Board meeting at St. Demetrios Church. Discussion and updates on construction, First Health Care meetings, marketing, and fundraising. Frank Macnick was hired as marketing director based on the recommendation of First Health Care. Construction report: Some rooms need re-tiling of floors and walls at the contractor's expense. The telephone line has not yet been hooked up. Many visitors are stopping by the property causing both delays and potential safety hazards. Initial rates established: Double occupancy $145/day, Private room $165/day, Alzheimer's/Dementia $165/day.
- September 24: Board meeting at St. Demetrios Church. Financial, fundraising, and construction reports are on the agenda. Furniture delivery is scheduled for October 22.
- October 22: GANHC Board meeting at Saints Peter & Paul Church. Focus on planning for the November fundraiser and discussing the technological needs of the facility.
- November 19: Board meeting at St. Demetrios Church. Construction update. Mr. Maggio is not making progress per the timeline and a meeting will be held with him on November 20 to discuss this. If that fails, we may need to pursue legal remedies. Mr. Maggio has seven days to proceed with plans for us to obtain the Certificate of Occupancy. The sprinkler system is leaking, which is not uncommon when first installed. The Wheeling Fire Department inspection was passed. The Village of Wheeling, Illinois Department of Public Health, HUD, and nurses' organization's inspections are still to come. The committee to establish the chapel convened: Fr. Massouras, Presbytera Skoulas, and Maria Mueller. Fr. Massouras has a list of items needed for the chapel. Mr. Maggio sent a $1,000 donation. Dr. Dochios said this is the most beautiful she has ever seen.
- November 30: GANHC-First Health Care Team meeting. Discussion on hiring progress and building status. Deposit of $1,900 for dishes and silverware. The Greek translation of documents.
- December 14: GANHC Executive Board meeting to discuss the selection of vendors, rearranging furniture, and hiring progress for dietitian and dietary manager.

On November 25, 2001, the GANHC held a gala banquet, "The Dream Comes True," at Crystal Palace Banquets. The tone was subdued given the

"A Dream Comes True" invitation cover. November 25, 2001. John Psiharis collection.

recent September 11, 2001, terror attacks. The special guest of honor was Dr. Mary Dochios Kamberos, GANHC's first "Super Mega Donor." The invocation and benediction were offered by Metropolitan Iakovos of Krinis, Presiding Hierarch, Diocese of Chicago. Music by the Linardakis Band. The menu consisted of avgolemono soup; Crystal Palace salad; bon filet, broiled salmon, or vegetarian plate; oven-browned potatoes, vegetables du jour, dinner rolls, wine, ice cream, assorted pastries, fresh fruit and coffee, and tea. A champagne toast kicked off the evening. Sofia Marousis was the general chairperson and Bette Brown and Theresa Tzakis were co-chairs. Net income from the event was $214,541.

A post-event article entitled "Greek-American Nursing Home Fundraiser Nets $214,500," in the February 7, 2002, issue of the *Greek Star* reported:

> The Chairperson of the event Sofia Marousis welcomed the 900 guests. The theme of the evening, 'The Dream Comes True,' celebrated the completion of the construction and furnishing of the Greek-American Rehabilitation and Nursing Centre located in Wheeling, IL.
>
> After thanking her dinner dance committee and the governing board of the Greek-American Nursing Home Committee (GANHC), Marousis introduced the speakers of the evening: John H. Secaras, Dr. Theodosis Kioutas, and Chris Tomaras.
>
> The treasurer, Secaras, congratulated Marousis and gave a brief report stating, among other things, that further initial operating funds were still needed. The full amount recommended was $3 million, of which $2.3 million had been raised. He also thanked

all donors, particularly the evening's super mega benefactor, Dr. Mary Dochios Kamberos; and the mega benefactors, Hellenic Women's Philanthropic Association, 'Soteria,' and the Greek American Restaurant Association (GARA). Other noteworthy contributors ($100,000 or more) were thanked by Secaras in alphabetical order: AHEPA, Georgia Boolookas, Jim and Rita Christie, William and Mary Kakavas, Dr. Theodosis, and Anna Kioutas, and Chris Tomaras. During the evening, the Eisenberg Foundation for Charities contributed an additional $38,000, adding its name to the list of noteworthy contributors.

Dr. Kioutas introduced his officers and governing board, commending each for his/her help. He also thanked the entire Greek-American community of Chicago, without whose help this dream would not have come true. Fundraising was handled by Tomaras and $214,500 was netted from all the proceeds of the dinner dance.

The highlight of the evening was a special presentation to Dr. Kamberos, the first million-dollar donor to the nursing home. Flanked by the officers and governing board of the committee, she was presented with a crystal piece etched with the nursing home building and logo. Dr. Kamberos was referred to as the 'American Hellenic Philanthropist of the Decade.'

Among the dignitaries present were Metropolitan Iakovos of Krinis, Counsel General of Greece Gabriel Coptsidis; Illinois State Senator Adeline Geo-Karis, AHEPA 13th District Governor, John Dalapas; and AHEPA Governor Stash Betzelos.

A December 2001 article in the *Greek Star* highlighted the economic impact of this project.

Over $20 million will be added to the local economy by the Greek American Rehabilitation and Care Centre annually. Due to open in the first quarter of 2002, the Centre will employ in excess of 165 professional staff. The Greek American Care Center will provide rehabilitation, nursing, and Alzheimer's care to 204 people when fully occupied.

Annual purchases of food, medicine, supplies, and equipment made locally by employed staff will create a positive financial impact on the greater Chicago area. Total staff salaries alone are estimated to be between $4.54 and $5 million annually.

Staff will include registered nurses, licensed practical nurses, nursing assistants, therapists, trained Alzheimer's care specialists, social workers, and activities personnel. In addition, the Greek American Centre will employ a complete range of support staff in dietary, maintenance, and housekeeping, and a

> full complement of office and accounting personnel. Volunteers in various areas will also be welcome.

An article by Christopher Ganos entitled "Greek-American Nursing Home Opens," appeared in a 2001 issue of the *Chicago Greek Circle*:"

> Wheeling, Illinois, is home to the first Greek-American rehabilitation and nursing facility in Illinois and the second such facility in the United States. After 16 years of tireless effort by the Greek-American Nursing Home Committee and nearly five decades since the need for such a facility was identified, the Greek American Rehabilitation and Nursing Centre opens its doors this fall.
>
> In the early 1900s, Chicago was the destination for many Greek immigrants who journeyed to the United States to pursue the 'American Dream." Through the first half of the 20th century, these Greek pioneers steadily achieved success in business. They built comfortable homes for their families, as well as churches in their communities. While many of those who came to the United States thought that they would eventually go back to Greece, far more stayed in America permanently. After World War II, the need for a facility to care for aging Greeks became apparent.
>
> In the 1950s, the Hellenic Woman's Philanthropic Association, Inc., "Soteria," began raising money for a nursing home. Their vision was for a facility that would address the physical and medical, as well as the cultural and social, needs of its residents. This goal was very specific, and they did not waiver [sic] in their commitment. Over the years many organizations asked Soteria for donations to various causes. None of these fulfilled their criteria until the Greek-American Nursing Home Committee presented them with their proposal. Soteria donated their entire treasury of $330.000. Many other donations followed. To date, the largest donation by an individual ($880,000) was made by Dr. Mary Dochios Kamberos, and the largest donation by an association ($306,000) was made by the Greek American Restaurant Association (GARA).
>
> After much deliberation, an eight-acre building site with a pond was chosen near Dundee Road and Milwaukee Avenue in Wheeling. Although the residents of Wheeling were very receptive to the idea, and the zoning board voted unanimously to approve the nursing home plans, the committee had to clear one last hurdle before breaking ground for this state-of-the-art facility: obtaining a certificate of need from the State of Illinois. Illinois had placed a moratorium on building nursing homes in certain areas. Despite this moratorium, a certificate of need was requested and a variance by ethnic group was granted after a study determined that 230 Greeks required nursing care during a

one-year period. Thus, the Greek American Nursing Centre was built.

The building's Greek ethnicity is immediately apparent – from the Greek Key design that was used in the masonry to the stately columns that flank the entrance and rear patio. Every effort is being made to provide for the cultural, as well as the professional, needs of the residents. A chapel built in accordance with Orthodox tradition will be available 24 hours a day for residents to visit. Orthodox clergy will conduct services, celebrate special holidays, visit residents, and be part of the nursing center community. The committee is also seeking bilingual staff for residents who prefer to speak Greek. This staff, to the extent available, will be both in administration and resident care positions. Greek meals will be routinely served, to the extent medical needs permit.

In addition to long-term care, the 204-bed Greek American Nursing Centre will offer respite care for loved ones when caretakers are away on vacation or tending to their own emergency, or when an individual simply needs a period of rejuvenation. A fourth-floor wing will provide compassionate specialized care for those with memory loss (including Alzheimer's disease and other forms of dementia). Rehabilitation services, including physical and occupational therapy, and hospice care will also be available.

Even after residents from throughout the Midwest move into the Nursing Home Centre, the Greek American Nursing Home Committee will continue its efforts to provide for the success of the facility. What was once just a dream has now become a reality through the dedication of these individuals and the support of the Greek community.

The Last Mile

Greeks have been involved with medicine since the days of Hippocrates, continuing in the desire to assist and aid the ill is the basis for a dream come true. Today, the Chicagoland Greek American community has accomplished one of its greatest goals set over 50 years ago - the construction of a center to care for the elderly. This new center proudly boasts of another Greek truism, '*filoxenia*.' In Greek, the word '*filoxenia*' literally means 'friend of a stranger.' The Greek American Rehabilitation and Nursing Centre is set to open its doors in March and beckons friends and neighbors of all ethnicities and creeds to experience Greek hospitality and quality care in a truly beautiful setting. (*Greek Press* editorial, February 24, 2002).

With a soft opening planned for March 2002, there was little time for rest. Construction was in the final stages, and the broader economic impact of our project was significant. In December, it was revealed that the center would employ more than 165 professional staff. Annual purchases of food, medicine, supplies, and equipment made locally will add to the positive financial impact of the area. Total staff salaries alone were estimated to be between $4.54 and $5 million.

First Health Care selected Susan Barbian to serve as administrator. Although she wasn't Greek, Susan had served as an administrator and as a director of nursing in other nursing homes. In addition to being a licensed nursing home administrator, she was also a registered nurse. Personality-wise, some of us sensed she was not a good fit, and once we opened several conflicts occurred between her and the board and staff members.

Based on the management company's recommendation, we contracted out the provision of physical and other therapies to outside providers. I, and others, were uncomfortable with outsourcing so many functions to outsiders, but the urgency of these matters weighed heavily on us. We had to create a nursing home from scratch in every way, and although each of us brought our unique backgrounds and skill sets to the table, we needed professional help. There was no room for error and no time to waste. Sub-contracting services to outside providers seemed the best route at the time, although we planned to internalize these functions in the coming years.

Key hires included the director of nursing, admissions director, marketing director, social services director, dietary director, activities director, and housekeeping supervisor. Efforts were made to reach out to the Greek community to fill these positions but to limited success. Although we preferred to hire Greek speakers, when possible, the decision was based on qualifications. There was a balance of both Greek and non-Greek-speaking employees along with some who spoke Spanish, Tagalog, and other languages.

It became apparent that we needed to encourage students of Greek descent to pursue degrees in nursing, social work, physical therapy, and related fields since there was not a large pool of qualified Greek-speaking applicants to consider from these disciplines. We discussed that down the road, the GANHC should consider adopting a scholarship program of some sort to help with this and that GACS create employment and training programs to funnel qualified job seekers to the nursing home.

For a time, it seemed like almost everywhere I went I encountered questions about working for the new facility. I referred some people to apply for employment. These were people that I had encountered either through GACS or in Greek or professional circles.

Perrie Veremis Hayes was hired as marketing director to lead a two-pronged marketing plan that focused on both the Greek and broader communities as well as targeting physicians, hospitals, trust officers, and other potential referral sources. An emphasis was placed on outreach to Greek doctors, especially those who were affiliated with nearby hospitals. We began marketing months before the actual opening of the facility to facilitate patient referrals. Within the Greek community, efforts were focused on those who had loved ones in need of care or who might consider transferring a patient from another facility. These marketing efforts also complemented our fundraising.

Soon the inspections began. First were local officials including the Wheeling zoning and fire departments followed by others including plumbing, electrical, building, and elevator inspections. Then state inspections including the Illinois Department of Public Health and Office of the Fire Marshall occurred. On a few occasions, tweaks needed to be made to be approved. I recall problems with toilets and patient call signals that needed to be corrected. In all, the project came in at about what was budgeted without any significant deviations or difficulties.

Once structural inspections concluded, another round of inspections came into play. The certifying agencies including H.U.D., Medicare, and Medicaid (Illinois Department of Public Aid) began their due diligence. At some point, we were granted a provisional license by the state to begin operations. It allowed us to open our doors on a limited basis with several patients as residents. In effect, it was a trial run.

In February the GANHC began offering exclusive pre-opening tours to benefactors and other supporters. This included VIP tours provided by board members for Metropolitan Iakovos, AHEPA leaders, Philoptochos societies, organization presidents, and major donors. On March 3, Metropolitan Iakovos and the GANHC board hosted an *Agiasmos* (Blessing of the Waters) service and a preview tour. More than 400 were in attendance. Metropolitan Iakovos proclaimed the nursing home a "five-star hotel for seniors." The facility was state-of-the-art. There was tremendous enthusiasm within the community that this long-held goal had been achieved.

A headline on the front page of the Sunday, March 3, 2002, *Daily Herald* proclaimed, "New Nursing Home Good for Greeks and Suburbs." The article by staff writer Cass Cliatt reported:

> Six years in the making, the Greek American Rehabilitation Nursing Centre is set to open the doors of its lavish Wheeling campus.
>
> A small lake, walkways, and a 204-bed facility on North First Street will attract Greek-Americans from throughout the

Northwest suburbs and Chicago, Wisconsin, Indiana, and even as far as Idaho, administrators said.

The area could see the benefit of $20 million a year moving through suburban towns, Executive Director Susan Barbian said.

Wheeling Economic Development Director William D. Whitmer said it's difficult to gauge the exact financial impact of a specialty business such as a nursing home, but the village can't help but benefit from the added services.

The center will provide clients with long-term nursing care, rehabilitation services, and respite care, becoming only the third in the United States to cater its services to a large Greek-American community.

'We try to be good citizens and do business with local people as best we can,' Barbian said. 'That's important because we're a part of this community, and we want other people to succeed in this community as well.'

The center will bring about 175 jobs to the area, using a bilingual staff and a menu to cater to a Greek population that numbers about 180,000 in metropolitan Chicago, administrators said.

Still, the success of the nonprofit center will depend on the services it can provide to clients of all nationalities throughout the area.

The center began its struggle to open in the 1950s when a committee of Greek-Americans led by Dr. Theodosis Kioutas of Wilmette decided the local Greek population needed a place to care for its ailing relatives [sic]. *

'This is a need for the Greek community, especially for families of the elderly people who came many years ago here, and they have some language difficulty,' Kioutas said. 'When they get older, even if they speak English, they revert to the mother tongue.'

The Greek American Rehabilitation Nursing Home Committee became registered with the state 15 years ago, gaining the ability to open a nonprofit facility.

The committee bought its site in Wheeling in 1994 and spent years raising $4 million before breaking ground in June 2000. The U.S. Department of Urban Development provided a loan for the remainder of the $14 million project.

Now, the center is ready for a blessing ceremony today with His Eminence Metropolitan Iakovos of Krinis.

> 'We have a total of 85 people waiting on a list to get in,' Barbian said. 'They inquired as early as a year ago about coming in.'
>
> Wheeling's Whitmer expects the village will benefit from the families and employees using the facility in the village.
>
> 'The employee base will be spending their dollars in Wheeling,' Whitmer said. 'Whether they're local residents or whether they're commuting here, we'll be able to capture some of the associated expenses of going to work and eating lunch.'
>
> Administrators think the location of the center in Wheeling is ideal for its proximity to the growing number of families who attend Greek Orthodox churches in Des Plaines, Elmhurst, Glenview, Lincolnshire, Niles, Palatine, and Chicago.
>
> The Greek-American Nursing Centre will hold a public open house and tour for families interested from 2 to 4 p.m. on March 17 at the center, 220 N. First St.

*The article inaccurately reported that Dr. Kioutas started Soteria in the 1950s. He was not involved with Soteria before their support of the GANHC. GACS was founded in 1982, and the nursing home committee was launched thereafter. GANHC was formally incorporated in 1985. Dr. Kioutas was part of GACS and the GANHC beginning in 1982.

A front-page story on March 4th, by Eileen O. Dady, correspondent to the *Daily Herald* newspaper, entitled "Generations-old Dream Finally Realized Sunday," covered the grand opening event:

> A dream started generations ago by Greek American women after the end of World War II came to fruition Sunday in Wheeling.
>
> Daughters and granddaughters had tears in their eyes as the leader of the Greek Orthodox Church in the Midwest, Metropolitan Iakovos of Krinis, dedicated the new Greek-American Rehabilitation & Nursing Centre in Wheeling.
>
> 'This is such a big day. I called people back in Greece to tell them,' said Tina Spiratos of Glenview, whose mother saved for this day.
>
> Nearly 100 guests gathered in the chapel of the new facility for the blessing. They included members of the surrounding Orthodox clergy, board members, and major donors; along with descendants of the Greek-American women's organization.
>
> The bishop sang a litany of Greek prayers and blessed the gathering with incense, before performing a formal sprinkling rite to portions of the four-story building itself.

One week ago, the facility admitted its first two patients. Another 85 are on the waiting list, officials said, but they are waiting for their next public health inspection before admitting more patients. They hope to begin admitting 15 at a time, they said.

'Their dream came true,' said Theresa Tzakis of Vernon Hills. 'It's a big day for us.'

Tzakis' mother joined with other women to form the Hellenic Women's Philanthropic Association 'Soteria,' which means 'savior' in Greek, back in the 1950s. They began saving for a healthcare facility for elderly Greek American residents.

'It started with 50-cent lunches,' Spiratos said, 'and that grew into $320,000. Once they obtained this property, and with the certificate of need from the state of Illinois, we turned over our bank accounts to them.'

Dr. Theo Kioutas, a Wilmette physician who is credited with spearheading the drive to open the healthcare facility, credits the women's organization with starting the movement to obtain the $4 million they started with to construct the facility. The U.S. Department of Urban Development provided a loan for the remainder of the $14 million project.

'They were the momentum,' Kioutas says of the women. 'After they made their donation, everything started to come together.'

Guests toured the skilled nursing care facility, taking in all the amenities on the first floor, brightly decorated with framed prints of Greece. The upper floors included semi-private and private rooms, with dining rooms on each floor overlooking the large pond. The fourth floor will care for Alzheimer's and dementia patients. 'People in our ethnicity don't have a facility for the elderly,' Kioutas said. 'For people that came here so long ago, and don't go back to the old country, they can stay here. It will mean a lot to be able to share Greek food, religious services, and even some of the language with others.'

Kioutas and admissions officials stressed the facility is open to anyone from the community, of any denomination. 'We're all Americans,' he added.

On March 6, the GANHC hosted lunch and tours for 50 guests from the neighboring Wheeling Senior Center.

Elizabeth Poulos and Nia Adinamis Canning hold the distinction of being the first two residents of the new Greek-American Rehabilitation & Nursing Centre. This soft opening allowed the home to get up and running and to work out any kinks before additional patients moved in. Inspections were frequent and examined all facets of the operations including health care, dietary, financial, recordkeeping, and compliance with applicable standards and policies at the federal, state, and local levels. Findings were addressed or corrected.

We were then allowed to expand our census to 22. While the facility was fully staffed and operational, revenue was limited to 22 patients. Although these costs were factored into the financial plan, they were still significant. After another round of inspections, we were granted final approval to open the doors.

In time, a long-term grand vision emerged. It foresaw the nursing home as the first phase of what was informally referred to as a "Greek Village." As imagined, the village would be a hub for our community's older adults, at whatever level of care they may require, and provide for easy transitions between these care options as warranted. It incorporated adult day care and assisted living on an expanded campus offering seniors a spectrum of interconnected long-term care options from which they could seamlessly transfer as care needs changed. It envisioned the nursing home kitchen providing meals to these programs, as well as for a meals-on-wheels program serving homebound seniors within the community. Charity care would be available for those in need so that no one is turned away.

Red Carpet Roll Out

The official ribbon cutting was held on Sunday, March 17, 2002. Although we were not able to enroll more than two trial residents until the operating license from the state was received, the ribbon-cutting was the official opening.

A pre-opening VIP reception for benefactors, key supporters, elected officials, and community leaders was held on Friday, March 15. About 300 guests attended this elegant event featuring a string quartet, harpist, and bouzouki player. Each guest received a rose and souvenir program booklet on arrival. A buffet table was adorned with delicious offerings provided by Master Caterers.

The menu featured:

- Smoked Salmon. Thin sliced boneless smoked salmon, lemon wedges, and capers served by a uniformed chef.
- Whole roast beef au jus and roast turkey breast are carved for miniature sandwiches by a uniformed chef.
- Croissant rolls, silver dollar rolls, multi-grain rolls, deli-style mustard, mayonnaise, whipped cream cheese.

The Greek American Nursing Home Committee

invites you to attend

The Grand Opening

of the

Greek American Rehabilitation and Nursing Centre

220 N. First Street • Wheeling, Illinois 60090

(Milwaukee Ave. 1 block N. of Dundee Rd. to Strong Ave. W. to First St. S.)

Friday, March 15, 2002

Wine and Hors d'oeuvres 5 - 8 p.m.

Please respond by March 12th 847-459-8700

GANHC VIP Grand Opening invitation. March 15, 2002. John Psiharis collection.

- Chilled grilled fresh vegetable display overflowing out of terra cotta pots. Zucchini, eggplant, mushrooms, sweet onions, carrots, sweet potatoes, and red and green peppers. Balsamic vinaigrette reduction.
- Honeydew gazebo toppling over with fresh grapes, strawberries, and whole and cubed cheeses in an artful display which may include Feta, Kefalograviera, Kasseri, Sharp Cheddar, Kalamata olives (no pits) and served with assorted crackers.
- Jumbo tail on shrimp with cocktail sauce and lemon wedge.
- Hot appetizers. Homemade spanakopita, tiropita, miniature souvlaki (pork brochette), Grecian chicken souvlaki, and Grecian meatballs.
- Sweet table. Assorted mini-pastries and assorted homemade Greek mini-pastries. Silver coffee and tea service.
- Beer, wine, and soda bar. Heineken Beer, Miller Lite, chardonnay, Greek white wine, white zinfandel, and merlot. Assorted sodas.

The menu for the Ribbon Cutting and Grand Opening celebration held on the 17th was more restrained and featured: Fresh fruit trays with cantaloupe, honeydew, watermelon, strawberries, kiwi, and red and green grapes. Assorted miniature pastries. Assorted homemade Greek pastries. Silver coffee and tea service and champagne punch.

The Greek American Nursing Home Committee

invites you to attend the

Grand Opening

of the

Greek American Rehabilitation and Nursing Centre
220 N. First Street ¥ Wheeling, Illinois 60090
(Milwaukee Ave. 1 block N. of Dundee Rd. to Strong Ave. W. to First St. S.)

Sunday, March 17, 2002

Ribbon Cutting, Open House and Tours 2-4p.m.

Please respond by March 12th 773-561-8865

GANHC Grand Opening invitation. March 17, 2002. John Psiharis collection.

GREEK-AMERICAN NURSING HOME
Committee Newsletter
Volume 3, Number 1, Spring 2002

BLESSING

On Sunday, March 3, 2002 the Blessing (Agiasmo) and Preview Tour of the GARNC were held. His Eminence Metropolitan Iakovos of Krinis conducted a blessing service at which clergy of the diocese and an estimated 150 laity were present. Following the Agiasmo, His Eminence spoke and congratulated Dr. Kioutas and his committee for the exceptional job they did while praising the nursing home, comparing it to a five star hotel. Tours were held and refreshments served.

GRAND OPENING

On Sunday, March 17th the official Grand Opening of the Greek American Rehabilitation and Nursing Centre was held with appropriate ribbon cutting. The ribbons were cut by Mr. Greg Klatecki, the President of the Village of Wheeling, Dr. Theodosis Kioutas and the home's Executive Administrator, Mrs. Susan Barbian.

Following the ribbon cutting, a wing was dedicated in honor of Theodosis Kioutas, M.D. by the GANHC and a grateful Greek American Chicagoland Community.

Following this presentation, over 600 people were given a tour of the facility and enjoyed the music and the refreshments that were offered. All attendees were pleased with what they saw and were very complimentary regarding the entire home.

Additional information regarding our nursing home can be obtained by visiting our website at http://www.ganh.org/

The *Greek-American Nursing Home Committee Newsletter*. Volume 3, Number 1. Spring 2002. Elaine Thomopoulos collection.

More than 500 guests attended this celebration. Enthusiasm and pride in this monumental achievement were apparent and those so inclined made donations on the spot or inquired about the admission process for family members. Doctors and health care professionals were also present.

The back page of the April 25, 2002, issue of the *Greek Star* featured full-page coverage of the grand opening celebrations, reading in part:

> From the beginning of the formation of the Greek-American Nursing Home Committee, the Greek community continues to support this philanthropic project. Over $3 million was raised from the grassroots campaign within the Greek community.
>
> Greek Americans from throughout the United States have stepped forth to assist in the development of this healthcare facility.
>
> The great benefactor of the center is Dr. Mary Dochios Kamberos who remembers both her parents and the Idaho Greek community for supporting her medical education. Other key donors include The Greek-American Restaurant Association and Soteria Women's Philanthropic Organization.
>
> One of the first Hellenic organizations to come forth after the committee was formed was the Greek-American Restaurant Association (GARA). GARA followed in the spirit of the pioneering Greek restaurateurs who built their businesses, raised families, and were instrumental in the development of Greek churches and schools.
>
> Under the leadership of Matthew Manavis, GARA president, GARA stepped forward to become one of the largest donors to the project. GARA has contributed in excess of $300,000 for the center's kitchen and two dining rooms.
>
> According to Manavis, 'With the state-of-the-art kitchen in the nursing home, over 1,000 meals can be prepared at one time. We are proud to be part of this exciting project and wish the committee continued success.'
>
> After World War II, Greek-American women formed the Hellenic Women's Philanthropic Association 'Soteria.' They began saving for a healthcare facility for elderly Greek Americans. What started with 50-cent lunches, grew to $330,000 that was donated to the Greek-American Nursing Home Committee. In honor of their donation, an entire wing on the second level is named for 'Soteria.'
>
> The creation of this center united the Chicagoland Greek Americans as no other project or cause has in these times. Other supporters include The Philoptochos Ladies Societies, the AHEPANS, the regional Greek societies, like the Tageatic Women's League, Enosis Demovaltetsioton, and the Hellenic Society of Constantinople; and the Hellenic professional

associations like the Greek Women's University Club, Hellenic Professional Society, and Hellenic League; charitable organizations like the Eisenberg Foundation and many, many individuals.

> The Greek-American Nursing Home Committee is grateful for all the individuals and organizations that have supported the development of this Centre.
>
> Though the dream within the Greek community was alive since the late 1940s and 1950s, it wasn't until the mid-80s that the project for the development of a Greek American nursing home was launched. The Greek-American Nursing Home Committee was organized in 1985.
>
> 'As a primary physician I noticed a need for a nursing home,' said Dr. Theodosis Kioutas, chairman of the committee, 'Others saw this need as well and this is how we got the group together.'
>
> Since 1985, Dr. Kioutas has persevered in the development of the Greek-American Rehabilitation and Care Centre. Dr. Kioutas admits many voices raised doubts about whether it could be done. He does, however, credit those Greek-Americans who realized it could be done.
>
> 'It developed a confidence with the community,' he said. 'People started to believe in and contribute to the project.'
>
> 'This is a dream come true,' said Dr. Kioutas, who hails the centre as a 'majestic building.' The Greek-American community has Dr. Kioutas and his committee to thank for making this a success.

Enrollment picked up as word spread. Although our focus was elderly of Greek descent, we welcomed every resident with open arms. We benefited from being the newest nursing home in the state since we had just opened, which appealed to some families choosing a home for their loved ones.

The GARNC accepted private pay residents as well as those covered by Medicare and Medicaid. Since our inception, we believed that no Greek elderly should be prohibited from the home, regardless of their ability to pay. Once the facility opened, the GANHC continued efforts to raise money for a charity fund that would be tapped as needed to cover expenses in caring for those who had limited or no ability to pay.

The state-of-the-art nursing home featured an ice cream parlor on the first floor along with physical therapy, a beauty shop, and a large activity room with divisible side rooms. The large space was used for resident activities as well as gatherings and meetings. The breakout rooms could be used for private resident-family dinners, parties, or meetings. Board meetings were usually in one of these rooms. Off the big room was a sliding glass door that went onto a secure outdoor patio overlooking the duck pond. The pond was named Arcadian Lake in honor of the Pan Arcadian Federation, a major supporter of the GANHC. A chapel consecrated "The Entrance of the Theotokos" by Metropolitan Iakovos, was on the first floor. Administrative offices and a reception desk were also located on the first floor, as was an office for the GANHC.

Patient rooms with a total of 204 beds were located on the second, third, and fourth floors. A nurses' station was in the lobby of each floor with hallways and rooms extending out from there. Activity rooms and dining areas were on each floor. Rooms were configured mostly as single bedrooms, but there were several suites on each floor. The fourth floor was designed to meet the special needs of memory-impaired residents. The laundry, kitchen, and HVAC were in the basement.

The activity staff planned a varied schedule of activities that appealed to Greek residents, while being mindful of those who were not Greek. The menus offered residents both Greek and American cuisine. Churches, Philoptochos societies, Greek schools, and other organizations scheduled visit days for their members and students. Some made weekly visits while others visited monthly or quarterly. Ethel Kotsovos, as volunteer coordinator, arranged these activities.

On June 9, the Midwest District of the Pan Arcadian Federation hosted its annual dinner dance at the Chateau Ritz. The event, chaired by John Andrews, raised $20,000 to benefit the GANHC. An article by George Chiagouris entitled, "Arcadians Salute Young and Old at Annual Dinner Dance; Proceeds for the Greek-American Nursing Home," that appeared in the June 6, 2002, edition of the *Greek Star*, reports in part:

> The Pan-Arcadians recognize the contribution, dedication, and sacrifices that the elder Hellenes have made here in the United States. The subsequent generations have been able to reap the benefits of the road that was paved by the blood, sweat, and tears of our forefathers. They believe that it is time that our generation, which has achieved the American dream of fame, education, and prosperity, give back to those who helped us realize our dreams.
>
> Many Greek-Americans, including Arcadians, have donated on a personal basis towards the construction of the Greek-American Rehabilitation and Nursing Centre in Wheeling, IL. The Midwest District of the Pan-Arcadian Federation has decided to raise additional needed monies. The centre has thirty residents. Additional funds are needed at present by the nursing home to assist in reaching its occupancy goals and defray some of the operating costs.

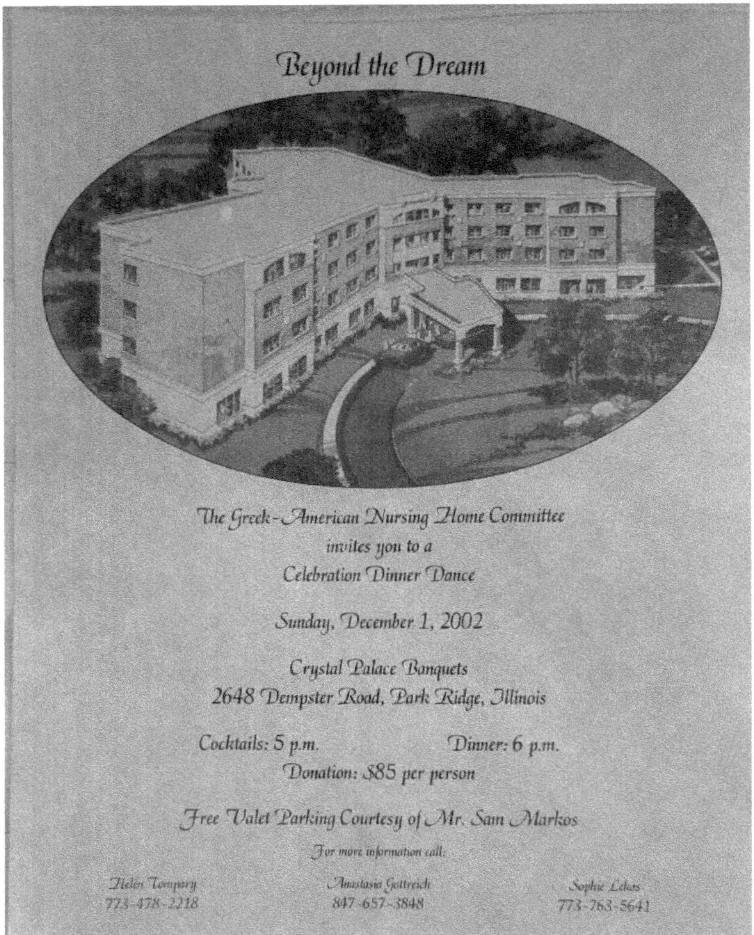

"Beyond the Dream" invitation. December 2002. Elaine Thomopoulos collection.

Other notable 2002 fundraisers included:

- October 12: The Holy Apostles Philoptochos Society hosts "Touched by an Angel," a luncheon and fashion show with the proceeds benefitting the GANHC.
- October 14: GANHC hosted a Columbus Day Radiothon on the Sotiris Rekoumis radio program. $50,000 was raised. Special recognition was given to Dr. Kioutas, Catherine Fasseas, Chris Tomaras, John Secaras, John Andrews, and Bill and Mary Kakavas for their efforts in this endeavor.
- October 20: American Hellenic Society of Berwyn 42nd Anniversary Dinner at Skylite West. Tickets are $35 per person.
- December 1: GANHC hosted the "Beyond the Dream Celebration Dinner Dance" at the Crystal Palace Banquets in Park Ridge. Tickets are $85 per person. Net income $157,686.

605 tickets sold. Radio personalities Vicky Kournetas and Kiki Vale were mistresses at the ceremony. John Linardakis's Band performed. Catherine Fasseas was the dinner chairman.

A GANHC press release promoting the "Beyond the Dream," event, explained the evening's theme and issued a rallying call to the community. "We must go beyond the original dream for a Greek-American Nursing Home, which began over 16 years ago. Though the Greek-American Rehabilitation and Nursing Centre opened in March, we as a Greek community cannot rest on our laurels. It is imperative that we all support this worthwhile effort to provide a place of caring, a place of dignity, and a place of hospitality for our elderly. We must 'go beyond,' to assist in offsetting the initial operating expenditures until the center becomes self-sufficient."

During the event, the Metropolis of Chicago Philoptochos Board presented a check for $9,250 to the GANHC. Of the total, $6,750 was designated for the altar of the Centre's chapel and the balance for facility operating expenses. The proceeds were raised during their annual September luncheon.

That evening, the Educational Society of Sellasia also presented a donation of $5,000 to the GANHC. Panos Giannakopoulos, president of the society, stated "On behalf of the Educational Society of Sellasia and the executive board it is our pleasure and honor, as an organization, to contribute the amount of $5,000 to be used for the needs of the nursing home."

GANHC ended the year with a New Year's Eve celebration at McMahon's Arena Restaurant and Steak House in Northbrook, IL. The evening featured Las Vegas-style Big Band music by Ed Collins and a live Vegas band. Greek music is provided by a disc jockey. Owner Gus Cappas provided an open bar, champagne, and party favors. The event was chaired by Eleni Bousis, and tickets to the event were $100 per person.

I was elated that this project had finally come to fruition. A journey of 18 years had come to an end and a new chapter was about to begin. The GANHC was the little engine that could. Despite many challenges and hurdles, the dream so many had worked for so long to achieve had finally come to fruition. We felt the exhilaration of a mission accomplished. It is hard to put into words the sense of pride and accomplishment I had walking through the doors of the new facility knowing the difficulties encountered and the backstory, and that I had played a part in this success. But it was more than that. There was a sense of vindication that many of us felt. The naysayers who through action or inaction and those who created obstacle after hurdle for 18 years were proven wrong. We persevered and accomplished what some felt was unachievable. I was proud to be a part of the Greek American community. A community that showed time and again the true meaning of *philotimo, philoxenia,* and respect for its elders.

Unfortunately, the time to bask in this success and celebrate was short-lived. Beyond the horizon, storm clouds were gathering.

The Cookie Crumbles

Soon after the nursing home opened, major problems began to emerge and take center stage. During the balance of my time on the board, our energy, resources, and efforts were laser-focused on the home's survival and overcoming the dire financial crisis that we were in.

Updates presented during the October 2002 board meeting revealed that the patient census had risen to 88 residents with three bed-holds (residents who were in the hospital but would return). Seventy-seven percent of the residents were Greek. Most residents were covered by Medicaid. We were advised that the breakeven point was 173 patients and until that time, there would be an ongoing need for fundraising to make up the difference. Including all payment categories, GARNC generated $883,575 in revenue between March and August of 2002. We were owed $330,000 from Medicaid and $63,850 in Medicare. Private pay outstanding balances were $40,000. In the coming two weeks, $217,000 was needed to meet payroll and vendor expenses.

An emergency board meeting was held on November 18 to discuss nursing home operations and the financial crisis we were facing. From my notes of the meeting: "We have collected $17,000 from the Radiothon thus far. Dinner Dance: as of Nov. 10, 2002, there is $50,000 in underwriting and 245 reservations. Discussion on finances includes Mary Kakavas expressing her frustration that no one has billed for resident care. Dr. Kioutas feels that the nursing home is overstaffed, and the Administrator isn't doing her job. Tina questions why the management company isn't doing anything. Elaine Thomopoulos asks for consensus to fire the present Administrator. Jim Pirpiris states that people who do not do their job should be fired on the spot – 'Don't wait, they can do more damage.'"

We concluded that many of these problems were related to the management company and its handpicked administrator being ineffective in their performance and thus seriously jeopardizing something we had worked so hard to achieve.

During two pre-opening inspections, the first with two residents, and the second with 22 residents, we had critical findings due to very basic violations, including incomplete charting and documentation such as failing to chart an insulin shot on a patient's record. The purpose of the phased opening process was to allow a new nursing home a chance to get its footing and work out any deficiencies. Once corrected, we passed the inspections and were granted Medicare approval. This delay in obtaining certification resulted in the further cost of some $360,000 in lost revenues.

Among the problems that were uncovered: Headhunting firms had been hired at a cost of at least $70,000 to help fill key leadership positions without the board's knowledge or consent. Morale was low, and overtime expenses were nearing $25,000 per month. Although the home opened in March, we discovered that no billing for any residents occurred well into October. By the time the board became aware of the situation, nearly $350,000 was deemed uncollectable due to a lack of data, aging, and deaths of residents.

A payment was made for property taxes that were not due. Even though other bills went unpaid, $70,000 was paid to the Cook County Treasurer for taxes on an exempt property that did not owe property taxes. Through the personal intervention of Cook County Treasurer Maria Pappas and Deputy Treasurer Peter Karhalios, the funds were reimbursed in a somewhat timely fashion. Nonetheless, this tied up $70,000 at a critical juncture and contributed to the overall crisis we were in.

Susan was an employee of the management company, and they did not want to replace her. When we decided to replace her, the management company saw it as a cancellation of our agreement. A protracted legal battle evolved between First Health Care and the nursing home. The board eventually negotiated terms, reached a settlement, and terminated the contract.

A nursing home cannot be without a licensed nursing administrator in charge for more than 24 hours. We identified an acting administrator and appointed her on an interim basis. At the same time, the board launched a search process to fill the administrator position permanently. On Monday, December 16, 2002, the board, acting as a committee of the whole, held the final round of interviews. We met with two finalists, each of whom spent more than an hour interviewing. Before the interviews began, Dr. Kioutas distributed and read aloud to the board the following statement:

> I called this special meeting because I believe we have reached a special point in our history of eighteen years. To use an expression from our fundraisers, the dream came true. We want it to be a good one. We do not want it to turn into a nightmare. Some of you have been with me and this project from the beginning! Others have come later, but to all of you, I am repeating my extreme determination that this project continues to stay alive and serve the ones it is designed to serve for the next 100 years.

The Dream Comes True

The Greek-American Rehabilitation and Nursing Centre Dinner Dance

Louis G. Atsaves, board members Mary and Bill Kakavas, and Senator Adeline J. Geo-Karis

Treasurer, John Secaras; Honoree, Dr. Mary Dochios Kamberos; President, Dr. Theodore E. Kioutas

Consul General, Gabriel Coptsidis; Medical Director, Nicholas Papanos; Bessie Papanos; Dr. Lynn Kantzavelos; John Papanos; Dr. Katherine Kioutas Katsoyannis

Chris Tomaras applauds the additional money raised during the evening

Chicago Greek Circle Winter 2002 29

The *Chicago Greek Circle*. Winter 2002. Elaine Thomopoulos collection.

I will allow nothing to sidetrack me! Not personal feelings, not pride, arrogance, ignorance, blind ambition, lack of respect or consideration. To me, the obligation to the needy is first but also to the community and the individuals who supported us with their money is paramount.

Again, I wish to remind all of you that as a physician who practices Internal Medicine and Geriatrics by evolution, I have extensive knowledge, experience, and contacts in the industry. I refrained from imposing my opinions and let the management company, with input from some of our members, run things.

I am also giving you a copy of the letter from the management company. It is stating facts which we have to have checked for accuracy to settle our 'accounts' with them. I am only going to make one comment regarding our census. Before we opened our

> doors, we had a list of almost ninety prospective residents. Due to the extremely slow processing process (not industry standard), we lost most of them as revenue-generating residents. The other accomplishment? We have to check them with our records and industry standards including the operating standards at the manager's other facilities. To be fair to them as well as to us.
>
> One thing is certain, though. As soon as we get an administrator who can run this place, we should discontinue our relationship with the management company. We cannot afford to have them! We can accept their offer to withdraw and use them only as consultants if the need arises.
>
> With all this said, I wish to call the first candidate for the interview.

The outcome of the three-hour-plus meeting was the hiring of Burton Behr. Once Behr took over, things seemed to settle down and the complaints were fewer. Dr. Nicholas Papanos, who was also a GACS board member, became the medical director, replacing Dr. Katherine Katsoyiannis who had held that position. Dr. Papanos worked hard to reach out to his fellow doctors to encourage referrals. Improved resident comfort and care standards were implemented.

A new director of nursing and other staff were brought in. Attention was laser-focused on billing private pay, Medicaid, and Medicare residents. The initial patient mix had most of our residents covered by Medicaid. Medicaid was by far the lowest rate of reimbursement, and it took a very long time to receive payments. This long delay exacerbated the dire circumstances we faced. At the time we were most in need, the state was seven months behind in paying its bills. Hundreds of thousands of dollars were in the pipeline.

Medicare, on the other hand, covered the full cost of care and paid faster than the state. Private pay families were for the most part prompt payers, but combined, these two categories made up about 30 percent of our monthly revenue. The balance was owed by the state. This was the same problem that GACS was having with the state but with a different department and on a larger scale.

Another complicated matter was the bifurcation process for the building. Up until this point, both the building and operations were under the GANHC umbrella. This made it difficult for us to obtain a line of credit for the home's operations. A separate entity, Greek-American Nursing Home, LLC was created as a wholly-owned subsidiary, and the property and building were transferred to the LLC. The bifurcation was completed in April 2003. and the mortgage payments of $90,000 per month as well as $10,000 per month for a repairs and maintenance fund were now directed

Some of the members of the Greek American Nursing Homoe Committee. Seated are executive committee members Dr. Elaine Thomopoulos, Dr. Kioutas, Helen Georges. Standing, from left, are George Lekas, Theresa Tzakis, John Rassogiannis, Tina Spiratos, Gerry Garbis, Bill Kakavas, Harry Tompary, John Secaras (treasurer); and Toni Panos. Photo by Furlas Studios.

Some GANHC board members at an event at GARNC. Seated: Dr. Elaine Thomopoulos, Dr. Theodosis Kioutas, Helen Georges. Standing from left are George Lekas, Theresa Tzakis, John Rassogianis, Mary Kakavas (not included in the above caption), Tina Spiratos, Gerry Garbis, Bill Kakavas, Harry Tompary, John Secaras, and Toni Panos. Circa 2003. Photo by Furlas Studios. Elaine Thomopoulos collection.

to the LLC. This made it possible for us to qualify for a line of credit based on our receivables unencumbered by the building costs. It also shielded the building from daily operations of the home in the event there were any future lawsuits regarding the nursing home.

As a result of delayed payments from the state and mismanagement by the hired hands, the mortgage was three months in arrears and technically in default. We were in danger of having the U.S. Department of Housing and Urban Development foreclose on us. There were fears that the front driveway of the home would be lined with ambulances waiting to transport residents to other nursing homes. A lot of time and effort was expended in dealing with Cambridge which had underwritten the loan. Eventually, we reached an agreement and became current on what was owed.

We began to learn more about the financial picture of the nursing home, and it wasn't pretty. In addition to management company fees, payroll, and mortgage payments, we owed several hundred thousand dollars to food, pharmaceuticals, physical therapy, medical supplies purveyors, and others.

The board worked tirelessly to stem the tide. Members of the Greek-American Nursing Home Committee and friends made personal loans to the

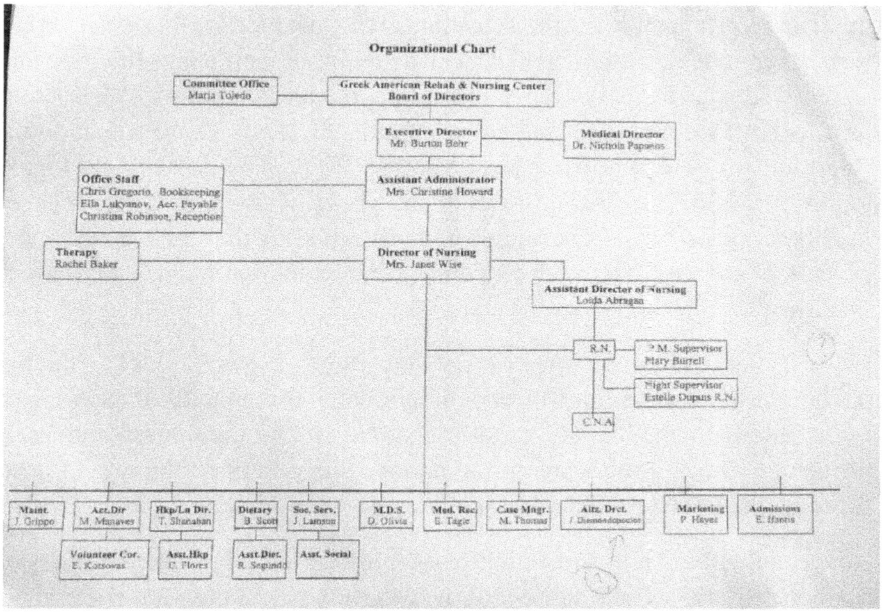

GARNC organizational chart. Circa 2003. Elaine Thomopoulos collection.

organization. Individual board members contributed, as did some key supporters. They included: James Christie ($25,000), Dr. Kioutas ($25,000), Chris Tomaras ($25,000), Dimitris and Eleni Bousis ($25,000), Demetrios Pirpiris ($10,000), Bill Kakavas ($10,000), Gerry Garbis ($5,000) and John Secaras ($5,000). Dr. Mary Dochios Kamberos donated an additional $60,000 above her $1,500,000 donation. A fundraising dinner planned for the first of December had 244 reservations at one point. It will be hosted by radio personalities Kiki Valos and Vikki Kornetas.

Bill Kakavas volunteered to work with kitchen staff to improve the quality of meals and reduce expenses. Helen Georges spearheaded collection efforts for private-pay clients who were in arrears.

Insurance costs were significant and amounted to approximately $350,000 during the first year of operation (including workers' compensation of nearly $63,000). As we dug deeper, the board discovered that the management company had obtained quotes for a "for-profit" facility rather than a non-profit. On renewal, we were able to reduce insurance costs to $237,000 and receive better coverage. We also modified our coverage to be an occurrence policy instead of a claim policy. This option was only available to the top one to two percent of nursing homes. Health Cap based in Michigan agreed to insure us under these terms which further reduced costs. However, we were not able to receive a refund of $123,000 that had been paid in error.

Attempts to expedite payment of past-due funds from the state were made. In a letter dated April 9, 2003, Representative Sandra Pihos (42nd district), the state representative for the Wheeling area, appealed to Illinois Governor Rod Blagojevich on our behalf, as well as for other facilities in the state that were owed significant amounts of state payments. According to her letter, payments were delayed anywhere from 90 days to seven months. Representative Pihos noted in her letter that "18 nursing homes were forced to close in 2002 and during the first six weeks of 2003, an additional six facilities notified the Department of Public Health that they were in the process of closing." Between November 2002 and March 2003, there were no payments received from the state.

Eleni Bousis attended the annual meeting of the Greek Orthodox Archdiocese Leadership 100 and individually distributed 40 packets of information on the nursing home to some of the wealthiest and most influential Greek Americans in the nation. She described the urgent need faced by the GANHC and several made generous donations.

Between the sheer will and determination of the GANHC, the generosity of our benefactors, and the support of the community and elected officials, we made it through this crisis. The state eventually paid some of the overdue money and through donations from major donors and personal loans from board members, as well as the ability to obtain an $850,000 line of credit after the bifurcation was finalized, the ship had been stabilized. But only for the moment.

Course Reset

In the spring of 2003, we celebrated the first anniversary of the nursing home. And it had been quite a year. GANHC was not out of the woods by any means, but we had put out the fire for the moment. There still was a critical financial crisis to deal with. Although we had averted foreclosure and met payroll, insurance, and utility bills; there was a backlog of debts owed to various purveyors, subcontractors, and the like.

GANHC assumed responsibility for the home and severed its relationship with the management company, hired a new administrator, and brought invoicing current. We significantly reduced overtime, food, and insurance costs and finalized the property tax exemption. In total, monthly expenditures were reduced by more than $30,000.

These were challenging times at every level, physically, mentally, and emotionally. Some weeks there were three or four different meetings, regarding various areas of concern. In looking over the minutes of some of those meetings they began at either 6:00 or 7:00 p.m. and sometimes didn't adjourn until 11:00 p.m. or later. There were many phone calls and a good number of breakfast or lunch meetings to discuss pressing matters. We regularly attended functions and fundraisers that either benefited the GANHC or were important to attend for one reason or another.

The board was actively engaged in the operations of the GANHC, contributing selflessly of their time, talents, and treasure. Dr. Kioutas devoted countless hours, over many years, to this effort and was supported by many board members including Gerry Garbis, who managed the building construction process; John Rassogianis, George Lekas, Elaine, and I handled publicity; Bill Kakavas, with the help of GARA members, oversaw the design and furnishing of the kitchen and food service operations; Father George Massouras was a liaison with Bishop/Metropolitan Iakovos and coordinated establishing the in-house chapel; Peter Karhalios, John Secaras, and Tina Spiratos provided legal guidance; Ethel Kotsovos coordinated office functions; and Helen Georges helped Dr. Kioutas to manage the many facets and activities of the organization. Theresa Tzakis, Kay Mourikes, and Tina Spiratos were liaisons with Soteria; Toni Panos and Eugenia Seifer were liaisons with the Daughters of Penelope, and Gerry Garbis and Jim Perpiris handled that role with AHEPA. Thomas Pappas and Tom Diamond coordinated with the Greek-American Restaurant Association, Dr. Chad Prodromos was a go-between with the Hellenic Medical Society, and Eleni Bousis represented the GANHC to the Leadership 100, major donors, and within the community at large and with fundraising. Elaine recalls going with Helen Georges to select wall art that was donated by a gallery.

As board members, we got to know each other better and grew closer. While some of us had known each other for years, others had more recently joined. Nonetheless, in this time of crisis, everyone jumped in to do what they could to steady the ship. I can't tell you how much respect and admiration I have for those who struggled with these situations. We worked together to save a dream that was on the verge of collapse. Each gave their all and did what they could, and despite occasional differences, came together to make it happen. It seemed there was an unspoken mantra that failure was not an option. We had come this far and intended to prevail over these difficulties and achieve the goal that many had labored towards for far too long. Success was within our grasp, and we needed to overcome any hurdles and finish the job.

In March, the GANHC held a series of events to celebrate the first anniversary of the nursing home. On March 2, a "Celebration Brunch" to celebrate the opening was held. Benefactors, clergy, organizations, society presidents, and other supporters were invited to this elegant event. We hosted two community open houses on Sunday, March 16, and Sunday, March 23 that were well attended. About 300 guests attended the first week and 200 the second week. The events included tours of the facility, health screenings, free ice cream sundaes, refreshments, and showings of *My Big Fat Greek Wedding* in the third-floor lounge. The Trovadouri Group of Chicago performed in full regalia. On the 30th of March, the GANHC had a visible presence at the Greek Independence Day Parade held in Greektown.

The GANHC April 2003 Easter fundraising appeal letter read in part:

> We are celebrating our first year as a fully licensed nursing and rehabilitation home.
>
> The good news **is** that the residents are smiling. They look forward to greeting each other each morning and to the activities planned. We have been very fortunate to have a group of committed volunteers to help residents with their routine, take walks outdoors, assist during mealtimes, help them participate in activities, and most importantly, visit with each resident, as needed. The food is good. Greek-style meals are served several times a week. Highlights are liturgy every Saturday in our beautiful chapel and the Wednesday visits of Father Makrinos, who hears confession, offers communion, and visits privately with residents. Special days are those when community groups, especially children, visit and entertain.
>
> Due to the weak economy, we are not receiving timely reimbursement payments for the majority of our residents from Medicaid and Medicare. Since June 2002, we have received one payment from Medicaid in February 2003 for the months of June through October 2002. According to the Medicaid schedule, we are not due another payment for November 2002 until the end of April! Medicare is not so sporadic but is several months behind.

During the first year, there were 200 admissions, and at the 12-month mark, the home had a census of 110 with two beds on hold. The GARNC launched *Ygeia* Health Education Programs, a series of health education lectures focused on the needs of older adults. A secondary goal was to introduce the facility to those who may be considering either rehabilitation or long-term care options. These included:

- April 22, 2002: First *Ygeia* Health Education Program. Dr. Kioutas was the speaker for the first program of the series and introduced Dr. Nicholas Papanos as the new medical director of the center.
- June 17, 2002: *Ygeia* Health Education Program on dementia with Dr. Katherine Katsoyannis.
- July 31, 2002: *Ygeia* Health Education Program discussion on skin cancer by Kathy Culiner, R.N. of the Kellogg Cancer Center.
- January 28, 2003: *Ygeia* Health Program lecture on glaucoma during Glaucoma Awareness Month by Dr. Christopher Kardasis.
- March 6, 2003: *Ygeia* Health Education Program lecture by Mary Lewis, Director of the Alzheimer's Department entitled "Caretaking for Individuals with Alzheimer's/Dementia: Understanding the Illness and Living with the Individual."

- April 10, 2003: *Ygeia* Health Education Program lecture entitled "Normal Aging – How Does It Affect Memory Loss" by neuropsychologist Dr. Michael Mercury.
- May 5, 2003: *Ygeia* Health Education Program lecture entitled "Aging with Grace – Maintaining a Positive Attitude" by Dr. Jack Hayes.
- May 10, 2003: *Ygeia* Health Education Programs lecture entitled "Hip and Knee Surgery? Get All Your Questions Answered" by Dr. Dan Kuesis.
- May 14, 2003: *Ygeia* Health Education Program lecture by Carol Drengenberg on Wellness.
- September 27, 2003: GARNC presents a health fair from 9:00 a.m. to 3:00 p.m. All screenings were held at GARNC.
- October 4, 2003: GARNC hosts an onsite health fair and bazaar with doctors on hand for questions or concerns. The craft bazaar was run by Friends of the Centre Auxiliary to help raise funds for the center.

By December 2003, the nursing home had a census of 160 residents with 24 Medicare, 48 private pay, and 86 Public Aid residents. The board continued cost-cutting efforts. During the December 2 meeting, we decided not to renew the contract with RXPERTS, which had been providing pharmacy services to the facility, due to higher prices and poor service. A decision was made to bring the accounting functions "in-house," and we approved a negotiated settlement with First Health Care to exit our agreement with them.

John Secaras, Tina Spiratos, and I were on the nominating committee and although there were impressive people interested in joining the board, there were no openings. In 2003, two members, James Mezilson and Steve Manta resigned from the board, providing two vacancies.

In recognition of Dr. Dochios-Kamberos' magnanimous support, she was unanimously voted onto the board. Bill and Mary Kakavas nominated two people, Peter Karahalios and Dr. Katherine Katsoyannis. Peter was an attorney who was deputy treasurer of Cook County under Maria Pappas. Katherine was a physician specializing in gerontology at Lutheran General Hospital and served as the medical director of Norwood Park Nursing Home. She was also Dr. Kioutas' daughter.

Our committee was lobbied by members who preferred one or the other of the nominees. After several conversations, we ultimately felt that Peter's background in law and finance was a skill set that was needed most on our board and he was nominated. At some point, an opening on the board occurred and Katherine was selected to fill that position.

GANHC Christmas card, circa 2003. John Psiharis collection.

On April 25, 2004, GARNC hosted an open house celebrating the second anniversary of the center. Special tours of the Memory Loss Village, Neighborhood Long Term Care, and the newly launched ReGenesis Rehabilitation Center were showcased. Entertainment was provided by the Macedonian Dance Troupe.

In the spring of 2004, it was decided to review and update the bylaws. Fifteen years had passed since the original bylaws had been written, and the nursing home was now in operation, so it was long overdue. The original bylaws were adopted during a GANHC meeting held on July 16, 1985, and provided for a board no larger than 21 members. Elaine and I had taken the lead in writing the original bylaws, and we were asked to help with this again. Helen Georges, Katherine Katsoyannis, and a few others were also on the committee. The new version increased the maximum number to 25, underscoring our commitment to providing care to those in need regardless of their ability to pay, recognized honorary board members, and established standing committees.

Although I knew Katherine and had worked with her on outreach for the adult day care center when she was a geriatrician at Lutheran General Hospital, I had my first extended encounter with her during an April 2004 meeting of the bylaws committee. We were sitting around a table in the nursing home office at GARNC, reading through proposed revisions to the bylaws. There were probably six to eight people there, more than I would have expected for a bylaws committee meeting. I arrived a few minutes late due to traffic. When I walked into the room, Helen Georges was reading through sections of the bylaws, deferring to Katherine for input on every section, and making changes with little input or even discussion by the other members. It seemed to me the rest of us were there as window dressing to rubber-stamp whatever had been decided.

I remember disagreeing about some matter being discussed and Helen visibly grimacing when I raised my point. How did a new board member have such sway over bylaws that had been in effect for 15 years? It was at this moment that I realized it was their intention for Katherine to be the next president of the GANHC.

During the April 29 GANHC meeting, the new bylaws were adopted, and conflict of interest and financial disclosure policies were enacted. The board unanimously voted to make Dr. Kioutas Honorary Chief Executive Officer as follows: "A lifetime personal position is hereby created for Dr. Theodosis Kioutas who was President of the GANHC from inception in 1985 to 2004. The Honorary Chief Executive Officer will be a mentor and consultant to the officers and Board of Directors of the GANHC. The Honorary Chief Executive Officer when present at a meeting of the Board will have the right to cast one vote." John Secaras reported that it would cost about $700 for a portrait of Dr. Kioutas, and a collection was taken from board members.

In February 2004, the board considered recommendations from Mary Lewis, director of the Village, the dementia care wing, to create a more comfortable and safe area for residents with memory loss. Neither Elaine nor recall which improvements were implemented. The suggestions included:

> Increased directional signage, softer lighting in hallways and dining room to minimize glare, matte finish for all floors, and partitions in the dining room to create a smaller environment for the dining experience. This will allow for those in the earlier stage of memory loss to eat in a quieter environment while those who require more assistance sit together. The partitions will allow more flexibility in activity programming. The activity needs of higher and lower-functioning residents are different. We also agreed to individualize the look of each hallway to make it easier for residents to identify where they live by painting each hallway a different color (light blue, light yellow, light green). Shower rooms will have a warmer feel by including shower curtains with valances in pretty prints, wreaths, and other wall hangings, baker's rack or other attractive shelving to hold towels, heating lights to keep residents warm, hanging plants, and equipping each shower stall with a fold-down seat. Other changes include securing stairwell doors, disguising exit doors and elevators with wallpaper and border the same as walls, and a keypad for elevators so that residents cannot press the button and go onto the elevator unattended.

During the April meeting, the board received a letter from the family of a resident that underscored the excellent quality of care the staff strived to provide to each resident:

> My husband entered your nursing home in October 2003 after having been in another nursing home for three years, He had Parkinson's disease, dementia, and bedsores acquired in the other nursing home; he required a great deal of care. However, with the diligent treatment from your nursing staff, the bedsore was soon cured, and he was made comfortable and content.
>
> The aides here are wonderful. They are obviously well-trained in all they do. They are efficient, exceptionally caring to the residents, and very cooperative with one another. They are always aware of a resident's abilities and disabilities and quick to respond to needs as they arise. They seem to approach their work with the desire to give the very best care that they can provide.
>
> From the warm greeting from the busy receptionist, the well-planned and delicious meals provided by your food service, the speech therapist who assured me that she had instructed the staff on how to feed my husband in order to cope with his swallowing problems, to all the hard-working housekeeping staff who keep everything immaculate, I have been impressed again and again with the quality of care that you provide. I know that such quality does not come automatically but depends upon excellent administration, and I want to thank you and all your staff for providing that for my husband and for all the other needy residents here.

In 2004, the GANRC hosted several lectures in May during Older Americans Month. They included:

- April 28: Dr. Van Stamos, an orthopedic surgeon, presents a lecture to those contemplating hip or knee surgery.
- May 20: Dr. Katherine Katsoyiannis, a GANHC board member and geriatrician at GeriCare Ltd., presents a lecture in conjunction with Older Americans Month with questions and answers on memory loss.
- May 22: George Reveliotis, an attorney specializing in real estate taxes and seniors speaks during an Older Americans Month lecture.
- May 28: Lecture on "Preventative Medicine and Anti-Aging Techniques" by Violet Bawolsky of Ancient Healing and Jerry Kolcan. It is an Older Americans Month lecture.

Notable fundraising activities that occurred during this period included:

- The American Hellenic Society of Berwyn held its annual fundraiser with proceeds benefiting the GANHC. In April, President Gus Flessor presented a check for $5,100, the proceeds from their Forty-Second Anniversary Dinner Dance. This donation completed the organization's $20,000 pledge for a room on the second floor. The society was founded by Nicholas Economos, Gustav Rassogianis, and James Papadimitriou, and chartered on April 24, 1960, with 58 members.
- On June 14, 2003, the GANHC received proceeds from the Arlington Park Greek Fest, co-sponsored by *Greek Circle* magazine and held at Arlington Racetrack.
- On July 31st GARNC hosted a "Celebrate Summer" event. According to the invitation, "The patio of the GARNC is transformed into an outdoor café reminiscent of Greece or Greek Town. Enjoy lakeside views as you partake in the festivities. Let your mind take you away to a Greek Island with music, including *rembetika* music from 1 p.m. to 5 p.m. featuring Andreas Georgas, and the Hellenic Five performing popular music from 5 p.m. to 8 p.m."
- On October 5th GANHC hosted the "Our Accomplished Dream Dinner" fundraising dinner dance at the Chateau Ritz Banquets, Niles, IL. Cost $100 per person. Chaired by Eleni Bousis and co-chaired by Chris Tomaras and Peter Karahalics. The event netted about $130,000.

There was a schism developing on the board, fanned in large measure by the crisis we were in. One faction was the Dr. Kioutas supporters. They were longtime members and included Elaine Thomopoulos, Helen Georges, Toni Panos, John Rassogianis, Dr. Kamberos, and John Secaras. I was usually in this camp. The second group was composed primarily of newer members including Eleni Bousis, Bill and Mary Kakavas, Jim Christie, Theresa Tzakis, and Tina Spiratos. They believed that Dr. Kioutas was responsible in part for the crisis we were in because of failed oversight of the management company.

Dr. Kioutas had begun to experience health problems. Initially, he experienced a severe case of food poisoning that required hospitalization. It occurred during a February 2000 anniversary brunch hosted by husband-and-wife Dr. Angelo Christopoulos and Dr. Maria Balkoura, that was attended by several doctors. One physician who was stricken died within a few days. Later, we learned that Dr. Kioutas had an inoperable brain tumor. Although they attempted chemotherapy and radiation, neither approach was successful. Thus, some felt a sense of urgency to get Katherine elected president of the GANC board. Elections were to occur in June.

Changing of the Guard

Around this time, the board learned that nearly $2 million in taxes, including employee withholdings, were delinquent. We, as board members, were under the impression these payments had been made. In a review of the meeting minutes, there was mention that Dr. Kioutas said he had a check for $200,000 and would be taking care of the past-due taxes. Elaine and I recall these conversations. For whatever reason, the taxes were not paid. Elaine remembers, "I think Dr. Kioutas might have had the undiagnosed tumor when all the crisis with non-payment to the IRS and state was happening. I think at some point we were informed about what was happening but did not have the money to pay. I don't think we realized how serious not paying this was."

The IRS began contacting board members for interviews, and some hired lawyers at personal expense to advise them. These were tense months as we feared that HUD would have cause to foreclose on the home. Several meetings were held between officers of the board, GANHC attorneys, and the IRS. We were hesitant to commit to an installment plan since payments from the state were unpredictable. In time, a settlement and payment plan were arranged, and the crisis was averted.

Eleni's efforts to solicit donations from wealthy Greek Americans were successful in a big way. A generous East Coast benefactor gave $200,000 and made monthly donations thereafter to pay off the tax debt. His support at this critical moment was vital to the survival of the home. He also provided additional funding to cover other pressing expenses. As a condition of his support, he requested strict anonymity.

Members of the board received anonymous mailings at our homes detailing alleged improper actions involving Behr at previous nursing homes he ran. Other mailings included occurrences of timecard fraud and reports of theft from the kitchen.

As the board elections approached, there was a lot of back and forth between board members about this situation. Katherine was going to be nominated for president. Those who were in opposition, led by Bill Kakavas, planned to nominate Eleni Bousis for president from the floor. There was lobbying going on behind the scenes. I recall one evening when John Rassogianis had stopped by my home after a meeting to visit Tornie, the GACS resident cat who came home with me when I left GACS. I unexpectedly received calls from Dr. Kioutas, Helen Georges, Theresa Tzakis, and Bill and Mary Kakavas. Although none knew that John was visiting when they called, the calls came one after another. I put the calls on the speakerphone so that John could also participate. He was also on their call lists. We spent nearly three hours on these calls. The board felt the full weight of this decision and the ramifications of making the wrong choice. There was a lot of back and forth about the candidates. On other days, I received calls from Jim Pirpiris, Tina Spiratos, Ethel Kotsovos, and others. Some were for Katherine, others for Eleni, and a few were undecided, including John and myself. We were conflicted. There were compelling reasons for and against each of them.

In a May 18, 2004, letter sent to GANHC Board members, Katherine wrote:

> I am addressing this communication to you in an effort to make myself absolutely clear and my motives understood with regard to the upcoming elections of the Greek-American Nursing Home Committee.
>
> I am aware, and like many in the Greek community, very appreciative of your personal contributions, services, and sacrifices toward the establishment of the Nursing Home but you, as well as the whole community, know that the greatest sacrifice and the biggest effort was extended by Dr. Theodosis Kioutas, my father. I don't believe that there is anyone else that could have been as effective in bringing together the many diverse and distinct facets in accomplishing this dream. He was unwavering in his support and guidance and always acknowledged the whole community in this success.
>
> My father dreams that this institution will survive for many more years and decades. That is why I am hoping you will support the nominating committee's slate of officers and in particular my election to the office of President.
>
> As you can see in the resume sent with the slate, I have devoted my professional career to caring for the elderly. I have developed a very successful practice and established myself as a long-term care consultant. I have also, consistent with my father's example, served on many boards and committees voluntarily sharing my skills and knowledge.
>
> It is this knowledge and professional experience I propose to bring to the facility at this point in time. My purpose is to ensure the continued success and survival of the institution during a very difficult time in the long-term care industry.
>
> I have been told that my being a Geriatrician involved in the management of the home may cause some people to question a possible conflict of interest. This is not the case. I attend many patients in many different facilities, including the Norwood Park Home, which has been in existence for over 100 years and on whose board, I have sat and offered my expertise for five years. There is no conflict of interest because the facility only benefits to the extent that I refer patients to the facility. I do not and have never received compensation in any form from the Greek-American Nursing Home.
>
> The long-term care industry is very specialized and lately highly competitive. All nursing homes have a period of negative cash

> flow initially and all need very careful and knowledgeable handling in order to survive.
>
> I am stepping forward to offer my knowledge and expertise in steering this ship into the future. I am doing this for the seniors of the Greek Community and for my father.
>
> The nominating committee deliberated and drafted a slate to carry us to the next phase. We should all come together in support of their work and for the best interest of the home.

Dr. Kioutas was the epitome of a leader within the Greek American community and played a huge role in both GACS and GANHC. I had nothing but the highest respect and admiration for him. He had done an amazing job of leading us to where we were. It's doubtful anyone else would have persevered to the extent he did to bring this dream to reality. Our success in large measure was due to his passionate, valiant, and indefatigable leadership, however, in my view, we were in crisis and everything we worked so hard to achieve was in serious jeopardy. We had major issues with the management company that should never have happened and were amid an IRS problem of which we were not initially aware. Irrespective of personal feelings, this was serious, and we needed to address the situations we found ourselves in.

Kathrine in my view represented the continuation of the status quo. I respected her, and under normal conditions, she may have been the right person for that role, but these were not normal times. We were in a crisis. In my mind what we needed to save the home was money and fundraising. We already had a competent medical director and many doctors within the community to call upon.

Eleni was involved with GACS, and I had always been impressed by her fundraising prowess. At GACS, she served on the advisory board, chaired dinner dances, and led a successful $500 per-ticket event at the Metropolitan Club. Eleni was able to attract new supporters to GACS. In all, she had raised hundreds of thousands of dollars for various charities including the nursing home. Her efforts in gaining the support of the Major East Coast Donor to cover past due taxes were vital to turning things around.

I hadn't forgotten the April meeting where Katherine and Helen took over the bylaws process. It was as though it was a preordained conclusion that Katherine would become the next president. I felt this nursing home belonged to the community, not to any one family. John told me he felt the same way. He told me that he would take his lead from me since I was a founder and he believed that I had the best interests of the nursing home at heart.

On May 24, 2004, the evening of the meeting, you could feel the tension in the room building as we worked through the agenda items. Dr. Kioutas came late, so in her role as first vice president, Helen Georges chaired the meeting. When it came time to vote and the ballots were passed out, John, who was sitting next to me, asked if I still intended to vote for Eleni, and I replied yes. We completed our ballots, and they were collected and counted. Eleni had won by four votes. Katherine's supporters were in shock. They did not expect this outcome. Some gazed around the table and you could tell they were trying to figure out who jumped ship. Meanwhile, Eleni's supporters seemed relieved that this was over. Dr. Kamberos, who gave her proxy and was participating in the proceedings via speakerphone, angrily proclaimed "That's a shitty vote!" and hung up. Dr. Kioutas and Katherine were visibly upset and walked out of the meeting.

The minutes for this meeting taken by Elaine detail the evening's proceedings:

> Dr. Katherine Katsoyiannis, chair of the nominating committee, presented the slate the nominating committee recommended. Voting was done by secret ballot and was monitored by Tina Spiratos and John Secaras, who were appointed by Helen Georges.
>
> Katherine Katsoyiannis had been on the slate presented by the nominating committee as President. Eleni Bousis was nominated from the floor by Mary Kakavas, and she was elected. Eleni received thirteen of the twenty-two votes.
>
> Peter Karahalios, nominated as Vice-President by the nominating committee, was elected Vice-President. Katherine had been nominated from the floor but declined the nomination.
>
> Dr. Elaine Thomopoulos, who had been nominated as Second Vice-President by the nominating committee, withdrew her name from consideration. John Psiharis was nominated from the floor but declined the nomination. Jim Pirpiris was nominated from the floor for the position and was elected.
>
> Theresa Tzakis, nominated for the position of Secretary by the nominating committee, was elected.
>
> Mary Kakavas, who had been nominated for the position of Assistant Secretary by the nominating committee, withdrew her name from the election. Tina Spiratos was nominated as Assistant Secretary and was elected.
>
> The following people were nominated by the nominating committee and were elected: Jerry Garbis as Treasurer and George Lekas as Assistant Treasurer.

The newly elected officers were Eleni Bousis, president; Peter Karahalios, vice president; Demetrios Pirpiris, second vice president, Gerald Garbis, treasurer; George Lekas, assistant treasurer; Theresa Tzakis, secretary and Christina Spiratos, assistant secretary.

I congratulated Eleni and left. This meeting drew a larger number of guests and observers than usual and as we walked out there was a buzz outside the meeting room and into the hallways among the guests and employees who had gathered to await the outcome. Some seemed surprised by the results.

A New Day

As a result of his declining health and the results of the vote, Dr. Kioutas resigned from the board. Katherine also resigned.

On June 13, 2004, the GANHC Annual Meeting and Reception was held at the nursing home, and the new executive board was introduced. The board felt that it was critical to provide the community with a complete and transparent update and to set the record straight. There were many rumors in the community, most of which were not true, and this was an opportunity to report the facts.

The meeting was standing room only with overflow into the hallways and lobby. Eleni provided a detailed report on our progress as well as the problems that we were addressing. The emotions were still raw in some circles, and a few in the audience booed at times. A lively question-and-answer period followed. A portrait honoring Dr. Kioutas was unveiled in the lobby during the meeting, and Dr. Kioutas and his family were there.

In her remarks to the assemblage, Eleni stated: "Thank you for entrusting us to carry on the dream. With humble love and dedication, we pledge to make every effort to uphold our mission, to provide superior care to the aged, ill, and needy of the Greek-American community. Our mission draws strength from that which binds us: our culture, our language, our church, and our steadfast desire to provide exceptional care for the seniors and disabled in a 'state of the art' facility that is both familiar and comfortable. We pledge to make every effort to promote the vitality and success of this most important institution for generations to come. Please stand by us, we need your support, dedication, and love as we undertake this mission to preserve Greek dignity for ages to come."

As the event ended and the crowd dispersed, I saw Dr. Kioutas in the lobby. I extended my hand and began to congratulate him on the portrait, but he withdrew his hand, glared at me, and walked away. Unfortunately, this was the last time I saw Dr. Kioutas. I considered attending his wake and funeral but given his reaction to me, I did not want to cause the family any additional pain or discomfort by attending.

The first board meeting after the elections was held the next day, June 14. We discussed the challenges of negotiating a settlement for the FICA taxes when the state was behind and erratic in paying Medicaid vendors. If we negotiated a payment plan, we needed to keep up with the payments, or we risked default and could lose the nursing home.

Eleni reported that she had received several resumes from individuals who were interested in joining the board, and they were passed on to the nominating committee (John Secaras, chairman, John Psiharis, Tom Pappas, George Lekas, and Christina Spiratos). The board discussed building security, particularly during the overnight hours, and the need for board members to be onsite, especially during nights and weekends to better understand what was going on.

During the July 12 meeting, we discussed resident care matters and the administrator's performance in executive session before opening the meeting to our guests. John Secaras presented the Nominating Committee's report. John Secaras, chairman, John Psiharis, Tom Pappas, George Lekas, and Christina Spiratos: James Angelopoulos and Jean Kaporis stepped down from the board per their wishes. Father George Massouras would soon be leaving the board but will continue to serve as liaison to his eminence. To fill two of the three board vacant seats, the committee nominated Gus Bahramis, CPA, and Faye Pantazelos of New Century Bank. They were unanimously approved. According to the minutes, "Gus promised to be on the job by tomorrow afternoon and stated, "Let's get some responsibility and accountability." At this meeting, we approved the launching of a website for GANRC. Eleni also reported that singer Anna Vissi, a friend of hers, had offered to give a benefit performance for the GANHC. The Rosemont Theater was one possible location; it had a seating capacity of 5,000 to 6,000. An ad book was also planned for the event to raise additional dollars.

In her July report to the board, Eleni summarized the problems that the executive committee had identified and the actions that were taken to address them:

1. **What We Found**

   Mortgage consistently late by one month, thus incurring a late charge every month. Federal and state withholding taxes haven't been paid since December 8, 2003.

   Over $1 million passed due to vendors. Some are now demanding COD.

   Overtime was running at $10,000 per bi-weekly pay period ($260,000/yr.).

Billing our accounts receivable was haphazard and late.

Food costs run at $7.00/res/day. The industry average runs $3.50 - $4.50.

2. What Has Been Done

Brought in outside help to speed up bookkeeping and accounts receivables.

Directive to stop all overtime provided we would not be in violation of state statutes by doing so.

Hired a security firm to patrol the building overnight and stand by the employee exits for two of the three shifts.

Sending all overdue private pay accounts "final chance to pay before the account is turned over to a collection agency" letters.

Have a greater presence by board members being present every day.

Held meetings with key staff and nurses.

Held meetings off-site with knowledgeable persons in the industry.

Directive to hold food costs to a maximum of $5.00/res/day.

On the 23rd of July, the Committee sent out an urgent community appeal to supporters. The response card in bold lettering displayed the tagline: "Financial Crisis – Please Help Us! For this Greek American Project!!!" By August 2, $13,000 had been received in response to this appeal. In total more than $50,000 was collected.

In her August 2, 2004, report to the board, Eleni noted that the GANHC owed approximately $800,000 in federal and state taxes, $700,000 to various vendors, and $485,000 to the physical therapy provider. It was also found that private pay residents owed $370,000. Two-thirds of the residents were on Public Aid. The board was advised that if we continue to provide care for Public Aid and charity cases, it needed to raise at least $500,000 per year.

During the September board meeting, which lasted over three hours, we addressed service quality matters and concerns expressed to us by employees, residents, and their families. These matters included: time spent on dinner service, slow breakfasts, and patient care matters. We were advised by Bob Kagda, our accountant, that the financial picture had improved by 36 percent over the last period. Our monthly shortfall for September was $22,000. Eleni asked me to prepare a handout providing new board members with a brief history of the early days of the GANHC, which I presented during the meeting.

"Razzle Dazzle" fundraiser flyer. December 2, 2004. Elaine Thomopoulos collection.

The November 10 meeting focused on the selection of an IT system. Based on staff and board member recommendations, we approved purchasing the Vista Care system for a cost between $60,000 and $75,000. There were updates on the upcoming Razzle Dazzle (Smoker) Dinner to be held on December 2 and a discussion on the search for a new administrator.

Notable fundraising in 2004 included an October 10 GANHC "*Yia Yia and Papou*" Benefit Dinner at The Westin-O'Hare hotel and a December 2 Razzle Dazzle Dinner Benefit organized by AHEPA-13th District at the Wellington Banquet Halls in Arlington Heights, IL. Of the 300 tickets available at $125 each, 122 were sold and the event raised $15,200.

On November 14, GANHC hosted an "Open Meeting" at the Chateau Ritz to report to the public on our progress and finances. We continued to believe that being transparent with the community was critical to overcoming our problems. The Greek community was sometimes known for gossiping and spreading rumors that were not always grounded in fact. To address this, the board was proactive in communicating with the community and keeping them apprised of developments. As was the case with the June annual meeting, this meeting was well attended with a lively discussion and a questions and answers period following reports from Eleni, Peter, Gerry, and others. Some polarization lingered from the recent elections but overall, the meeting went well, and several donations and pledges were received.

By the end of the year, the census had grown to 175 residents. Accounts receivable of over $900,000 were owed by the state. We focused on the need to get an accounting staff in place and in strengthening our collections efforts.

At this time, there was also a parting of the ways between the board and administrator Burton Behr. I was asked to serve on the search committee for his replacement, along with Eleni, Tina, Gus, and one or two others. After two rounds of meetings with several candidates, the board settled on John Koch as administrator. He had been an assistant administrator and acting administrator of a nursing home operated by Holy Family Hospital. John began in January 2005 and became the third administrator in three years.

The GANHC 2004 Christmas appeal letter from Eleni stated in part:

> We are currently faced with a $2.5 million deficit along with an $11.5 million mortgage. Through our appeal letter for financial help, a loyal and humble Christian Orthodox humanitarian responded to our appeal and is in the process of negotiating our IRS deficit. Truly this individual is worthy to be called 'Axios' and 'Agios.' We are indeed honored and privileged to know him. We are praying that many will be touched and follow this great man's gesture and kindness.
>
> Besides our deficit and mortgage payment, we are constantly sinking deeper into financial instability due to the fact that we have embraced 100 public aid residents who have no financial income. The state government pays $105 daily per public aid resident. The cost of a resident is approximately $170 per day. As you can see, we are in desperate need of financial support to provide these residents with appropriate quality care in a warm, secure, and safe environment.
>
> I contacted a consultant to help us determine the cause of this problem and advise us on how to resolve this severe problem. What he told us was very compelling and upsetting to my board and myself. He advised us of two options: either close the door to public aid residents and turn this home to private and Medicare-only residents or inform the community, organizations, and foundations of this critical matter. He suggested that we inform the community of the need to raise

> $500,000 yearly through different fundraising events, so we can compensate for the difference to assure our survival. We have to preserve Greek dignity in honor of those who have left and those who are here with us today.

Art Stamos and I served as co-chairs of the Operations Committee. In this capacity, we had regular Saturday morning meetings at the facility in conjunction with other committees that met at the same time to address their areas of responsibility. These committees focused on finance, food services, fundraising, medical, and legal matters.

The Operations Committee spent a lot of time talking with staff regarding their concerns and ideas. In time, we were able to address several of them. The committee recommended the purchase of a Bio-Metric palm reader to eliminate improper timecard procedures. Art Stamos paid for the equipment as a donation to the home. We suggested the hiring of a security company to provide overnight security to ensure the safety of our employees and reduce theft. We also reviewed options for security cameras in the kitchen and certain other areas.

Dr. Nick Papanos, the medical director, chaired the Medical Committee composed of several respected medical professionals. They represented an array of specialties and helped to promote the facility within the medical community. At the time, Glen Brook Hospital was our receiving hospital and special attention was placed on building relationships with them.

The Food Services Committee, chaired by Bill Kakavas, was able to reduce food costs by changing our supplier to Sysco from US Foods and by taking advantage of pricing promotions and other efficiencies. A dietary consultant was brought in to revamp the menus and offer more Greek meals.

The Legal Committee addressed concerns related to finances as well as resident and employee-involved matters. Given the gravity of the decisions we were making, their careful study and recommendations were valued by the board.

The Financial Committee, chaired by Gus Bahramis, had the difficult task of dealing with the finances. Their priority was to address issues in our billing processes to ensure that we billed promptly and correctly. They also prioritized the need for a line of credit collateralized by our accounts receivable.

The Fundraising Committee was busy planning fundraisers as well as working with organizations and others who pledged financial support to the project. This work included:

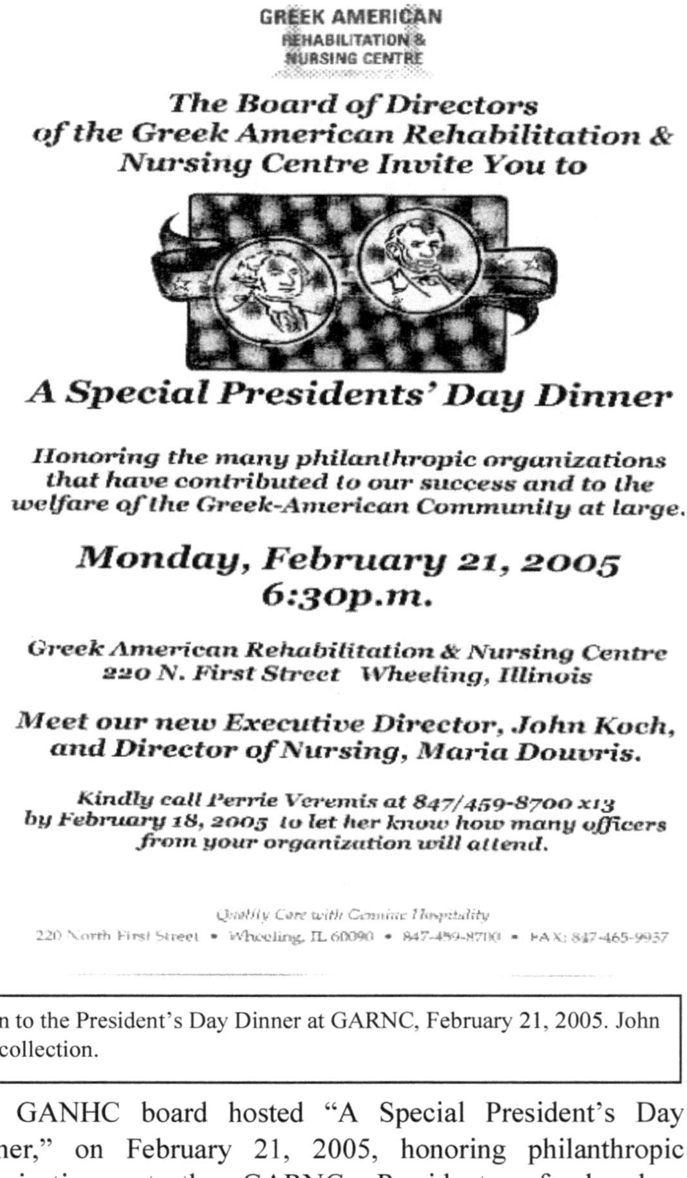

GREEK AMERICAN
REHABILITATION &
NURSING CENTRE

The Board of Directors of the Greek American Rehabilitation & Nursing Centre Invite You to

A Special Presidents' Day Dinner

Honoring the many philanthropic organizations that have contributed to our success and to the welfare of the Greek-American Community at large.

Monday, February 21, 2005
6:30p.m.

Greek American Rehabilitation & Nursing Centre
220 N. First Street Wheeling, Illinois

Meet our new Executive Director, John Koch, and Director of Nursing, Maria Douvris.

Kindly call Perrie Veremis at 847/459-8700 x13 by February 18, 2005 to let her know how many officers from your organization will attend.

Quality Care with Genuine Hospitality
220 North First Street • Wheeling, IL 60090 • 847-459-8700 • FAX: 847-465-9937

Invitation to the President's Day Dinner at GARNC, February 21, 2005. John Psiharis collection.

- The GANHC board hosted "A Special President's Day Dinner," on February 21, 2005, honoring philanthropic organizations at the GARNC. Presidents of churches, Philoptochos societies, professional organizations, and fraternal societies that supported the GANHC were invited to attend.
- The GANHC Mardi Gras Gala was held on March 5 at The Westin- O'Hare. The event featured world-renowned singer Anna Vissi, Jimmy Damon, Ellen Karis, and Robin Simone. CBS News journalist John Davis served as master of ceremonies. Gina Christie was chairlady of the Gala. Vicky Palivos chaired the silent auction and Jim Pirpiris served as chair of sponsors. Eleni hosted Anna and her two bodyguards throughout their stay. The event raised $262,930.

THURSDAY MARCH 24, 2005

PAGE 5

Greek American Rehabilitation & Nursing Center Spring Gala Extravaganza is a resounding success

Greek pop icon Anna Vissi visits seniors during karaoke party at the Greek American Rehab and Nursing Centre

The *Greek Star*, March 24, 2005. Elaine Thomopoulos collection.

- In April, Toni Panos, Emily Hayes, and Elaine Thomopoulos presented a check for $600, proceeds from a raffle held during the Daughters of Penelope Homer Chapter #98 fashion show luncheon.

  A "Memorial Day Picnic on the Nursing Home Grounds" was held on May 30. Purveyors, as well as others within the community, donated food, refreshments, and supplies. Musical entertainment, face painting, a clown, and other activities were available. Local residents were encouraged to attend with their families. A special $500 per ticket raffle was organized with the drawing held at the end of the picnic. In total 462 tickets were sold totaling $231,000. The grand prize was a Mercedes valued at $30,500. The National Philoptochos Society donated $25,000 during the picnic.

- December 7: AHEPA-13th District Smoker to benefit the GANHC at the Chateau Ritz in Niles. Gerry Garbis was the event chairman. Tickets for the evening of dinner, gambling, and raffle are $25 each.

Full back-page coverage in the March 24, 2005, edition of the *Greek Star* heralded Anna Vissi's benefit performance and visit to the GARNC. Due to the poor quality of the photo, here is the content:

> The Greek American Rehabilitation & Nursing Centre celebrated its third anniversary this March with a Mardi Gras Gala. The gala was held on March 5, at the Westin O'Hare, which was brimming with over 900 attendees. The event was sold out three weeks prior due to all the anticipation with the star line-up of performers. The center is a not-for-profit skilled nursing home providing short-term rehabilitation, long-term care, memory loss care, and hospice/respite care to the elderly, ill, and disabled who come from throughout the United States.
>
> The center accepts individuals of all ethnicities and religious affiliations.
>
> This charity benefit was undertaken by Northbrook resident and Board President Eleni Bousis with Long Grove resident and Chairwoman of the event Gina Christie raising over $250,000 for the rehabilitation center. Co-chairwoman Cathy Demos and Victoria Bousis set the room in Mardi Gras style glimmer and included colored lighting effects with masks on every wall, artistically created centerpieces, and beads for everyone.
>
> The evening's entertainment was introduced and highlighted by emcee John Davis (noted journalist formerly with CBS Chicago). The Mardi Gras Gala was kicked off with a silent auction during

"Mardi Gras Gala" flyer. March 5, 2005. John Psiharis collection.

cocktail hour, a five-course dinner, and was followed by a spectacular display of entertainment. East Coast comedienne Ellen Karis warmed up the crowd before the dance floor was lit up.

The entertainment extravaganza provided something for everyone. The dance floor was packed with revelers the entire evening. Many were fans of the world-renowned diva Anna Vissi. For the local crowd, Chicago's Frank Sinatra—Jimmy Damon, and sultry jazz singer Robin Simone provided familiar tunes to dance the night away. The Hellenic Five band accompanied all the performers with live music for dancing. It truly was an unforgettable evening. and sultry jazz singer Robin Simone provided familiar tunes to dance the night away. The Hellenic Five band accompanied all the performers with live music for dancing. It truly was an unforgettable evening.

The proceeds of the event will be utilized to offset the operational expenditures of this not-for-profit home (501 C3 corporation). For additional information, please contact the Greek American Rehabilitation & Nursing Center at 847/459-8700x13 or see www.greekameriecancare.com."

[CAPTIONS] [LEFT-TOP] Anna Vissi performs. [LEFT-BOTTOM] Guests dancing. [RIGHT-TOP]. Jimmy Damon sings for the crowd. [RIGHT-BOTTOM] Board Vice President, Peter Karahalios and family with Eleni Bousis and Robin Simone.

Greek pop icon Anna Vissi visits seniors during karaoke at the Greek American Rehab & Nursing Center

Renowned Greek and international pop icon Anna Vissi surprised the senior residents at the Greek American Rehabilitation and Nursing Centre in Wheeling, IL on Friday afternoon, March 4. Her visit created tremendous excitement among the elderly residents.

Vissi, revered as the most iconic figure in the Greek community, gave back to her fans not only by surprising the elderly residents at the Centre with a thrilling visit but also by performing at the Mardi Gras Gala that benefitted the Centre on Saturday, March 5.

Vissi visited with the residents and performed a few songs during the weekly karaoke party. In addition to Vissi, the other entertainers, John Davis, Robin Simone, and Jimmy Damon, stopped by to meet and greet the residents.

John Davis led the staff and residents in a traditional Greek dance. The afternoon of stars and the caring that they showed the residents will remain forever etched in their minds. Many friends, relatives, staff, and board members joined in the festivities. At the end of the program, board president, Eleni Bousis along with the Executive Board members provided each entertainer with an appreciation gift to recognize their dedication to the center and its residents.

Anna Vissi is dubbed the 'Madonna of Greece' because of the unprecedented longevity of her career and her evolving trend-setting style. Hailed by *The New York Times* as an 'irrepressible entertainer,' Greece's number one female artist has amazed audiences worldwide with her powerhouse voice and stage

> presence. Vissi performed a song called 'Eleni' named in honor of a young girl who died of Cooley's Anemia (thalassemia).
>
> [CAPTIONS] [LEFT-TOP] Renowned Greek and international pop icon Anna Vissi surprised the senior residents at the Greek American Rehabilitation and Nursing Centre in Wheeling, IL on Friday afternoon, March 4. [LEFT-BOTTOM] From left, Jimmy Damon, Robin Simone, John Davis, Anna Vissi with Eleni Bousis. [RIGHT-TOP] Anna Vissi greets the residents. [RIGHT-BOTTOM] John Davis leads the Greek dance.

An Easter fundraising appeal letter dated March 21, 2005, summarized the progress made to that point:

> Through the combined efforts of our friends and supporters, we were able to raise over $200,000 with our Mardi Gras Gala. We commend each and every one of you for this great success. This will be a great aid in assisting with the financial recovery of our center.
>
> But my friends, our mission and goals are not fulfilled. Although we have accomplished resolving a vital crisis facing our home, we have many obstacles to overcome.
>
> Since June 2004, when the new executive board took office, we have been working on a plan to turn our bleak picture around. First, we looked inward and evaluated our systems, and here is our progress to date:
>
> - In December 2004, we hired a new executive director, John Koch, who has over 20 years in the healthcare industry. He is well-versed in all areas of finance and operations and is in the process of evaluating staffing, any duplication of staff effort, and expenses while maintaining the quality of care.
> - Mr. Koch has already reduced the kitchen staff and will replace line cooks with a chef and assistant to cut expenditures in the dietary department. Meals will {sic} are now being cooked fresh versus using many canned and prepared items. We are evaluating food purveyors and are looking at savings of 15%-20% from our current purveyor.
> - In January, Mr. Koch hired a new Director of Nursing, Maria Douvris. Ms. Douvris comes to the center with over 20 years of experience in nursing management. Ms. Douvris is implementing quality assurance and education of the nursing staff. She will also be working with the administrator to evaluate supply costs with an expectation of achieving savings of $60,000 to $75,000 annually.

- The board along with Mr. Koch is evaluating the property, liability, and health insurance contracts. We foresee a sizable reduction in both contract prices.
- Mr. Koch has also proposed that we develop an in-house Physical, Occupational, and Speech Therapy Department. At the current time, we have a contract with an outside therapy firm, Select Rehabilitation. As a result of developing an in-house therapy team, it is estimated that the facility will increase its net profit by $500-$700,000 annually.
- We are in the process of refinancing our mortgage with Capital Source. Our Treasurer, Jerry Garbis; Board member and Attorney, Art Stamos; and Vice President and Attorney Peter Karahalios, are personally working on the negotiations. They have entered into an agreement with Capital Source, which should realize a savings of $200,000 per year in reduced debt service payments. These savings will go toward our operating budget.
- Our Medical Director, Dr. Nicholas Papanos, has established a Medical Advisory Team that meets quarterly. It is of utmost importance that we have open communications with the physicians of the community and address their issues and concerns. A meeting was held on January 26th that resulted in discussions on improving referrals.
- We are conducting a fundraising campaign to raise awareness of our plight. There are many concerned supporters. A very humble individual has successfully underwritten a two-year payment plan with the IRS.
- We are re-evaluating our identity as a nursing and rehabilitation center and are developing new marketing strategies and publications.
- We have created a website, and we invite you to take a virtual tour of this wonderful facility at www.greekamericancare.com.

We believe the combination of these efforts, with the support of our fellow leaders in the Greek American community, will result in a successful mission to save our beloved Home. To proceed with our fifth effort, we must first pay off our $600,000 debt to our current therapy firm, Select Rehabilitation. We will raise this money by having a Memorial Day Picnic on May 29, 2005 (hosted by AHEPA) on the grounds of the center. We will be selling 600 - $500 raffle tickets to raise $300,000. Our attorneys, Mr. Art Stamos and Mr. Peter Karahalios, are negotiating the balance with Select Rehabilitation. We are counting on seeing you at the picnic.

In April, there were 163 residents with 24 Medicare and five bed holds. During the April 11 board meeting, Toni Panos, Emily Hayes, and Elaine

Thomopoulos presented a check for $600, proceeds from the Daughters of Penelope Homer Chapter #98 raffle held during their luncheon fashion show. The nominating committee presented their recommendations for new board members: Thomas Skallas, Tom Diamond, Jack Mitsakopoulos, Peter Kopsaftis, Chris Tomaras, and Dr. George Sianas. With two vacant slots to fill, the board voted to approve Jack Mitsakopoulos and Peter Kopsaftis. The others will be considered when openings arise.

In June the resident census was 163. Of the total, 26 were covered by Medicare. In July there were 166 residents. By mid-August, we reached 175. Those numbers were consistent throughout the rest of the year. Approximately 80 percent of the residents were of Greek descent, and more than 65 percent were on public aid.

In August, GANHC formalized its relationship with the Greek Orthodox Metropolis of Chicago. The Diocese ensured weekly services in the chapel from a local priest at no cost. Accounts payable were $1,282,630, down slightly from the $1,563,585 we owed in June.

After much conversation and consideration, the board decided to change the name of the facility. Until then, the facility was called the Greek American Rehabilitation and Nursing Centre. Some felt it was not reflective of the facility as a whole and felt that the term "nursing home" did not always have the most positive connotation. A few of the names considered were Hellenic Home, Hellenic Village, Hellenic Glory, Hellenic Light of Care, Hellenic Embrace, Hellenic Life, and Hellenic Rehabilitation and Care Centre. On September 19, the board voted 13 to two to change the name of the facility to Greek American Rehabilitation and Care Centre. We left open the possibility that the name might be changed in the future if a major contribution were received.

I stepped off the board in June 2006 when my term came to an end. It was a long and wild ride! Being part of this effort was an enriching, exciting, and transformative experience.

After 20-plus years of GACS and the GANHC, a break was long overdue. I was worn out. The crises that each organization faced were challenging at best. Combined, they were overwhelming. With the Centre open and on a path to success, and a new leadership team in place, it felt like the right time to step down. I was confident the nursing home was now on the right track and in good hands, and steady progress was being made in operations, finances, and fundraising. Our group built and opened it! Mission accomplished! It's up to current and future leaders of this institution to carry this mission forward and take it to the next level.

To this day, I am grateful to have had the opportunity to be part of this monumental endeavor. I will forever cherish the memories, experiences, and lessons learned, and hold those who played a part in this story in the highest esteem.

The organization that was launched in the back room of the Elysion Restaurant on that December evening in 1982 achieved something few would have thought possible… the second Greek American nursing home in the United States! This little group grew into a movement that forever transformed the *omogenia* of Chicago!

The GARCC Wall of Honor on display in the lobby reception area. September 13, 2018. Photo by John Psiharis. John Psiharis collection.

Epilogue

By spring 2007, the deficit had been reduced by $2.8 million, and with current census levels, the home was able to meet monthly expenses. A debt of approximately $1 million remained. The annual gala, held on May 19, raised $773,550. The event, theme, "An Enchanted Evening," featured performances by Aggelos, Stelios, and Diamandis Dionisiou, and "our own Frank Sinatra, Mr. Jimmy Damon, a dedicated friend of the Home."

On November 18, 2010, the GARCC hosted its second annual Yiayia and Papou Dinner Dance, "Generations Coming Together," at Fountain Blue Banquets and Conference Center in Des Plaines, IL Musical entertainment for all ages including selections from the roaring 1920s to the present. Children's entertainment included a magic show, face painting, and a balloon artist. Tickets were $75 for adults and $30 for children 12 and under.

On April 28, 2012, the GARCC hosted a gala celebrating its 10th anniversary featuring performances by Eleni Dimou, Konstantinos Christoforou, and Christos Sevastos, accompanied by the Enigma Band.

On November 18, 2017, The Hellenic Legacy Gala event celebrated the 15th anniversary of the opening of the GARCC. Held at the Westin–O'Hare Hotel, the gala featured performances by Giorgos Tsalikis and Yiannis Kritikos and was attended by nearly 700 guests.

In January 2018, the facility achieved a Five-Star rating from the Centers for Medicare and Medicaid Services (CMS) and was designated one of the

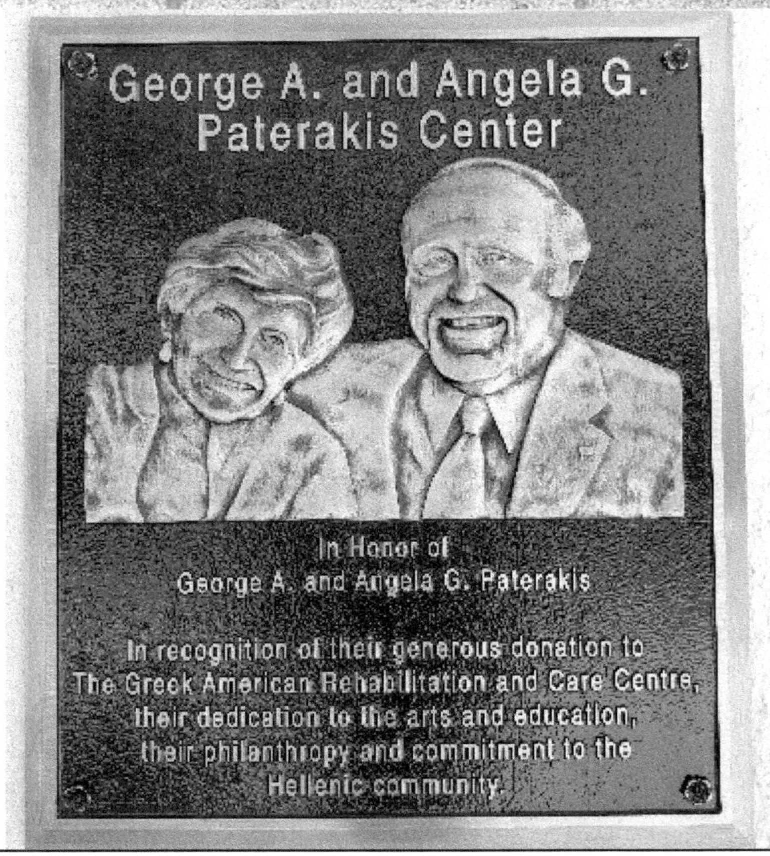

Top: Nicholas J. Bouras Center commemorative plaque. **Bottom:** George and Angela Paterakis Center commemorative plaque. June 11, 2020. Photos by John Psiharis.

outstanding nursing homes in Illinois. The GARCC also achieved certification from Vohra Wounds Physicians as a Vohra Center of Excellence for Wound Management in 2018.

That same month, the GARCC purchased two adjacent properties through generous donations from the Nicholas J. and Anna K. Bouras Family Foundation and the George A. and Angela G. Paterakis Trust. This includes the building that housed the Wheeling Senior Center, with plans to open an outpatient rehab program in the building, and the Wheeling Professional Building, which currently houses medical offices. It is heartening that the vision we set forth from the earliest of days, a Greek Village composed of a nursing home, adult day care, assisted living, childcare, and congregate activities on one campus, may come to fruition in the not-too-distant future.

Over the years several renovations have occurred, including converting the ice cream parlor into the "Bird's View Café and Gift Shop." The entire fourth floor is now a specially designed memory care unit. An Internet café is available to the residents.

The facility still maintains a resident census that is about two-thirds Medicaid, and the state remains delinquent in its payments, but with robust fundraising efforts and community support, the facility is financially stable. A waiting list of prospective residents exists. Presently, GARCC offers short-term and long-term care, specialized dementia care, outpatient physical and occupational therapy, cardiac and pulmonary therapy, wound care and pain management, respite care services, and hospice care.

This book chronicles the early years of the nursing home, but the need for community support is ongoing. A 2018 Christmas appeal letter from Eleni and Peter highlighted the continued need to raise funds to upgrade or replace systems and equipment that we initially installed 20 years ago.

Among the needs were new nurse calls light system (still needed $99,369), elopement monitoring call system ($66,818), Point Click Care Electronic Medical Records Software ($20,700 installation, $5,000 monthly maintenance), Medicare/Rehabilitation room renovations (11 rooms – approximately $450,000), and a new air conditioning system (approximately $250,000).

On May 18, 2019, a benefit gala dinner benefitting the GARCC was held at The Westin-O'Hare Hotel. The "Hellenic Legacy Gala," featured exclusive performances by Glykeria and Kostas Karafotis. The $300 per ticket event was a big success.

An October 2019, ranking of the "Best Nursing Homes in Illinois in 2020," by *Newsweek* magazine, ranked the Greek-American Rehabilitation & Care Centre number 14 on the list of the top 30 nursing homes in the state. In 2019, according to the Illinois Department of Public Health, there were

BEST NURSING HOMES 2021
Newsweek
statista

Certificate

Based on the results of an independent analysis, Newsweek recognizes

Greek American Rehabilitation & Care Centre

as one of the

Best Nursing Homes 2021

in the state of

Illinois

The following parameters were taken into consideration:

Key performance indicators on health inspections, quality measures, and staffing

Recommendations from experts

COVID-19 Response

Nancy Cooper
Global Editor in Chief
Newsweek

Manuel Mörbach
CEO
Statista Inc

Newsweek statista

Certificate designating GARCC one of the best nursing homes in Illinois in 2021. From the *Yasou* GACS Facebook page. Posted on October 13, 2020.

approximately 1,200 long-term care facilities in Illinois serving more than 100,000 residents. GARCC was again named one of the best nursing homes in Illinois for 2021 in the *Newsweek* ranking. The August 10, 2022, edition of Newsweek ranked GARCC number 17, placing the home in the top 2.4 percent in Illinois.

These years later, I continue to believe that the votes that John Rassogianis and I cast to help elect Eleni as president were the right thing to do. John felt the same. In my view, we needed a dynamic fundraiser to lead us out of this crisis. It is doubtful that the GARCC would be here today without the leadership and fundraising prowess that Eleni provided.

As of December 2023, Eleni remains chairman of the board and Peter Karahalios is president. Dr. Lisa Palivos is vice president, Peter Kopsaftis is treasurer, and Paula Tolan-Francis is secretary. Theresa Tzakis continues to serve on the board and is the longest-serving member. After John Koch left the administrator role, he was succeeded by Eleni Ifantis, Mark Murphey, and Dino Varnavas, who is the administrator as of 2023.

The GARCC website, (accessed on March 25, 2020), announced the planned summer opening of Compassionate Love Day Care, a children's day care program. The program serves children of employees, resident families, and the neighboring community (ages six weeks to six years). The COVID-19 pandemic upended those plans, but the program did open in 2022 and is housed in the Paterakis Center within the Bouras International Campus. Intergenerational visits with nursing home residents are a regular part of the daycare schedule.

In 2021, the GARCC board announced a restructuring of the organization to comply with IRS fundraising regulations for not-for-profit organizations. The GARCC is now under the auspices of the newly created Greek American Health Services Foundation (GAHSF). All fundraising efforts were transitioned to the newly incorporated parent organization and the nursing home operates as a subsidiary of the GAHSF.

More recently, a March 2022 Easter appeal letter from the GAHSF signed by Eleni Bousis and Peter Karhalios, provided an update to the community about the challenges of running a nursing home in the pandemic era. It read in part:

> As we are celebrating our 20th year of operations, we are facing enormous costs which must be addressed, including updating worn-out furniture and other fixtures within our facility. Costs for nursing and daily supplies for the residents have increased dramatically.
>
> Additionally, like so many other healthcare service providers, in order to retain our wonderful and dedicated nursing staff and be able to stay competitive, salaries for Certified Nursing Assistants and Nurses needed to be increased by 30%. This was <u>absolutely</u> necessary to provide health care services to our treasured residents and your beloved Family members and for the nursing home to maintain its 5-star rating by the Federal Government.
>
> Consequently, as a direct result of the financial challenges caused by the Pandemic, there has been a 30% increase in healthcare services salaries and the necessary 5% overtime (as we all know, healthcare professionals are exhausted requiring the use of expensive health care staffing companies), intense competition for recruiting nursing staff, and an increase in the cost of medical supplies which were as follow: 2019 - $155,019; 2020 - $190,538; a huge jump in 2021 to $353,800; and is estimated to double in 2022.
>
> However, the most daunting and important issue we face is our $9 Million Dollar [sic] mortgage which threatens the future and legacy of all immigrants who each added value to your Nursing Home. Although we have been able to reduce the original $ 17-million mortgage balance, we know with certainty that the nursing home will be protected by the elimination of this mortgage balance.

Because of all the above facts, we are initiating a **Mortgage Elimination Campaign** which will begin with the Easter Appeal in hopes to resurrect your Nursing Home from this deficit as our Lord resurrected for our Salvation. Our goal is to ELIMINATE this mortgage to assure [sic] the sustainability and longevity of your beloved nursing home which is a safe haven for our most vulnerable population. Since its inception over 40 years ago of establishing the Greek American nursing home, we have accomplished much and want to assure it will be here for the next 100 years for all those in need. All of this was accomplished by your ongoing generosity. We are appealing to you to put your hand on your heart and be generous with your donation.

Our most recent accomplishment has been the opening of the children's day care, Compassionate Love Day Care, which opened to our staff and the community earlier this year. Located at the Paterakis Center, this early learning center brings us one step closer to our vision of creating the Bouras International Campus.

Our vision is to create the Bouras International Campus which will be a beacon of pride and the Crown Jewel of the Greek Community of the United States. Within this Bouras International Campus, we have the Greek-American Nursing Home, The Compassionate Love Day Care Center, and The Wheeling Professional Building (medical office building), and we hope to build an Assistant [sic] Living Facility in the near future.

As many of you know, this expanded international campus was purchased by the late Mr. and Mrs. Nicholas J. and Anna K. Bouras of blessed memory, excluding the day care building which was generously donated by the late Mr. and Mrs. George A. and Angela G. Paterakis of blessed memory. Mr. Bouras' ongoing generosity continues to keep the nursing home afloat by paying many of our daily expenditures.

In order to undertake any future expansions including an Assisted Living facility, we need to focus on reducing and eliminating our mortgage so that your nursing home will be around for many more generations.

As a not-for-profit organization with 70% of our resident population on Medicaid, the Board of Directors, staff, volunteers, and residents humbly implore you to include us in your Easter offering. Please give generously to your home so we may continue to protect, embrace, and serve the elderly and needy in our community. Your support and love are critically needed and undeniably appreciated."

The Greek-American Rehabilitation and Care Centre. September 13, 2018. Photos by John Psiharis.

Top: Entrance to the Greek American Rehabilitation and Care Centre, May 25, 2018. **Bottom:** The Dochios Memorial Campus, June 11, 2020. Photos by John Psiharis.

Top: Arcadian Lake as seen from the rear terrace. **Bottom:** Second pond with Wheeling Tower/ One Milwaukee Place, a senior citizens' residence, in background. On the right is the Paterakis Center. May 25, 2018. Photos by John Psiharis.

Top: George A. and Angela G. Paterakis Center. **Bottom:** Two GARCC vehicles used to transport residents. May 25, 2018. Photos by John Psiharis.

This elegant and impressive Wall of Honor in the nursing home lobby greets all who enter. The wall recognizes founding, past, and current board members, and major donors. A few errors are apparent: Irene Antoniou and Connie Gountanis-Rigas were neither founding board members nor board members of the GANHC. Emilee and George Alexandrou, Eleni Bousis, Frances Kuchuris, and Christina Spiratos were not founding members of the GANHC, but did serve on the board at various times. Polyzoes Gavaris was a founding board member of the GANHC. September 13, 2018. Photo by John Psiharis. John Psiharis collection.

GANHC Who's Who

Board of Directors

Emilee (Argiris) Alexandrou was a member of the GANHC board. With her husband George, they helped with fundraising efforts and chaired a couple of fundraising events. Emilee was also a board member of GACS and heavily involved in fundraising for Little City, which cared for her special needs child. Emilee and George ran Little City Bingo Nights that were held at a bingo parlor on Lincoln Avenue north of Foster. Early on, the GANHC benefited from a couple of bingo nights they organized for us.

George Alexandrou was a member of the GANHC board. George was the original owner of the Psistaria Greek Taverna and later the None-better Ice Cream Company. He was also a past president of St. Haralambos Greek Orthodox Church. Along with his wife Emilee, they helped with fundraising efforts and chaired a couple of fundraisers. They were also supporters of GACS and heavily involved in fundraising for Little City. George and Emilee ran the Little City Bingo Nights that were held at a bingo parlor on Lincoln Avenue north of Foster. Early on, the GANHC benefited from a couple of bingo nights they organized for us.

James Angelopoulos joined the GANHC board on March 27, 2000, as a representative of the Greek American Restaurant Association.

Chris Tomaras and Eleni Bousis during a Greek-American Community Services Advisory Board meeting at the Barclay-Chicago Hotel. Date unknown. John Rassogianis collection.

Constantine Bahramis became a member of the GANHC board in July 2004. He had a background in accounting and as chair of the finance committee applied these skills toward improving collections and accounting practices.

Eleni Bousis is GARCC chairman as of December 2023, after having served as president since 2004. She became a GANHC board member in 1996 and organized several successful fundraising events. Eleni led efforts that raised millions for the facility. She was also a member of the GACS Advisory Board where she chaired several successful fundraising events. Eleni and her husband, Dimitri, own Cermak Produce, a chain of produce and grocery markets in the Chicago area. They are benefactors for the Little City Foundation and other organizations here and in Greece. Eleni is a founding board member and currently chairs the Hippocratic Cancer Research Foundation (HCRF). Further information about Eleni Bousis can be found on page 198.

Christine Burbulis was a board member of GACS and joined the GANHC shortly after it was created. She chaired the real estate committee which led the search for potential properties including our eventual home in Wheeling. Christine was a real estate professional who oversaw property acquisitions for the Midwest Region of the U.S. Department of Housing and Urban Development. She resigned from the board in April 1998 in protest of the selection of the project architect. Photo on page 188.

James "Newport" Chiakulas was a GANHC board member in the mid-1990s. A labor attorney by profession, he was director of region 36 of the Illinois Education Association, and the long-time president of the Chicago Council for Justice on Cyprus, as his father before him had done. Jim was on the Bylaws Committee when it reviewed and revised the bylaws. He unsuccessfully ran for Chicago alderman of the 49th Ward against Alderman Joe Moore and for Congress against Representative Sidney Yates, a long-serving incumbent. He had previously played saxophone in jazz clubs with the stage name of "Jimmy Newport."

(L-R): Stella Adinamis-Cuthbert, GACS President Evangeline Mistaras, unknown, and Maria Paleologos during the Second Annual Greek-American Community Services Heritage Awards Dinner. Fountain Blue, Des Plaines, IL. April 22, 1988. John Psiharis collection.

James Christie was the owner of Bon-Ton Food Services, a poultry company located in Wheeling that serviced food service establishments and restaurants. He became a member of the GANHC board in April 1999 and served for several years. During a time of extreme need, Jim loaned money to help the GANHC through a difficult period. Jim also donated food for several picnics and open houses. In total, he donated more than $200,000 to the GANHC. Further information on James Christie can be found on page 198.

Stella Adinamis-Cuthbert was an early board member of both the GANHC and GACS, and as a lawyer, helped with the bylaws, incorporation, and tax exemption process. Stella was commissioner of the Illinois Department of Employment Security under Governor James Thompson.

John Davis joined the GANHC board shortly before I left and subsequently became vice president of the nursing home board. He and his wife Maria were involved in fundraising before they joined. They were also active in the Hellenic Museum and Cultural Center. John was a news anchor and reporter for CBS (WBBM TV Channel 2).

Toula Dernis was elected to the GANHC board in July 2005 and was active in fundraising. She was also a member of the Macedonian Society of Chicago. Her husband was Dr. Dimitris Dernis.

Thomas Diamond became a GANHC board member shortly before I left the board. He was co-owner of Fountain Blue Banquets and Conference Center in Des Plaines, IL, and Concorde Banquets in Kildeer, IL. Tom was elected president of the Greek American Restaurant Association in November 2002 and was a GARA representative to the GANHC.

Connie Dumas briefly served as a GANHC board member in the 1990s. Connie was a member of St. Peter and Paul Greek Orthodox Church in Glenview, IL.

Bertha Facklis became a member of the board after Soteria pledged its support to the GANHC. We invited Soteria to have two board seats. Bertha and Theresa Tzakis came on board. Bertha was a founding member of Soteria and served as president for 29 years. This was in addition to Thalia Jameson and Jean Kaporis who were also active in Soteria. Bertha was older and was not able to attend many meetings. At a certain point, she stepped aside and was replaced by Christine Mourikes. Bertha passed away at the age of 90 in February 1999.

Efthimia Galetsis was elected to the GANHC board in July 2005. In November 2006, Effie transitioned to the staff and became the chief financial officer of GARCC.

Gerald Garbis joined the GANHC board on February 15, 1999, and subsequently became treasurer. He was a retired civil engineer for the Metropolitan Water Reclamation District. Gerry, an AHEPA member since 1968, was past president of AHEPA Chapter #380, and secretary of the AHEPA Scholarship Committee. He acted as the liaison between the board, the architect, and the contractor during the construction process. Gerry co-chaired the 2000 GANHC picnic and a 2005 AHEPA fundraising smoker.

Polyzoes Gavaris was a founding member of both GACS and the GANHC. As the owner of the Elysion Restaurant, he donated meeting space and coffee for many meetings. In the beginning, Pol served as the registered agent for GACS but disagreed with the decision to separate into two organizations, and as a result, resigned from the GANHC. He remained on the GACS board for several years. Pol was active in the Pan Laconian Federation.

Helen Geocaris was a founding member of both GACS and the GANHC. She served on both boards until health concerns precluded her from participating. Helen served as co-chairman of the membership committee and co-chaired several fundraising events. She was involved with the Daughters of Penelope and helped to coordinate the Daughters' pledge commitment to the GANHC. Her husband, John, was the 40th Ward Democratic Party Committeeman.

(L-R): John C. Geocaris receives the Greek-American Community Services Heritage Award from John Psiharis as John Rassogianis and Elaine Thomopoulos look on. GACS Third Annual Heritage Awards Dinner. Diplomat Banquets, Chicago, IL. September 22, 1989. John Psiharis collection.

John Geocaris was a board member of GANHC in the early years and was the first co-chairman of the committee when it was part of GACS. He was the 40th Ward Democratic Party committeeman, at the time, the first elected Greek American in Chicago and one of only a few in Illinois. John was also deputy commissioner of the Chicago Department of Streets and Sanitation, a supporter of GACS, and active in AHEPA.

Helen Georges was an early board member of GACS and a founding board member of the GANHC. She was the GANHC's first vice president from inception through 2004 and was actively involved in most facets of the project. Helen had been an administrator for the Illinois Department of Public Aid. Photo on page 184.

Joanne Giannopoulos, PharmD., became a board member shortly before I left. She was a pharmacy professor at the University of Illinois at Chicago and worked at Swedish Covenant Hospital.

Metropolitan Iakovos of Krinis became honorary chairman of the GANHC in 1996 and retained this title until his passing in 2017. His representative on the board was Father George Massouras. His Eminence was enthroned as Bishop of the Greek Orthodox Diocese of Chicago in 1979 and elevated to Metropolitan in 1997.

Thalia Jameson was a founding member of both GACS and the GANHC. She was a member of Soteria and helped shepherd their support of the

(L-R): Seated: Unknown, Louis Malevitis. Standing: Unknown, Mary Kakavas, and Helen Georges at a GANHC fundraiser. Date unknown. John Psiharis collection.

GANHC. Thalia was an elementary school teacher at Chappell School. She passed away in 1994.

George Jameson was briefly a member of the GANHC board in the early days. His background in real estate was helpful.

Mary Kakavas was a supporter and board member of both the GANHC and GACS. She joined the GANHC Board in 1985 and stepped off in 2005. Mary served as GANHC board secretary, succeeding Toni Panos. Along with her husband Bill, they owned Thirteen Colonies Banquets at Belmont and Cumberland in the Thatcher Woods Mall in River Grove IL. Mary and Bill were generous and early supporters of both organizations and remained active with them for many years. In total, they donated more than $150,000 to the GANHC and thousands more to GACS. Mary was a member of the Supreme Board of the United Hellenic American Voters of America and AHEPA Chapter #311 – Zoe. She was also a board member and past officer of the Megalopolis Society. Further information on Mary Kakavas can be found on page 201.

William Kakavas was a passionate supporter of the GANHC since its earliest days and served as a board member for many years. Bill was also a GACS board member. Bill and his wife, Mary, owned Thirteen Colonies Banquets at Belmont and Cumberland in the Thatcher Woods Mall in River Grove, IL. Early on they pledged their hall and hors d'oeuvres for a series of fundraising cocktail parties benefiting the GANHC and underwrote many such events over the years until they sold the business and retired. As

Mary Dochios Camberos
Supports Greek-American
Nursing Home Project
By John Rassogianis

Dr. Mary Dochios Kamberos and John Regas. *The Greek Star*. Date unknown. Elaine Thomopoulos collection.

a popular location for community events, Bill and Mary knew many within the community, enjoyed their trust, and appealed to them for support. He was a terrific fundraiser and generous benefactor. Once the facility opened, Bill took responsibility for working with dietary to improve the quality of the residents' meals. In total, Bill and Mary donated more than $150,000 to the GANHC. Further information on Bill Kakavas can be found on page 201.

Mary Dochios Kamberos M.D., was the first "Mega Benefactor" of GANHC, having donated more than $1.5 million to the project. In recognition and appreciation of her support, Dr. Kamberos was elected to the board in 2003. She was older and lived on the far south side, so she seldom attended but occasionally called into board meetings from her home. Dr. Kamberos was a pediatrician for 50 years and spent much of that time providing care to juveniles in detention. The campus of the Greek American Nursing and Rehabilitation Center is named in honor of her parents, Chris N. and Helen D. Dochios. Further information on Dr. Kamberos can be found on page 201.

Jean Kaporis was a founding member of both GACS and the GANHC and served as assistant treasurer of the nursing home committee. She was instrumental in garnering the support of Soteria and helped with fundraising. Jean was also an active member of the Annunciation Cathedral and was president of its Philoptochos Society for a time, she was the point of contact when we held meetings or other activities at the church.

Peter Karahalios J.D. joined the GANHC board in 2003 upon the recommendation of Bill and Mary Kakavas and became vice president in 2004. A lawyer by profession, Peter was chief deputy treasurer of Cook County. He had also been an enforcement attorney for the Illinois Department of Securities. Peter helped with several legal entanglements that resulted from the financial crisis we were experiencing and offered free legal services to anyone who wanted to prepare a will or other planned giving instruments benefiting the nursing home. As of 2023, Peter is the GARCC board president.

Anna Kioutas J.D., served as a GANHC board member for a short period in the early years. She stepped off due to concerns about a husband and wife both serving on the board. Anna continued to serve as a legal advisor to the board. She was an accomplished attorney and volunteered her services as needed from 1982 through 2004 including helping us with the purchase of the property, financing, and other legal matters. Further information on Anna Kioutas can be found on page 202.

Dr. Theodosis Kioutas. Date unknown. John Psiharis collection.

Theodosis Kioutas M.D. was a founding and long-time board member of both GACS and the GANHC. Initially, he served as the chairman of the GACS Nursing Home Committee. When GANHC spun off onto its own in 1985, Dr. Kioutas served as president of the organization from its inception through 2004. His indefatigable spirit, drive, and endless passion for both organizations were key to their success. Dr. Kioutas passed away on January 26, 2005. More detailed information on Dr. Theodosis Kioutas can be found on page 202.

Katherine Katsoyannis M.D. was a board member of the GANHC from 2003 to 2004, shortly after the facility opened. Katherine specialized in geriatric medicine and was affiliated with Lutheran General Hospital. She was Dr. Kioutas' daughter. Her father and others had hoped that she would succeed her father as president. After narrowly losing the vote to succeed her father to Eleni Bousis, she resigned from the board.

Peter Kopsaftis became a GANHC board member in April 2005. He owned Paaris & Associates, a real estate investment and development company now known as Blackwater Assets. He is treasurer of the board as of August 2021.

Ethel Kotsovos was a member of the GANHC board from inception through June 1996, when she became office manager, and stepped off the board. Once the nursing home opened, Ethel became the volunteer coordinator. Ethel had been a social worker at the Hellenic Foundation and then moved to GACS, first as coordinator of the GACS Ethnic Elderly Needs Assessment Project, then as director of the Community Aging

Eleni Bousis greets Jim Kozonis, as Dr. Theodosis Kioutas looks on. Greek-American Community Services Advisory Board dinner meeting. June 1992. Photo by John Rassogianis. John Psiharis collection.

Network, and as a social worker in the adult day care center. Further information on Ethel Kotsovos can be found on page 196.

Demetrios Kozonis was a member of the GANHC board and a financial supporter of the project. He helped coordinate a donation from the Federation of Sterea Hellas. Jim was a successful developer of strip mall shopping centers on the northwest side of Chicago. He was also a member of the GACS Advisory Board and chaired the GACS building fund drive. Jim resigned from the GANHC in 1999.

Frances Kuchuris was a member of the GANHC board for a few years and was a financial supporter of the project. Her late husband owned Mary Ann Baking Company, Alpha Baking, and East Balt Commissary, among others. The company was a major purveyor of hamburger buns for McDonald's. Her son Frank took over the business upon the passing of his father. Frank was a member of the GACS Advisory Board. Frances resigned in April 1998 in protest of the architect selected. Photo on page 199.

George Lekas became a GANHC board member on February 15, 1999. He also served as assistant treasurer, working with treasurers John Secaras and Gerald Garbis, and was a member of the nominating committee. George retired as a science teacher for the Chicago Board of Education after 39 years. He was a member (and past president) of St. Demetrios church. George also helped to coordinate publicity including the GANHC newsletter.

(L-R): Christine Burbulis and Anna Manos at a GANHC event. Date unknown. John Rassogianis collection.

Dee Louchios was a GANHC board member for a brief period in the early 90s.

Anna Manos was a founding member of both GACS and the GANHC. She served as the first treasurer of GACS and as the corresponding secretary of the GANHC. Anna was a legal secretary at Hollobow and Teslitz, a downtown law firm, and lived around the corner from the Elysion Restaurant.

Steven Manta was a member of the GANHC board between 1999 and 2003 and was a long-time member of AHEPA. He served as supreme president of AHEPA in 1997-1998 and co-owned JL Manta, an industrial painting contractor company.

Sam Markos was a member of the GANHC board for a brief period representing the Greek American Restaurant Association. He was the owner of Crystal Palace Banquets and had previously owned Diplomat Banquets and co-owned Diplomat West in Elmhurst.

Rev. George Massouras served as a board member of the GANHC and as a liaison to Metropolitan Iakovos. He was the protopresbyter of Assumption Greek Orthodox Church and his wife Despina (Des) was the GACS social worker for a time. At a certain point, Father George retired from ministry and the Metropolitan assigned Father Demetrios N. Treantafeles of St Nectarios Church as his liaison. It was the closest church in proximity to the Centre.

James Mezilson was a member of the GANHC board and served as treasurer during the time we were negotiating the North Park Village and Rosehill locations. He was an Archon of the Ecumenical Patriarchate of Constantinople and a member of both the Annunciation Cathedral and Sts. Constantine and Helen churches. Jim was a founding member of the Hellenic Museum and Cultural Center and had worked for former U.S. Senator Paul Douglas. He was a journalist by profession beginning his career in 1939. For more than 50 years, Jim's column "Mez," appeared in the *Greek Press* newspaper.

James M. Mezilson speaks after receiving the Greek-American Community Services Heritage Award. September 22, 1989. Diplomat Banquets. John Rassogianis collection.

Harry Milakis was an early member of the GANHC board and the first chairman of its fundraising committee. Harry was regional director for the City of Hope and had an extensive background in fundraising. Before joining the City of Hope, Harry was director of the Southwest YMCA. He passed away after a struggle with cancer.

Jack Mitsakopoulos became a board member in April 2005. He was co-owner and president of the Chicago Fish House.

Andy Nichols was a GANHC board member in the early 1990s. He was recommended by Jean Kaporis and helped with publicity.

Kay Mourikes joined the GANHC board as a representative of Soteria, replacing Bertha Facklis who stepped off the board. At some point, Kay stepped off the board and was replaced by her daughter Tina Spirates, an attorney by profession.

Maria Paleologos was an early board member of the GANHC and helped with fundraising. She traveled each year and spent six months in Chicago and six months in Greece, so she was not always present. Maria was a member of St. George Greek Orthodox Church and active in their Philoptochos Society. Photo on page 181.

John Psiharis and Toni Panos ringing a ship's bell on the Odyssey cruise ship. Lake Point Tower is the background. Circa 1994 or 1995. Photo by John Rassogianis. John Psiharis collection.

Toni Panos was a founding member of both GACS and GANHC and served as recording secretary of the GANHC board during its early years. She was a medical secretary for a doctor in the western suburbs.

Toni lived in Oak Park and was a member of the Assumption Greek Orthodox Church. She was longtime friends with the Thomopoulos and Rassogianis families. Toni eventually moved to Lombard. She was involved in the Daughters of Penelope and helped to guide the Daughters' pledge commitments to the GANHC. Toni resigned from the GANHC board in December 2004.

Faye Pantazelos briefly became a GANHC board member in July 2004. She was also a board member of GACS for a short time. Faye, whose background was in banking, worked for the Bank of Ravenswood and other financial institutions before starting New Century Bank. The bank was closed by the FDIC in April 2010 because of the Great Recession that began in 2008.

Timothea Papas was elected to the GANHC board in July 2005. She attended St. Andrew Greek Orthodox Church.

Thomas Pappas was a Greek American Restaurant Association (GARA) representative on the GANHC board and owner of Market Square

John Rassogianis in his first-floor office at Greek-American Community Services. Date unknown. John Psiharis collection.

Restaurant in Wheeling, IL. Market Square was a frequent destination for pre- or post-meeting meals, coffee, and conversation.

Demetrios Pirpiris was a GANHC board member for several years and served as second vice president. He was a member of AHEPA, helping to coordinate their support of the project. Jim chaired a couple of fundraising events including annual smoker benefits through his AHEPA chapter. He owned Pirpiris Insurance Agency and provided us with guidance when we dealt with insurance matters.

Nicholas Pishos was elected to the GANHC board in July 2005. He was a funeral director associated with Cumberland Chapels, among others. Nick encouraged his clients to designate memorial donations to benefit the GANHC.

Chadwick Prodromos M.D., served on the GANHC board for a short time. He was an orthopedic surgeon who specialized in sports medicine and was affiliated with the Stamelos Clinic.

John Psiharis was co-founder first president, and executive director of GACS, a founding member of the GANHC, and a board member from inception through 2006. At different times, he served as assistant treasurer, and as co-chair of the bylaws, operations, and nominating committees.

John Rassogianis joined the GANHC board shortly after he became involved with GACS in 1987 and served through 2004. As publicity chairman, John was instrumental in coordinating the publicity efforts of the GANHC for many years.

Eugenia Seifer and John Rassogianis at a GANHC fundraising event. Date unknown. John Rassogianis collection.

John Regas was a board member of the GANHC. A noted interior designer, he owned a historic mansion on Astor Street that was designed by David Adler. John hosted an exclusive cocktail party fundraiser at the mansion that raised more than $80,000 for the GANHC. In April 1998, he had a falling out with the board over the selection of the project architect and resigned from the GANHC. Photo on page 185.

Peter Regas was a member of the GANHC board and a real estate attorney with Regas, Frezados, & Harp. His brother was John Regas. Peter resigned from the board in April 1998.

Nick Romas was a member of the GANHC board in the early 1990s, around the time of the North Park Village property effort. Nick, along with his brothers, owned several restaurants, including Mayor's Row, State & Lake, and Marina City Restaurants. He was also a donor and fundraiser for Mayor Richard M. Daley.

John H. Secaras was a board member of the GANHC and at various times served as both treasurer and co-treasurer. He also chaired the nominating committee and for a time was the co-chairman of the fundraising committee. A lawyer by profession, John had been the regional solicitor at the Chicago Office (Midwest Region) for the U.S. Department of Labor.

Eugenia Georgoules Seifer was a GANHC board member for several years and helped with fundraising. She was a past president of both the

Greek Women's University Club and the Hellenic Foundation Women's Auxiliary. Eugenia also served as 13th district governor for the Daughters of Penelope and in that role helped to shepherd their pledge to the GANHC.

Christina Spiratos joined the GANHC board as a member of Soteria to replace Kay Mourikes, her mother. She was an attorney and a member of the legal and nominating committees.

Art Stamos joined the GANHC board in 2005. Art and I co-chaired the board's operations committee from 2004 to 2006. The committee was tasked with monitoring the facility's operations. He generously donated the funds needed to procure a biometric time clock to eliminate timecard fraud. Art was an attorney by profession.

Kathy Stathos joined the GANHC board shortly after its inception and served for a short time. She had been a social worker in the Hellenic Foundation's south side office.

Sofia Tassaras was a member of the GANHC Publicity Committee for a short time. I recall attending meetings at her River Forest home.

Elaine Thomopoulos, Ph.D., was co-founder, first vice president, and administrator of GACS and a founding member of the GANHC. Elaine served on the GANHC board from inception through 2004 and was the second vice president for many of those years. She was involved in many facets of the GANHC including fundraising, design and construction, and management of the facility once it opened. Twice, Elaine and I co-chaired the GANHC Bylaws Committee.

Harry Tompary was a GANHC board member and past president of the Hellenic Professional Society of Illinois. He was John Secaras' nephew.

Theresa Tzakis became a member of the GANHC board as a representative of Soteria and served on the board for many years. She became GANHC board secretary in 2004 and as of 2022 remains on the board. Theresa lived in Vernon Hills and often came to the meetings with her brother Sam, who photographed several of our events. As of December 2023, Theresa remains a board member and holds the distinction of being the longest-serving board member of the GARCC.

Key People & Supporters

Margaret Balabanos became director of volunteers after Ethel Kotsovos left the position. This was around the time that Burton "Buddy" Behr became administrator. She had previously worked at the Hellenic Foundation.

Susan Barbian, R.N. was the first administrator of the Greek-American Rehabilitation and Nursing Centre. She had a background in nursing and was a licensed nursing home administrator. Susan was recommended to us and employed by First Health Care Associates, the management firm GANHC hired to open and run the nursing home for the first year of operations. She began in August 2001 and her last day was January 10, 2003.

Burton "Buddy" Behr became the second administrator of the Greek American Rehabilitation and Care Centre on December 24, 2002.

Shael Bellows was president of First Health Care Associates.

Cambridge Realty Capital Ltd. of Chicago was the financial advisor who managed the bond sale to finance the construction of the nursing home.

Columbia National Bank of Chicago was a regular supporter of GACS through the support of Leon Xintaris, the bank's executive vice president. Columbia financed the mortgage for GACS and for the GANHC land purchase. Columbia was bought out by LaSalle Banks, which was eventually purchased by Bank of America.

James Dades, C.P.A. was the accountant who prepared the annual audited financial statements for both the GANHC and GACS. Jim was referred to GACS by Peter Maroutsos and then subsequently hired by GANHC. He formerly worked for the IRS and had his office on Main Street in Skokie.

Diversified Management Resources, a division of Bethany Methodist, was the first management company the GANHC selected to manage the nursing home. They managed Bethany Terrace Nursing Centre, Bethany Methodist Assisted Living Center, Methodist Hospital Skilled Nursing Facility, and Bethany Retirement Community, all in Chicago. For some reason, this did not come about, and First Health Care Associates was the management company that ultimately did this job.

The Greek American Centre Auxiliary was composed of residents, families, volunteers, and others who worked to raise funds in support of the nursing home. Among their projects was raising funds to purchase a wheelchair-accessible van for resident outings and arranging for volunteer staffing of the ice cream parlor.

Greek-American Nursing Home Real Estate, LLC was the legal entity that assumed ownership of the property and building once the bifurcation was finalized. GARNC made monthly payments to the LLC which then paid the mortgage.

Ethel Kotsovos receives the Greek-American Community Services Executive Director Award from John Psiharis. Date unknown. John Psiharis collection.

First Health Care Associates was the management company the GANHC engaged to guide us through start-up and manage the home for the first couple of years.

Pat Gerbanas was the marketing director of the GARCC and helped the board with fundraising, publicity, and special events. As of December 2023, she is still in that role.

Katherine Hall was GARNC's first housekeeping/laundry supervisor. She had previously been an assistant administrator, admissions director, and housekeeping supervisor at other long-term care facilities.

Perrie Veremis Hayes was marketing director for the GARNC preceding and immediately following the opening. She held a master's degree in marketing communications and oversaw marketing efforts geared to medical providers, the Greek community, and the broader community.

Christine Hoidas Howard, initially hired as a bookkeeper, became assistant administrator of the GARNC around the time Burton "Buddy" Behr was the administrator. She held a bachelor's degree in accounting and had worked as the office manager at St. John Greek Orthodox Church.

John Koch was the third administrator of the Greek-American Rehabilitation and Care Centre. He had been an assistant administrator at Holy Family Nursing Home before joining the GARNC.

Eleni Ifantis was the fourth administrator of the Greek-American Rehabilitation and Care Centre and the first to be of Greek descent. She holds a master's in gerontology degree. Eleni initially joined the staff as admissions director and became the administrator after achieving certification as a Licensed Nursing Home Administrator.

Ethel Kotsovos had been a board member of the GANHC since its inception. She also worked for GACS as director of the Community Aging Network and social worker for the adult day care center. Ethel left GACS to become the office manager for the GANHC. Since this was a paid position, she stepped off the board. Ethel then became the GARNC volunteer coordinator upon the opening of the home. Further information on Ethel Kotsovos can be found on page 186.

Anna Kourakis was the first director of recreational therapy (activities director) at the GARNC. She held a master's degree in educational psychology and had previously worked as a mental health therapist and as a counselor at a community college.

Mary Lewis was the first director of "The Village," the GARNC memory care unit.

Rev. Costa Makrinos was the pastoral director of the GARNC, having been selected by Metropolitan Iakovos for this role. Father Costa offered services every Wednesday, provided one-on-one pastoral counseling, and hosted small group discussions. The divine liturgy was held weekly on Saturday mornings, and special services for holidays were offered.

Maureen McGuire was a lawyer for the GANHC. Maureen was involved in helping us reach settlements with First Health Care Associates and other purveyors who were owed money by the GANHC.

A.J. Maggio General Contractors were the general contractors for the construction of the nursing home. They specialized in the construction of healthcare facilities.

Marilu Nelson, R.N., was the first director of nursing when the GARNC opened. She was a certified rehabilitation nurse who had worked in hospital management and acute rehab settings in hospitals.

Andy Nichols was hired to help with publicity early on. John Rassogianis assumed many of these responsibilities, and outside services were no longer needed. He was a friend of Jean Kaporis and handled the publicity for the annual Annunciation Cathedral Ball events.

Nicholas Papanos, M.D., became medical director of the GARNC in April 2002. Dr. Papanos specialized in geriatrics and internal medicine. He was affiliated with Northwest Community Hospital, Holy Family Medical

Maria Toledo in my downstairs office at Greek-American Community Services. Date unknown. John Psiharis collection.

Center, and Our Lady of the Resurrection Medical Center. He had offices in Arlington Heights and Chicago and served on the GACS Board.

Eugenia Pilafas was a member of the GANHC fundraising committee and a financial supporter. She retired from her federal government career where she had worked as a securities examiner.

Mark Shapiro, Vice President of Operations for First Health Care Associates.

Shayman, Salk, Aaronson, & Sussholz & Co. were the architects of the Greek-American Rehabilitation and Care Center. The GANHC worked closely with Arthur Salk. There were many meetings held at their offices in Northbrook. They had experience in healthcare facilities and had built 82 nursing homes and assisted living facilities throughout the Midwest. In the beginning, their firm provided services on a pro-bono basis until the project came to fruition when they were formally engaged by the GANHC.

Honey Jacobs Skinner was a partner at Sidley Austin specializing in representing health care providers before government agencies. Honey represented the GANHC during the Certificate of Need process. Her husband, Sam Skinner, served as U.S. secretary of transportation and White House chief of staff for President George H.W. Bush.

Pat Switzer was a consultant who assisted us in applying for the Certificate of Need. She guided us through the application process and hearings and helped ensure we complied with the terms of the agreement once approval was granted.

Maria Villalobos Toledo became a part-time secretary for the GANHC while also working for GACS. She eventually transitioned into full-time employment. Once the nursing home opened, the GANHC retained Maria as the committee secretary.

Angels, Benefactors & Major Donors

John and George Apostolou donated at least $50,000 to the project. The brothers were co-owners of the Giordano's Pizza restaurant chain.

The American Hellenic & Progressive Association 13th District (AHEPA) donated more than $100,000 raised through a variety of fundraisers at both the chapter and district levels.

Angelyn Boolookas donated $120,000 to the GANHC and the second-floor lounge is named in memory of her parents, Harry G. and Gianoula Boolookas, with four contiguous private rooms dedicated to each of their four children. Her father was a founder and developer who helped establish the character of Chicago's Belmont-Central Business District. Angelyn was a co-founder of the Greek Women's University Club.

Nicholas and Anna Bouras were "Mega-Benefactors" of the GARCC, and the Nicholas J. Bouras International Campus is named in honor of Nicholas and his wife Anna. He owned Bouras Industries, a leading manufacturer of fabricated steel components for commercial real estate, stadiums, skyscrapers, and similar buildings.

Dimitris and Eleni Bousis were instrumental in the success of the GARCC. Eleni became a member of the GANHC around 1995 and applied her fundraising prowess by organizing many fundraisers and obtaining the support of major donors. She became president of the GANHC in 2004 and as of 2022 is chairman of the board. They have donated much and raised more. Eleni was also active with GACS, serving on the Advisory Board and chairing several fundraising dinners. Further information about Eleni Bousis can be found on page 180.

The Chicago Diocese Philoptochos Society pledged $100,000 to the GANHC. This pledge was a collaboration with individual societies and the Diocesan Philoptochos.

James Christie owned Bon-Ton Foods, a poultry company based in Wheeling, that supplied many Greek-owned restaurants and grocery stores (and others) in the Chicago areas. He was a member of the GANHC Board and stepped in at critical moments to provide financial support. Jim donated at least $200,000 to the GANHC. Further information about Jim Christie can be found on page 180.

(L-R): Aphrodite Demeur and Frances Kuchuris during the Greek-American Community Services "A Touch of Love" cocktail reception at the Metropolitan Club, Sears Tower. May 20, 1994. John Rassogianis collection.

George and Esther Christopher were major donors to the GANHC, having donated more than $50,000. They were the owners of Illinois Armored, an armored car service.

Mary Christy donated more than $25,000 to the project.

Daughters of Penelope 13th District pledged $100,000 in support of the GANHC. Helen Geocaris, Toni Panos, Anna Manos, and Eugenia Seifer, who served as district governor for a time, were members of the Daughters and helped coordinate the efforts to fulfill their pledge.

Aphrodite Demeur was a benefactor of the GANHC. Mrs. Demeur donated at least $100,000 to the project and attended many of the fundraisers. She was also a major donor to GACS and donated the *Ya'Sou* 2 van.

The George M. Eisenberg Foundation for Charities donated $100,000 to the GANHC. The second-floor dining room was dedicated in honor of the Eisenberg Foundation gift. The check was presented to GANHC on July 26, 1999, by Foundation President James K. Marousis. In 2003, they donated $30,000. The Foundation was also an annual funder of GACS.

The Federation of Sterea Hellas (U.S.A. and Canada) supported the GANHC. Both Dr. Kioutas and Jim Kozonis had been past supreme presidents of the organization. The federation donated at least $50,000.

The Greek Orthodox Archdiocese Philoptochos Society donated at least $25,000 to the project.

Greek Orthodox Churches of Chicago collectively and individually were instrumental to the success of this project. Although initially, the bishop was slow to support the movement, some churches were supportive early on, and others came into the fold as it became apparent that the project would come to fruition. Among the most ardent church supporters were Annunciation Cathedral, Assumption Church, Holy Apostles, Holy Trinity, St. Andrew, St. Basil, St. Demetrios – Chicago, St. George, St. John, St Nectarios, and Sts. Peter and Paul.

Greek Orthodox Diocese (Metropolis) Philoptochos Society and Church Societies collectively and individually were instrumental to our success. Almost every church Philoptochos society within the Chicago Diocese provided financial support to the project, with many becoming major and ongoing donors or hosting fundraisers for our benefit. The Diocesan Philoptochos Society also provided significant financial support and funded the chapel. To this day, various societies continue to volunteer, visit with residents, and support the home financially.

Greek American Restaurant Association (GARA) was an association created by and for Greek American restaurant owners and food service purveyors. The intent was to leverage the buying power of the many Greek-owned restaurants and benefit from opportunities to pool resources or join forces. GARA donated more than $306,000 to the project during the years covered by this book.

The Hellenic Medical Society of Illinois donated to the GANHC and held or co-sponsored several fundraising events to benefit the effort.

The Hellenic Society of Constantinople, formerly the Hellenic Ladies Society of Constantinople, was a benefactor of the Greek-American Rehabilitation and Care Centre, donating funding for the dementia care activity room. They also supported GACS.

The Hellenic Women's Philanthropic Society "Soteria" was a women's organization founded in the 1940s to establish a Greek American nursing home. During the succeeding decades, they raised more than $270,000 for this cause. Although it was a significant accomplishment, they were well short of what it would take to launch a project of this magnitude. Additionally, many of the initial members were getting older and not able to participate. The society was in danger of losing its tax exemption from the IRS because it had not used the proceeds for its intended purpose. In 1987, the Soteria board voted to turn over the funds to the GANHC upon approval of the Certificate of Need application and securing financing for the project. With interest having compounded over the years, the final amount was about $330,000. Some GANHC members were also part of Soteria, including Christine Burbulis, Bertha Facklis, Thalia Jameson, Jean Kaporis, Christine Mourikes, Tina Spiratos, and Theresa Tzakis.

THE GREEK-AMERICAN NURSING HOME
With your help, make the dream come true
Board of Directors • Bill and Mary Kakavas
847-295-5840

A GANHC business card for Bill and Mary Kakavas. Circa mid-1990s. John Psiharis collection.

William and Mary Kakavas raised and donated more than $150,000 to the GANHC. They were passionate supporters of the project from the earliest days serving as board members for many years and were also on the GACS board. Bill and Mary owned Thirteen Colonies Banquets at Belmont and Cumberland in the Thatcher Woods Mall in River Grove. Early on, they pledged their hall and hors d'oeuvres for a series of fundraising cocktail parties. Directly or indirectly, they generously hosted many such events over the years until they sold the business and retired. As a popular location for community events, Bill and Mary came into contact with many community members with whom they discussed the project or appealed for financial support. They were passionate fundraisers and generous benefactors. Bill and Mary also donated a Baldwin piano to the nursing home. Once the facility opened, Bill took responsibility for working with dietary to improve the quality of the residents' meals. Further information about Bill and Mary Kakavas can be found on page 184.

Dr. Mary Dochios Kamberos. The *Greek Star*. Date unknown. Elaine Thomopoulos collection.

Mary Dochios Kamberos M.D. was the project's first "Mega Benefactor," having donated more than $1.5 million to the GANHC. In appreciation of her support, she was elected to the board. Dr. Kamberos lived on the far south side and seldom attended meetings but would occasionally call-in during meetings from her home. She was a pediatrician for 50 years and spent much of that time providing medical care to juveniles in detention. The campus of the Greek American Nursing and Rehabilitation Center is named in honor of her parents, Chris N. and Helen D. Dochios. Further information about Dr. Kamberos can be found on page 185.

Pauline Karalis from Minneapolis, MN donated at least $25,000 to the GANHC.

Theodosis and Anna Kioutas were benefactors of the GANHC and raised tens of thousands more. Dr. Kioutas was a founding member and chairman of the GANHC from inception through 2004. His vision and leadership were key to the GANHC achieving the goal many thought would never happen. Anna briefly served on the board and was a legal adviser for various matters. The Kioutas family were generous benefactors and their contributions exceeded $100,000. The entrance lobby has a portrait of Dr. Kioutas hanging on its wall in recognition of his leadership and efforts on behalf of the GANHC. Dr. Kioutas was a founding member of GACS and served on its board throughout its existence. Further information about Dr. and Mrs. Kioutas can be found on pages 185 and 186.

Arthur Langas donated $50,000 in support of the GANHC.

The Laconian Ladies & Misses Benevolent Society donated $50,000 to the GANHC. Eugenia Stathakis, president, and Beulah Iatropoulos, vice president and treasurer were supporters of the GANHC from its earliest days and were also longtime participants in the GACS Fabric Arts of Greece Program. It was during these classes that Eugenia and Beulah first discussed making this donation to the nursing home and the donation was eventually made during a GANHC fundraising dinner.

Panayiotis (Pates) & Sara Ferlis Ladas Estate bequeathed a charitable trust of $100,000 to the GANHC. They owned the Arlington Café and Arlington Grill in Arlington Heights, Illinois.

Louis Mitchell was the owner of Lou Mitchell's, a well-known breakfast restaurant on Jackson Street near Greektown. Famous for giving Milk Duds to each female customer waiting to be seated, he gave at least $100,000 to the GANHC.

John D. Nicholson M.D. bequeathed $250,000 to the GANHC. Dr. Nicholson was an ear, nose, and throat specialist.

Dr. John Nicholson accepts the Greek-American Community Services Heritage Award as Peter Lallas, John Psiharis, and Elaine Thomopoulos look on. Second Annual GACS Heritage Awards Dinner. Fountain Blue Banquets, Des Plaines, IL. April 22, 1988. John Psiharis collection.

The Pan Arcadian Federation at both the regional and national levels was a major supporter of GANHC. The pond on our property is named Arcadian Lake, in recognition of their support.

The Thomas Anthony Pappas Charitable Foundation, based in Belmont, Massachusetts, donated at least $10,000 to the project.

Peter Parthenis Family, owners of Grecian Delight Foods, donated more than $50,000 to the GANHC.

George A. and Angela G. Paterakis were "Mega Benefactors" of the GARCC. George owned a successful mergers and acquisitions business, and Angela was a professor at the School of the Art Institute of Chicago and an advocate for arts education locally, regionally, and nationally. They were also major supporters of the National Hellenic Museum.

Mary Strouzas donated at least $10,000 to the GANHC. She was a participant in the GACS Fabric Arts of Greece program. Mary's son, Father Dennis Strouzas, was a parish priest at St. Nectarios Greek Orthodox Church in Palatine, IL in the mid-1970s.

Chris Tomaras. Date unknown. Photo by John Rassogianis. John Rassogianis collection.

Thirteen Colonies Banquets, located in River Grove, was a frequent venue for fundraising events benefiting the GANHC. Owners Bill and Mary Kakavas were generous benefactors of the GANHC and provided their banquet hall at no cost so that we received the full share of what was raised. Bill and Mary were members of the GACS and GANHC boards.

Chris Tomaras was a benefactor of both GANHC and GACS. He attended many of the events and raised money through his connections within the Greek and business communities. At a minimum, he donated $100,000 to the project. Chris was the founder and owner of Kronos Central Gyros and was affectionately known as the "Gyros King." At some point, he sold most of his stake in the business and became a philanthropist supporting many Greek causes including the PanHellenic Scholarship Fund which he founded. He was also president for North and South America of the World Council of Hellenes Abroad (SAE).

Washington Square Health Foundation was a foundation created from the sale of the assets of the former Henrotin Hospital. Dr. Angelo Creticos chaired the Foundation's board and helped GANHC obtain several grants. They also supported GACS. The Foundation annually provided grants beginning in 1996 through the opening. Funds were used, in part, to prepare and disseminate information related to long-term care health services.

A Chronological History of the Greek-American Nursing Home Committee

Note: This timeline includes references to the Greek-American Nursing Home Committee (GANHC), which was the legal name of the organization that established the nursing home. In March 2002, the nursing home opened as the Greek-American Rehabilitation and Nursing Centre (GARNC). On September 19, 2005, the name was changed to the Greek-American Rehabilitation and Care Centre (GARCC). In 2022, an umbrella organization, the Greek American Health Care Foundation, was created and the GARCC is now a wholly owned subsidiary.

Unfortunately, few records exist for the years 1985-1994. Elaine hasn't been able to locate anything much and neither have I. Theresa Tzakis, who served as board secretary for a time, no longer has her records either. The GANHC was active during this period with many meetings (usually at the Elysion Restaurant or GACS) and fundraisers (both our own and those organized on our behalf). During this period GANHC was focused on the due diligence and negotiations related to the North Park Village and Rosehill Cemetery properties, and the early consideration of the Wheeling location. What has been found came from appointment books, calendars, documents, photos, and ephemera that Elaine and I had, a review of the *Greek Star and Greek Press* newspapers, and other print media, as well as the James Mezilson collection housed in the National Hellenic Museum.

1982–1984

Regular meetings of the Greek-American Community Services Nursing Home Committee occur, usually held at the Elysion Restaurant, 2800 W. Foster Avenue, Chicago, IL. These meetings include consultants and other specialists who spoke on matters of concern, as well as site visits to ethnic nursing homes including Villa Scalabrini, Lieberman Center, and the Altenheim nursing home. Please refer to the GACS timeline detailed in *Working to Preserve Our Heritage: The Incredible Legacy of Greek-American Community Services* for information on these meetings.

1985

March 14: GANHC meeting at Elysion Restaurant. Miro Sich, a pro-bono consultant to the GANHC and president of the North America Mortgage Association, speaks about financing options for this project at the behest of Anna Manos.

May 16: GANHC files incorporation papers with the Illinois Secretary of State for the Greek-American Nursing Home Committee.

July 16: GANHC meeting at Elysion Restaurant. Bylaws are unanimously adopted by the Board of Directors.

September 18: GANHC is officially incorporated in Illinois as a not-for-profit organization by Jim Edgar, Illinois Secretary of State.

November 19: GANHC holds the first community meeting to introduce ourselves to the community at the Annunciation Cathedral. Speakers are Dr. Theodosis Kioutas, Dr. Elaine Thomopoulos, Jim Mezilson, Bertha Facklis, Miro Sich, Christine Burbulis, and Helen Georges.

December 9: GANHC Board meeting, Elysion Restaurant.

1986

January 21: GANHC's second community meeting at the Annunciation Cathedral. The speakers are Stella Adinamis Cuthbert, Dr. Theodosis Kioutas, Dr. Elaine Thomopoulos, Bertha Facklis, Christine Burbulis, and Harry Milakis.

April 14: GANHC launches a sustaining membership drive co-chaired by Jean Kaporis and Thalia Jameson.

May 27: GANHC receives the final 501(c) 3 tax exemption determination from the Internal Revenue Service.

July 18: GANHC submits a formal letter to Paul Karras, Chicago Commissioner of the Department of Public Works, expressing interest in the North Park Village location.

August: Angelo Geocaris, a businessman who was a close friend to Chicago Mayor Harold Washington, writes a letter to Paul Karras, commissioner of Public Works, in support of the nursing home being included within the North Park Village Plan at 5801 N. Pulaski Road.

October 20: GANHC announces a pledge by the Soteria Society to donate funds (approximately $270,000) it had raised over several decades for a nursing home to GANHC, once a Certificate of Need (CON) is received and financing is approved. Also announced is the creation of a speakers' bureau to visit churches and organizations to raise awareness and support for the nursing home project.

December: A year-end fundraising appeal signed by Dr. Kioutas and Harry Milakis, fundraising chairman is sent to the growing mailing list. They report that to date more than 50 Greek and Greek American organizations have given written endorsements in support of the nursing home project.

December 15: GANHC establishes a Building Fund Account at the National Bank of Greece to collect donations for the capital project. The

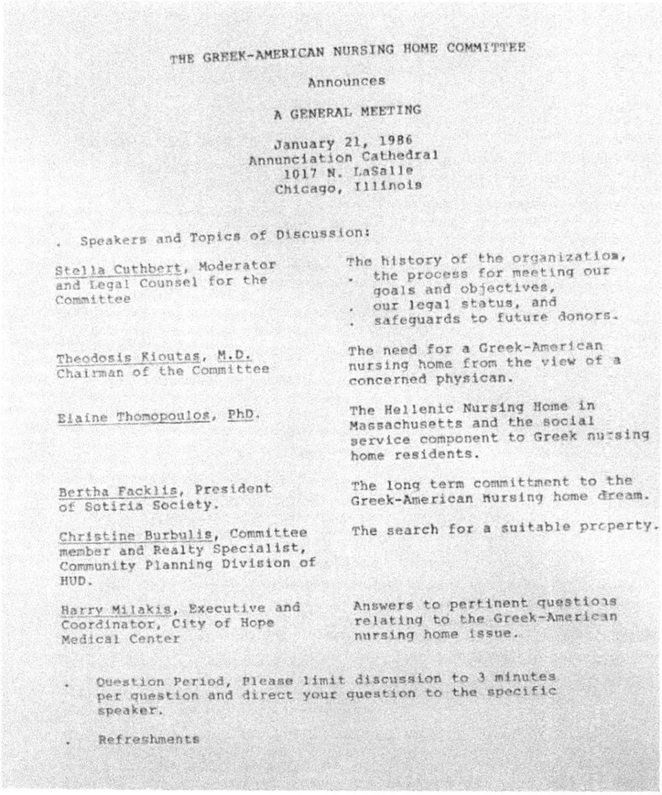

THE GREEK-AMERICAN NURSING HOME COMMITTEE

Announces

A GENERAL MEETING

January 21, 1986
Annunciation Cathedral
1017 N. LaSalle
Chicago, Illinois

. Speakers and Topics of Discussion:

Stella Cuthbert, Moderator and Legal Counsel for the Committee	The history of the organization, . the process for meeting our goals and objectives, . our legal status, and . safeguards to future donors.
Theodosis Kioutas, M.D. Chairman of the Committee	The need for a Greek-American nursing home from the view of a concerned physican.
Elaine Thomopoulos, PhD.	The Hellenic Nursing Home in Massachusetts and the social service component to Greek nursing home residents.
Bertha Facklis, President of Sotiria Society.	The long term committment to the Greek-American nursing home dream.
Christine Burbulis, Committee member and Realty Specialist, Community Planning Division of HUD.	The search for a suitable property.
Harry Milakis, Executive and Coordinator, City of Hope Medical Center	Answers to pertinent questions relating to the Greek-American nursing home issue.

. Question Period, Please limit discussion to 3 minutes per question and direct your question to the specific speaker.

. Refreshments

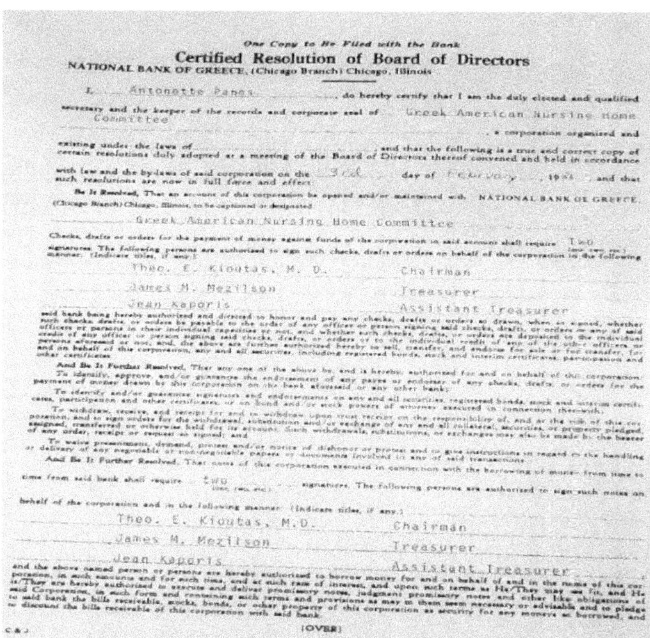

One Copy to Be Filed with the Bank

Certified Resolution of Board of Directors

NATIONAL BANK OF GREECE, (Chicago Branch) Chicago, Illinois

I, Antonette Panos, do hereby certify that I am the duly elected and qualified secretary and the keeper of the records and corporate seal of Greek American Nursing Home Committee, a corporation organized and existing under the laws of ______, and that the following is a true and correct copy of certain resolutions duly adopted at a meeting of the Board of Directors thereof convened and held in accordance with law and the by-laws of said corporation on the 3rd day of February, 198[illegible], and that such resolutions are now in full force and effect:

Be It Resolved, That an account of this corporation be opened and/or maintained with NATIONAL BANK OF GREECE, (Chicago Branch) Chicago, Illinois, to be captioned or designated Greek American Nursing Home Committee

Checks, drafts or orders for the payment of money against funds of the corporation in said account shall require Two (one, two, etc.) signatures. The following persons are authorized to sign such checks, drafts or orders on behalf of the corporation in the following manner: (Indicate titles, if any.)

Theo. E. Kioutas, M. D.	Chairman
James M. Mezilson	Treasurer
Jean Kaporis	Assistant Treasurer

said bank being hereby authorized and directed to honor and pay any checks, drafts or orders so drawn, when so signed, whether such checks, drafts, or orders be payable to the order of any officer or person signing said checks, drafts, or orders or any of said officers or persons in their individual capacities or not, and whether such checks, drafts, or orders are deposited to the individual credit of any officer or person signing said checks, drafts, or orders or to the individual credit of any of the other officers or persons aforesaid or not, and, the above are further authorized hereby to sell, transfer, and endorse for sale or for transfer, for and on behalf of this corporation, any and all securities, including registered bonds, stock and interim certificates, participation and other certificates.

And Be It Further Resolved, That any one of the above be, and is hereby, authorized for and on behalf of this corporation:

To identify, approve, and/or guarantee the endorsement of any payee or endorser of any checks, drafts, or orders for the payment of money drawn by this corporation on the bank aforesaid or any other bank;

To identify and/or guarantee signatures and endorsements on any and all securities, registered bonds, stock and interim certificates, participation and other certificates, or on bond and/or stock powers of attorney executed in connection therewith;

To withdraw, receive, and receipt for and to withdraw upon trust receipt on the responsibility of, and at the risk of this corporation, and to sign orders for the withdrawal, substitution and/or exchange of any and all collateral, securities, or property pledged, assigned, transferred or otherwise held for its account. Such withdrawals, substitutions, or exchanges may also be made by the bearer of any order, receipt or request so signed; and

To waive presentment, demand, protest and/or notice of dishonor or protest and to give instructions in regard to the handling or delivery of any negotiable or non-negotiable papers or documents involved in any of said transactions.

And Be It Further Resolved, That notes of this corporation executed in connection with the borrowing of money from time to time from said bank shall require two (one, two, etc.) signatures. The following persons are authorized to sign such notes on behalf of the corporation and in the following manner: (Indicate titles, if any.)

Theo. E. Kioutas, M.D.	Chairman
James M. Mezilson	Treasurer
Jean Kaporis	Assistant Treasurer

and the above named person or persons are hereby authorized to borrow money for and on behalf of and in the name of this corporation, in such amounts and for such time, and at such rate of interest, and upon such terms as He/They may see fit, and He is/They are hereby authorized to execute and deliver promissory notes, judgment promissory notes and other like obligations of said Corporation, in such form and containing such terms and provisions as may to them seem necessary or advisable and to pledge to said bank the bills receivable, stocks, bonds, or other property of this corporation as security for any moneys so borrowed, and to discount the bills receivable of this corporation with said bank.

C & J

(OVER)

Top: Agenda GANHC General Meeting. January 21, 1986. **Bottom:** GANHC corporate resolution to establish account at the National Bank of Greece. December 15, 1986. John Psiharis collection.

signatories are James Mezilson, treasurer, Jean Kaporis, assistant treasurer, and Dr. Theodosis Kioutas, president.

1987

GANHC fundraising cocktail party flyer. November 20, 1987. John Psiharis collection.

October 4: "Clothes Encounter," a fashion show to benefit the GANHC. It is organized by the Daughters of Penelope – Harris Chapter #133 and held at the Diplomat Banquets. Toni Panos is the event chairman and Julia Mavrogianis is the chapter president. Tickets are $17.50 per person.

October 27: GANHC Board meeting at Elysion Restaurant. The agenda includes an update on the properties under consideration: Glenview, Harms, and Central (Emily, Jameson); Halsted and Van Buren; Holiday Inn property, and the McDade property. The balance of the meeting is spent planning for the November cocktail fundraiser and discussing the need for a newsletter.

November 20: GANHC Cocktail Fundraiser at Thirteen Colonies Banquets, River Grove, IL. The event is underwritten by the Kakavas family. Donation is $20 per person.

December 3: GANHC Board meeting at Elysion Restaurant. The agenda includes an update on properties being considered including one in Glenview and a property at Halsted and Van Buren in Greektown. A February fundraiser and a Christmas appeal letter for donations are also discussed.

1988

February 14: A "GANHC Valentine's Day Brunch Honoring Dr. John Nicholson," in appreciation of his generous bequest to the GANHC, is held at Thirteen Colonies Banquets in River Grove and hosted by the Kakavas family.

February 15: GANHC Board meeting at the Elysion Restaurant. The board considers five prospective northwest suburban locations for the nursing home: 7.3 acres near Milwaukee Avenue and Wolf Road in Wheeling. The approximate land cost is $1,240,000. 2.45 acres on Milwaukee Avenue between Sanders Road and Willow Road. The asking price is $550,000. Nine acres on Milwaukee Avenue, a half block from Wheeling Nursery and across the street from Pasta Prima Restaurant in Wheeling. The asking price is $3,136,320. 9.63 acres at Skokie Boulevard and Lake Cook Road in Northbrook. Fairview North School in Wilmette. 4.8 acres with a school building right off the Edens Expressway. To be sold at auction on April 10, 1988, with a minimum bid of $950,000.

February 19: GANHC Board meeting at Elysion Restaurant. The agenda includes the Treasurer's report, property, report on luncheon – Bertha, dinner dance on May 6, public relations, and restructuring of committees, real estate, finance, fundraising, legal, and advisory.

May 6: GANHC Benefit Dinner Dance at Thirteen Colonies Banquets, River Grove, IL. The keynote speaker is Helen Boosalis, former mayor of Lincoln Nebraska, and former director of the Nebraska Department on Aging. Music by Emeis. Tickets are $50 per person. The event is underwritten by the Kakavas family.

October 9: Cheiron Chapter #274, Daughters of Penelope (Glenview, Illinois) presents a "Grecian Soiree" Dinner Dance at the Terrace Restaurant, Wilmette Golf Course, Lake Avenue and Harms Road, Wilmette, IL. Music by Panos and Stratos orchestra. Donations are $30 per person. Proceeds benefit the GANHC.

December 22: GANHC Board meeting at Elysion Restaurant. Rev, Masaru Nambu, executive director of the Japanese American Service Committee speaks about his organization's experience in building a nursing home. In part, he states "Not until we purchased land, then people started responding."

1989

July 26: GANHC Board meeting at Elysion Restaurant. The agenda includes reports on property search efforts and the October fundraising event.

October 20: GANHC's Second Annual Cocktail Party at the Thirteen Colonies Banquets, River Grove, IL. The event is hosted by the Kakavas Family. Tickets are $20 each. Helen Geocaris is the event chair and Christine Burbulis is the co-chair.

1990

No information is available for this year.

1991

June 26: GANHC Board meeting at GACS. Status reports were provided for each of the properties under consideration at the time: North Park Village, Rosehill Cemetery, Martha Washington Hospital, and a location on Milwaukee Avenue in Niles.

1992

April 2 and April 8: GANHC board members attend and speak during two public community meetings to explain the proposed nursing home at North Park Village. The room is filled for both meetings and the outcome is favorable.

April 30: GANHC Board meeting at GACS.

July 3: GANHC and GACS leaders meet with members of the United Hellenic American Congress (UHAC) and Bishop Iakovos at the UHAC office.

July 21: GANHC Board meeting at GACS.

August 12: GANHC Board meeting at GACS.

1993

March 3: GANHC submits a formal bid to City of Chicago Commissioner of General Services Paul Karras for the North Park Village property located in the 5700 block of North Pulaski Road.

April 28: GANHC board meeting at GACS.

June 11: GANHC board meeting at GACS.

December 15: GANHC investigates a property on Milwaukee Avenue in Glenview adjacent to the Cook County Forest Preserve. The asking price is $1.9 million.

1994

January 6: GANHC revises the March 3, 1993, bid submitted to Benjamin Reyes, Chicago Commissioner of General Services for the acquisition of the "site currently occupied by the main power plant and other small structures." The letter states that an Environmental Report for the property indicates "extremely poor environmental conditions." The report states that it would cost more than $500,000 to clean up the site to an environmentally acceptable standard. GANHC revised the bid to one dollar for the property.

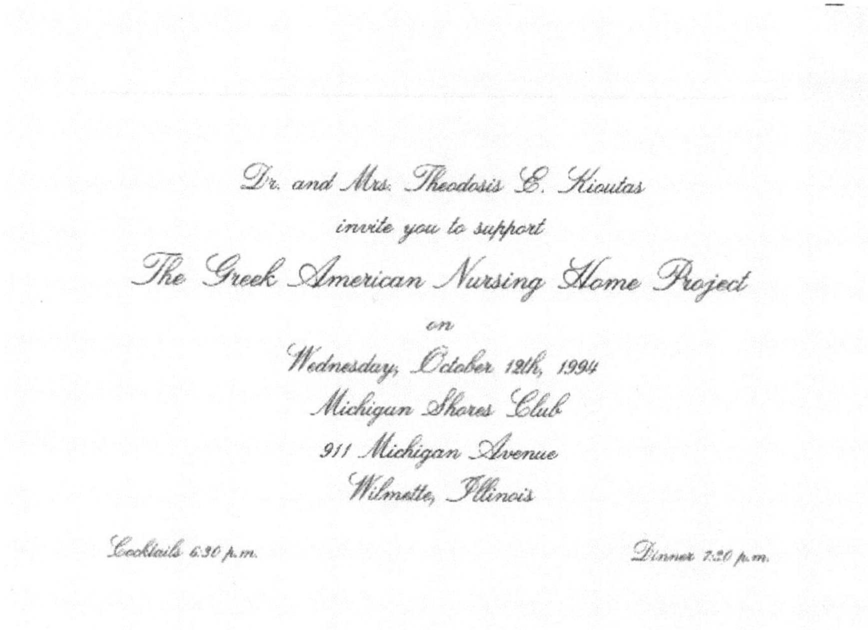

Dr. and Mrs. Theodosis E. Kioutas

invite you to support

The Greek American Nursing Home Project

on

Wednesday, October 12th, 1994

Michigan Shores Club

911 Michigan Avenue

Wilmette, Illinois

Cocktails 6:30 p.m. Dinner 7:30 p.m.

Invitation to the Michigan Shores Club fundraiser. October 12, 1994. John Psiharis collection.

January 12: GANHC board meeting at GACS. Agenda: Minutes, treasurer's report, property, old business, new business, public relations, and fundraising.

April 18: GANHC meeting at GACS to finalize and approve the purchase of the Wheeling property.

April 20: GANHC announces it has signed a contract to purchase the Wheeling property for $425,000. The eight-acre site is adjoined by a park and senior center and includes two ponds. $40,000 in earnest money is paid. Balance due on November 30.

May 2: GANHC Board elections are held. Officers are Dr. Theodosis Kioutas, president; Helen Georges, first vice president; Elaine Thomopoulos, second vice president; Toni Panos, recording secretary; James Mezilson, treasurer; John Psiharis, assistant treasurer; Helen Geocaris, membership chair; Christine Burbulis, real estate chair, and John Rassogianis as public relations chair.

June 2: "Be an Angel! Support the Nursing Home Contract to Purchase Land" cocktail party celebration hosted by the Kakavas Family at Thirteen Colonies Banquets, River Grove IL. Cocktails and sweets table. Music by Linardakis Band. Tickets are $25 per person.

August 9: GANHC Board meeting at GACS. Among the agenda items are discussions about the October Michigan Shores and November luncheon events and inviting other Orthodox faiths to take part in the project.

August 15: The Village of Wheeling approves the zoning request to "build a 90,000 square foot Greek American nursing home on 7¾ wooded acres at the Wolf Road site located at 199 N. First St. The land is vacant, in its natural state, and includes trees, vegetation, and two ponds. It lies west of the Pavilion Senior Center."

October 12: Dr. Theodosis and Mrs. Anna Kioutas host a fundraising dinner for GANHC in the Tudor Grand Ballroom at the exclusive Michigan Shores Club in Wilmette Illinois. Approximately 100 guests attend the $500 per person event featuring "Greek favorites emanating from the piano of maestro Vasilios Gaitanos."

November 11: GANHC obtains a mortgage of $210,000 from Columbia National Bank. The mortgage was paid off on April 30, 1996, allowing the release of the property free and clear.

November 12: GANHC bus tour to view the newly purchased eight-acre property in Wheeling.

November 13: Elaine Thomopoulos, John Psiharis, and John Rassogianis attend a meeting of the St. Demetrios Philoptochos society in the church community center. Angeline Eliakopoulos, Philoptochos president, introduces the GANHC representatives and pledges support to the effort.

November 13: GANHC Building Fund Benefit Luncheon at Thirteen Colonies Banquets hosted by Bill and Mary Kakavas. Tickets are $30 per person. More than 400 guests attended. The invitation reads: "The Greek American Nursing home will be built on eight rustic acres in Wheeling, Illinois. Under the terms of our contract, the balance of $385,000 is due by November 30, 1994. $40,000 has been paid in earnest money. This will be a full-service, state-of-the-art facility featuring a caring bilingual Greek staff. It will accept both Medicare and Medicaid."

November 30: GANHC closes on the purchase of 8.5 acres of land at 199 First Street Wheeling, Illinois as the site of the nursing home. The purchase price is $425,000. The GANHC pays $215,000 and obtains a mortgage for $210,000.

December 31: GANHC ends the year with $506,593 on the balance sheet.

1995

January 11: GANHC Bylaws committee meeting at GACS. The committee consists of Jim Chiakulas, Dr. Kioutas, John Psiharis, and Elaine Thomopoulos.

January 14: Benefit for GANHC at Thirteen Colonies Banquets, River Grove, IL. Hosted by the Kakavas family.

January 20: GANHC board members meet with members of the United Hellenic American Congress.

February: Chris Tomaras donates $10,000 to GANHC.

February 8: GANHC Board meeting at GACS.

February 13: GANHC Board meeting at GACS.

February 18: Roumeli Society fundraiser benefiting the GANHC at Thirteen Colonies Banquets, River Grove, IL.

March: The amount outstanding on the mortgage decreases to $170,000.

March 8: GANHC Board meeting at GACS.

April 5: GANHC Board meeting at GACS. Discussion on the process for obtaining pledges, a west side volunteer meeting, and the creation of a speaker's bureau are on the agenda.

April 11: GANHC Board meeting at Sauganash Restaurant.

April 12: GANHC presents an informational discussion, "The Greek-American Nursing Home: Its Progress and Plans," during the Lenten supper following the presanctified liturgy at Holy Apostles Church, 2501 S. Wolf Road, Westchester, IL. Elaine Thomopoulos, John Rassogianis, and Toni Panos represent the GANHC.

May: GANHC receives zoning approval from the Village of Wheeling.

May 3: GANHC Board meeting at GACS.

May 26: GANHC Benefit Dinner Dance hosted by the community's professional organizations at Thirteen Colonies Banquets, River Grove, IL. Tickets are $40 per person. Frank Columbus is the event chairman. The dinner is hosted by Bill and Mary Kakavas. The Society of Paleohorion Kynourias is a table sponsor and Consul General of Greece Nicholas Zafiropoulos attends. The presidents of each of the sponsoring organizations speak at the event: Elaine Barkoulies, Hellenic Professional Society of Illinois; George Alexopoulos, KRIKOS-Midwest; Barbara Javaras, Greek Women's University Club, and Chris Kuvalas, Orthodox Singles. Dr. Kioutas provides an update on the status of the GANHC.

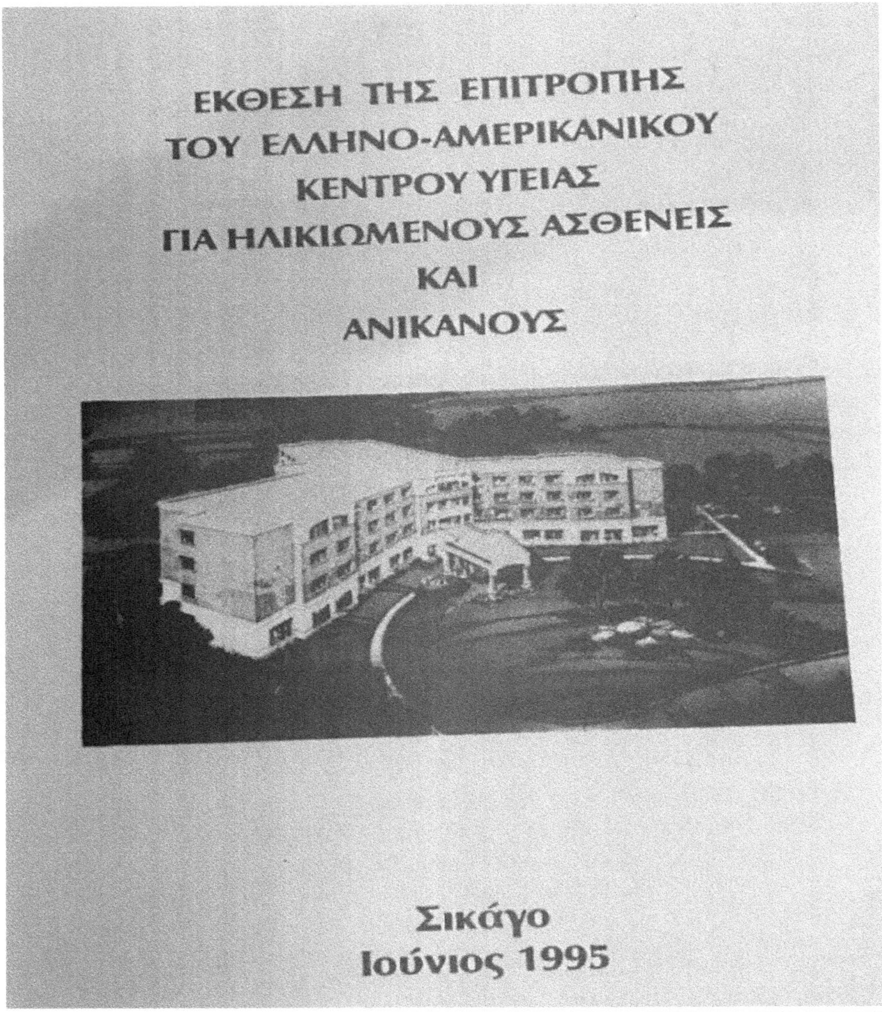
ΕΚΘΕΣΗ ΤΗΣ ΕΠΙΤΡΟΠΗΣ
ΤΟΥ ΕΛΛΗΝΟ-ΑΜΕΡΙΚΑΝΙΚΟΥ
ΚΕΝΤΡΟΥ ΥΓΕΙΑΣ
ΓΙΑ ΗΛΙΚΙΩΜΕΝΟΥΣ ΑΣΘΕΝΕΙΣ
ΚΑΙ
ΑΝΙΚΑΝΟΥΣ

Σικάγο
Ιούνιος 1995

A progress report on the GANHC written in Greek and distributed during the June 25, 1995, family picnic and to supporting organizations and individuals. Elaine Thomopoulos collection.

A benefit raffle offers the following prizes: Chicago Downtown Marriott Hotel Two for Breakfast Package; Alval Jewelers (Wheeling, IL), 14k yellow gold lady's ring with amethyst and blue topaz; Furla Family Portrait (Furla Photography, Chicago and Glenview); one case of assorted Greek wines (three prizes, various donors); European style silk flower arrangement in a natural vine basket (Catranis Florists); Family membership for one year (Hellenic Museum) and gift certificates to Billy Goat Tavern and Grill, Cote Rotie Restaurant, Greek Islands Restaurants, Pegasus Restaurant, and Petro's Dianna's Restaurant.

Gov. Edgar informed of the Greek-American Nursing Home developments

CHICAGO—Gov. Jim Edgar was recently briefed on Greek-American Nursing Home Committee (GANHC) progress by members of the Committee. From left, Maria and Bill Kakavas, GANHC; Toni Panos, Secretary, GANHC; Dr. Theodosis Kioutas, president of GANHC; His Grace Bishop Iakovos; Gov. Edgar; Andrew A. Athens, national chairman of UHAC; Faye Potakis, president of the Federation of Sterea Hellas, USA and Canada; Chris Tomaras, president of the Pan-Messinian Federation USA and Canada; Christine Burbulis, GANHC; Frank Mitropoulos, Gov. Dist. 13, Order of Ahepa.

The *Greek Star,* August 10, 1995. Pictured (L-R): Mary Kakavas, Bill Kakavas, Dr. Theodosis Kioutas, His Grace Bishop Iakovos, Governor Jim Edgar, Andrew A. Athens, Faye Potakis, Chris Tomaras, Christine Burbulis, and Frank Mitropoulos. Elaine Thomopoulos collection.

May 27: GANHC Board members speak about the project during a dinner meeting of Enosis Demovaltetsioton at the Hilltop Restaurant, 2800 W. Foster Ave., Chicago.

May 31: GANHC Board meeting at GACS. Discussion on the upcoming family picnic and a planned general meeting in June. Other agenda items include the creation of a speaker's bureau and office space.

June 14: GANHC Board meeting at GACS to review plans for the upcoming picnic.

June 21: GANHC Board meeting at GACS.

June 25: GANHC "First Annual Family Picnic and *Agiasmos*" on the nursing home grounds. The picnic hours are 1:30 p.m. to 7:00 p.m. and Bishop Iakovos of Chicago conducts the traditional Blessing of the Waters ceremony at 3:30 p.m. The event includes barbecues, refreshments, and music by the Linardakis Brothers.

June 27: Dr. Kioutas, Toni Panos, John Psiharis, John Rassogianis, John Secaras, and several other GANHC Board members meet with AHEPA leaders for a dinner meeting at the Greek Islands Restaurant, Lombard IL.

July 12: GANHC Board meeting at GACS. The agenda includes the treasurer's report, Nursing Home Picnic report (John Rassogianis), donations at the picnic, plans for the fall general meeting, fundraising, Daughters of Penelope report, public relations, and speakers' bureau (John Rassogianis), and determining a place to work from – computer.

August 2: GANHC Board meeting at GACS.

GANHC General Community Meeting at Annunciation Cathedral. September 26, 1995. Photo by John Rassogianis. John Rassogianis collection.

August 15: Wheeling Board of Trustees grants final approval to GANHC to construct a 204-bed skilled-care nursing home facility on our property.

September 14: GANHC Board meeting at GACS. The agenda is in part focused on the upcoming community meeting.

September 26: GANHC General Community Meeting at Annunciation Cathedral. The agenda includes Dr. Kioutas describing the Wheeling property and how the nursing home will operate. Helen Georges and Elaine Thomopoulos describe who is most likely to go into a nursing home. Christine Burbulis reports on the real estate search efforts, and John Rassogianis addresses the community's response and the need for volunteers. Dr. Kioutas then introduces the board members present and the floor is open for questions.

October 9: GANHC Board meeting at GACS.

October 14: Megalopolis Society Dinner to benefit the GANHC is held at Thirteen Colonies Banquets, River Grove IL.

October 29: Enosis Demovaltetsioton hosts a benefit for the GANHC to raise funds for paying off the balance of the mortgage on the property. It is held at Thirteen Colonies Banquets, River Grove, IL.

November 13: GANHC Board meeting at GACS. Balance of $85,000 remaining on the mortgage.

1996

January 23: GANHC Board meeting at GACS.

February 23: GANHC Board meeting at GACS. Discussion on results of 1995 fundraising efforts and plans for 1996 are discussed as well as collecting donations for Kostas Zografopoulos' medical bills. A picnic tentatively planned for June 2 and the need to hire a part-time secretary are also on the agenda.

March 2: The "Grand Ball to Benefit the Greek-American Nursing Home" is held at the Ambassador West Hotel. "United in Purpose for the Greek-American Nursing Home." Co-sponsored by the Hellenic Medical Society of Chicago (Chadwick C. Prodromos, president), Hellenic Professional Society of Illinois (Hara Anast, president), Hellenic American Dental Society (Dennis Costis, D.D.S., president), Greek Women's University Club (Barbara Javaras, president), Chicago Fine Arts Society (Don Dadas, president), and the Hellenic Bar Association (Leon Vainikos, president). Jimmy Damon sings "Ode to Liberty" and "America the Beautiful." Music and dancing are provided by the Al Sofia Orchestra and the "OPA" Orchestra.

March 3: 13th District AHEPA fundraiser to benefit GANHC. The *Yiayia* and *Papou Glendi* is held at Thirteen Colonies Banquets, River Grove, IL.

March 24: GANHC Board members attend an after-liturgy presentation and update on the nursing home project at Assumption Greek Orthodox Church. Among those in attendance are Dr. Kioutas, Fr. George Massouras, Toni Panos, John Psiharis, Elaine Thomopoulos, John Rassogianis, and John Secaras.

March 24: Pan Arcadian Federation dinner benefiting the GANHC at Thirteen Colonies Banquets, River Grove, IL.

April 5: GANHC pays off the remaining $30,000 balance of the mortgage to Columbia National Bank and now owns the property free and clear. Property ownership was placed in the name of the Greek-American Nursing Home Committee.

April 16: GANHC Board meeting at GACS. The Hellenic Medical Society sent $13,000 from their March fundraiser. The 13th District of AHEPA sends $12,915 from their March 3rd event. Pan Arcadian event proceeds are expected soon. Planning for an upcoming cocktail party. A motion is passed by a majority that His Grace Bishop Iakovos serves as the honorary chairman of the GANHC.

April 19: GANHC board members Bill and Mary Kakavas host a cocktail party benefit at Thirteen Colonies Banquets, River Grove, IL. Organizations are recognized for past, present, and future donations to GANHC.

May 16: GANHC Board meeting at GACS. Updates: Soteria will donate $200,000 once we reach $1 million in contributions. Esther Christopher pledged $25,000, St. Demetrios Philoptochos $10,000, and Annunciation Cathedral and Philoptochos pledged $25,000. Hearing at the Board of Appeals at the County Building concerning a $11,000 property tax bill.

May 31: GANHC audited financial statements report $584,531 in assets (including the land of $425,000, $42,050 in cash and cash equivalents, and $91,755 in pledges) and $23,004 in liabilities. Contributions totaled $176,707 with $370 in interest. Expenses of $52,072 (including $28,160 in property taxes that will be refunded).

June 13: GANHC Board meeting at GACS. Agenda items include a picnic report, a fundraising committee, a letter from the Regas family, a letter from Ethel Kotsovos, office space, a bylaws discussion, and planning for a display about the nursing home in the atrium of the James R. Thompson State of Illinois Building.

June 17: Representatives of the GANHC Board of Directors are invited to participate in a photo opportunity and provide an update to Governor Jim Edgar at the State of Illinois Building. Among those attending are Bill and Mary Kakavas, Dr. Theodosis Kioutas, Toni Panos, John Psiharis, Elaine Thomopoulos, Theresa Tzakis, and John Rassogianis.

June 30: GANHC Second Annual Family Festival on the Nursing Home Grounds. Free admission. Rain or Shine, 1:30 p.m. to 8:00 p.m. "Food, refreshments, live Greek & American music, courtesy of Markogiannakis Orchestra." Church bus sign-up deadline, Thursday, June 27, 1996. Jim Pirpiris, Picnic Chairman.

July 23: GANHC Board meeting at GACS.

August 1: GANHC Board meeting at Sauganash Restaurant.

August 8: GANHC Board meeting at GACS.

August 16: GANHC contracts with Patricia Sweitzer to work as a consultant on the Certificate of Need application process.

October: Students from Prototypon Greek School donate $400 that they raised for the GANHC.

October 14: Dr. Theodosis Kioutas, John Psiharis, and John Rassogianis are invited to a reception with U.S. First Lady Hillary Clinton to brief her on GACS and the GANHC. Chicago Hilton and Towers, 710 S. Michigan Ave., Chicago, IL.

October 20: The American Hellenic Society of Berwyn hosts a dinner dance in Plato Hall at Assumption Church to benefit the GANHC and the Plato Academy Scholarship Fund.

November 18: GANHC Board meeting at GACS. John Regas reports that he contacted three people who specialize in nursing homes and was advised that Pat Sweitzer is the best consultant for our certificate of need. Engaging her services was unanimously approved. Discussion on creating a GANHC Advisory Board. The Wheeling Parks District has offered to clear our property grounds of any debris up to the pond. A fundraising appeal letter in Greek will be crafted. Elections in January. A meeting with Bishop Iakovos will be scheduled. Dr. Kioutas, John Secaras, Christine Burbulis, and Bill Kakavas will attend.

December 7: "The Greek-American Nursing Home Benefit," at the John P. Regas Residence, 1406 N. Astor St., and hosted by the Regas Family. Cocktail buffet. Over $80,000 is raised.

December 16: GANHC Board meeting at GACS.

1997

January 20: GANHC Board meeting at GACS. New board member Peter Regas is introduced. John Regas reports that the December 7 event raised $83,540 with some expenses still pending. The board has hired Georgette Kendrick as part-time help in the GANHC office but Maria Toledo, the GACS secretary, should be kept in mind for a part-time secretary. The board voted unanimously to increase the size of the board by five to a maximum of 26 members to be filled as necessary. There are currently 22 members, including Father Massouras. The Soteria Association requests that Tina Spiratos, daughter of Kay Mourikes, be their representative on the GANHC board. All in favor. Pat Sweitzer, the CON consultant, reports that the data on Greek Americans in area nursing homes are outdated and that we need to gather current information.

February: Angelyn Boolookas donates $120,000 in memory of her parents Harry G. and Gianoula Boolookas.

February 1: In a written report to the 13th District of the Daughters of Penelope, Toni Panos, GANHC recording secretary and representative to the Daughters, reports that the 1995-1996 year is "spectacular." There were 14 fundraisers in this period that resulted in $147,000 being raised. This includes $400 raised by the children of Prototypon Hellenic School, 13th District Order of AHEPA and Daughters of Penelope, churches, professional and social organizations as well as the $80,000 fundraiser given by the Regas family. She further reports that GANHC has $322,642 in savings from prior donations and events, $4,088 in a checking account and that the property is owned free and clear at $425,000. Toni also asks

The Greek-American Nursing Home Committee
5758 North California Avenue
Chicago, Illinois 60659
773-561-8865

'PRESERVING GREEK DIGNITY'

February 6, 1997

Honorary Chairman
His Grace Bishop Iakovos
Bishop of Chicago

Chairman
Dr. Theo E. Kioutas

Governing Board
Eleni Bousis
Christine Burbulis
Helen Georges
Bill Kakavas
Mary Kakavas
Jean Kaporis
Demetrios L. Kozonis
Frances Kuchuris
Anna Manos
Rev. George Massouras
James M. Mezilson
Toni Panos
Demetrios Pirpiris
Dr. Chadwick Prodromos
John Psiharis
John C. Rassogianis
John Regas
Peter Regas
John Secaras
Eugenia S. Seifer
Christine M. Spiralos
Dr. Elaine Thomopoulos

TO: Board Members

RE: Board meeting - Monday, February 17, 7P.M.
3940 N. Pulaski, Chicago

AGENDA

1. Minutes
2. Treasurer's report
3. Dr. Kioutas - report on meeting with Bishop Iakovos and John Argudelis Feb. 4th
4. Report on CON statistic letters
5. C.D. interest rates
6. Old business
7. New business

SAVE THE DATES:

Sunday, March 9th - AHEPA Yiayia and Papou Fund Raiser, 13 Colonies

Saturday, March 15th, Ladies of Constantinople Half of the proceeds to Nursing Home

Theodosis E. Kioutas, M.D.
Theodosis E. Kioutas, M.D.
President

Admitted in 1996.

A not for profit organization dedicated to care.

A GANHC Board of Directors meeting agenda. February 6, 1997. The letterhead lists board members during that time. Elaine Thomopoulos collection.

for help in identifying 184 Greek American individuals who entered a nursing home or hospital extended-stay facility in 1996. We have already identified over 300 Greek Americans in nursing homes between 1992 and 1994. This also includes, for example, a patient who broke their hip and was placed in a rehabilitation center for therapy. Information to be obtained is the initials of the patient, zip code or home address, and the name and address of the nursing home.

February 17: GANHC Board meeting at GACS. Dr. Kioutas reports on his meeting with Bishop Iakovos and John Argudelis. Certificate of deposit interest rates and upcoming fundraisers are discussed.

March 9: AHEPA 13th District "*Yiayia* & *Papou*" Dinner fundraiser at Thirteen Colonies Banquets, River Grove, IL. The event honors His Grace Bishop Iakovos, Illinois Governor Jim Edgar, Illinois State Senator Adeline

Geo-Karis, and Andrew A. Athens. Proceeds to benefit GANHC. Those in attendance include His Grace Bishop Iakovos, Alec K. Gianaras, Illinois State Senator Adeline Geo-Karis, Supreme Vice President Steve Manta of the Order of AHEPA, Kathy Ferguson, grand secretary of the Daughters of Penelope, and Dr. Charles Kanakis, who represents Andrew Athens. The banquet is chaired by John Zane Argoudelis.

March 15: The Hellenic Ladies Society of Constantinople hosts a fundraising event with GANHC receiving half of the proceeds.

March 17: GANHC Board meeting at GACS.

April 14: GANHC Board meeting at GACS. Agenda items include GANHC certificates of deposits, the efforts to gather statistics for the Certificate of Need application, board member liability insurance, and fundraising.

May 9: GANHC Board meeting at GACS. The agenda includes a discussion on the progress of the Certificate of Need application process, GANHC certificates of deposit, and Dr. Kioutas' recent meeting with the Greek Restaurant Association. A list is compiled of Greek nursing home admissions in 1996 to help document the need for the facility.

May 31: GANHC audited financial statements show assets of $802,915 (including $425,000 in the land, $204,853 in cash and cash equivalents, and $48,237 in pledges) and liabilities of $23,843. Revenue totals $244,067 which consists of $233,266 in contributions, $6,000 dinner dance, and $4,801 interest income. Expenses: $33,070 (including $19,309 in property taxes that will be refunded).

June 12: GANHC board meeting at GACS. GANHC has raised $1,103,857 and has pledges of $210,775. A condition of receiving approval from the state is that there be at least $2 million committed to the project. Much has been done and plans were discussed to raise the remaining amount.

April 14: GANHC Board meeting at GACS. Agenda items include the Certificate of Need, fundraising, and public relations.

May 19: GANHC Board meeting at GACS. Discussions include an update on the Certificate of Need process and compiling the number of Greek patients that entered area nursing homes in 1996.

June 12: GANHC Building Fund status update reveals that GANHC has assets of $1,103,857, consisting of $408,857 cash in the bank, $270,000 from Soteria which will be donated once the CON is obtained, and as their certificates of deposits mature, and $425,000 paid in full for the property. The outstanding pledge balance is $210,775.

June 27: GANHC Board meeting at GACS. Treasurer's report: Checking, savings, operating accounts, and charity savings total $71,430.70. Total savings, money markets, CDs, and stocks are $845,940.58 (not including the Banco Popular CD to be transferred in July).

July 21: GANHC Board meeting at GACS. The agenda includes an update on efforts to gather statistics and data for the CON and a report from Dr. Kioutas about his recent meeting with the Greek American Restaurant Association.

August 17: The Certificate of Need application clears the first round. It is approved by Illinois Health Facilities Planning Board staff and is recommended to the IHFPB for final approval.

August 18: GANHC Board meeting at GACS. The agenda includes updates on the CON and the December fundraiser.

September 15: GANHC Board meeting at GACS. Agenda items include a grant from the Washington Square Health Foundation that Chairman Dr. Angelo Creticos arranged. Also, updates on the CON and the December fundraising dinner. Discussion about sending Christmas cards to our major donors and supporters.

October: Special GANHC Board meeting to review and sign the CON application at Costa's Restaurant.

October 20: GANHC Board meeting at GACS. A financial status update reveals that the GANHC has $332,943 in certificates of deposit at Broadway Bank ($82,943), Cole Taylor Bank ($50,000), St. Paul Federal ($100,000), and Western Springs Savings and Loan ($100,000). The operating accounts balance is $27,064. It is announced that Lou Mitchell pledged $100,000 to the GANHC. The board decides to procure board and officer liability insurance for an annual premium of $1,300. Frances Kuchuris donates the funds needed to obtain coverage.

October 21: GANHC obtains board and officer liability insurance coverage.

October 26: The American Hellenic Society of Berwyn hosts a dinner dance with proceeds earmarked for the GANHC Building Fund.

November: The GANHC Certificate of Need application receives a "positive reaction" from the staff of the Illinois Health Facilities Planning Board. on the CON.

November 15: GANHC combined accounts balance is $422,905 and pledges receivable is $503,385.

November 16: The GANHC is awarded a Heritage Award during the Eleventh Annual Greek-American Community Services Heritage Awards Dinner at Bristol Courts Banquets in Mount Prospect, IL. Dr. Theodosis

Dr. Theodosis Kioutas accepts the Greek-American Community Services Heritage Award on behalf of the GANHC. November 16, 1997. Bristol Court Banquet Hall. Pictured (L-R): Peter Maroutsos, John Rassogianis, John Psiharis, Athanasia Papadopoulos, and Dr. Kioutas. John Psiharis collection.

Kioutas accepts the award and most GANHC board members are in attendance.

November 17: GANHC Board meeting at Annunciation Cathedral. A key topic of discussion is the upcoming hearing on the CON application. $296,351 received in this period. Banks and CD balances of $451,0331. Total spending toward the $12.5 million CON cap is $333,784.

November 17–19: The AHEPA families of the 13th District organize "Jewel Shop and Share" days to benefit the GANHC. By shopping at any Jewel grocery store on these three days and presenting a coupon, Jewel donated five percent of total purchases, excluding taxes, to GANHC. The coupon was printed in the November 13, 1997, issue of the *Greek Star* with a message from Frank Mitropoulos, Past District Governor of AHEPA. Supporters were encouraged to do their Thanksgiving shopping on those days to maximize Jewel's donation to the GANHC.

November 20: Dr. Theodosis Kioutas, Father George Massouras, and GANHC board members light candles and offer prayers at the Assumption Church before embarking on their 130-mile trip to Champaign, IL for the following day's hearing on the Certificate of Need application.

THE GREEK STAR

Poinsettia Ball for the Greek-American Nursing Home proves to be a success

The Sotiria table.

The AHEPA table.

Poinsettia Ball guests register for tickets.

The *Greek Star,* December 25, 1997. Elaine Thomopoulos collection.

November 21: GANHC Board members and consultants attend the hearing of the Illinois Health Facilities Planning Board where the application for a Certificate of Need was under consideration. The CON is unanimously approved.

December 7: GANHC Poinsettia Ball held at Bristol Court Banquets in Mt. Prospect. Bertha Facklis, longtime president of Soteria, is honored. Tickets are $50 per person. The event has 392 guests and raises $49,687 in dinner tickets, donations, and pledges. Mary Betinis donates $15,000 during the dinner in memory of her husband.

December 15: GANHC Board meeting at Annunciation Cathedral. Among the agenda items is a report from the dinner dance committee and a discussion of financing options for the building including FHA, Fannie Mae, bond issues, and private markets. The Advisory Board consists of five committees: Fundraising, finance, construction, administration, and public relations.

1998

January 5: Special GANHC board meeting at Annunciation Cathedral with a panel of six guests. The minutes offer a synopsis of the meeting. "The meeting focused on the financing of the facility and the financial timeline that funds would be needed. Art Salk, who heretofore was the GANHC architect, as we considered North Park Village and produced the initial renderings of the Wheeling property, and Pat Sweitzer, a healthcare consultant who helped us prepare our Certificate of Need, were the primary speakers. Draper and Kramer, Artemis Capital, and First National Bank of Chicago representatives, each interested in handling the financing for the project, were present as well. Various financing options, construction schedules, and deadlines required by the CON were discussed. CON capped the project at $12,535,290. In time, the consensus moved towards a tax-exempt municipal bond sale backed by the Village of Wheeling. Cash on hand: $453,859, plus Soteria resolution ($270,000) and real estate ($425,000). Total ready assets are $1,148,859. Other assets are $182,615 in pledges receivable, $20,000 in bequests, and 123 shares of AT&T common stock."

January 19: GANHC Community Meeting at Annunciation Cathedral. This meeting includes a presentation by one of the architectural firms that bid on the project. A discussion on Advisory Board committees ensues. They are Administration, Finance, Fundraising, Construction/Architectural, and Public Relations. Kefalonia organization donates $5,000. Mrs. Aphrodite Demeur donates $25,000.

February 16: GANHC Board meeting at Annunciation Cathedral, 1017 N. LaSalle St. Committee reports are heard (administration, architect, finance, fundraising, and public relations/publicity).

February 21: The GANHC Architectural Committee meets to hear bidders present their credentials. Several firms indicated interest including Shayman Salk which had designed the initial renderings on a pro-bono basis.

February 23: The GANHC Board meets at GACS to review proposals and discuss the selection of architects for the project.

March 2: The GANHC Board meets at Annunciation Cathedral to discuss the selection of the project architect and consider hiring a financial consultant.

March 16: GANHC Board meeting at Annunciation Cathedral. The board votes to select SSAS as project architects and discusses hiring a financial consultant to obtain FHA insurance and subsequent mortgages, as well as help with regulations compliance. It is determined that the groundbreaking will be on either May 2 or 3.

March 24: GANHC formally contracts with Shayman, Salk, Aaronson, Sussholz & Co., as the project architects, although they have been assisting on a pro-bono basis since 1986.

March 30: GANHC Board meeting at Annunciation Cathedral. Treasurer Anna Manos reports $469,506.66 on hand as of March 30. The Poinsettia Ball raised $55,673.92. Annunciation Cathedral Philoptochos donated $4,300 from their March luncheon. Dr. Kioutas underwrote the expenses for the ball, so we received the full proceeds. Jensen and Halstead withdrew their proposal for architectural services. John Rassogianis moved that the executive board be authorized to hire SSAS and enter into a contract with them. All were in favor, except two members, one who abstained and one who voted no. John Secaras moved that we investigate hiring Cambridge Realty Capital as financial advisors. Hellenic Medical Society to donate a portion of the proceeds from their upcoming fundraiser to GANHC. John Secaras moves that the name of the nursing home be Greek-American Nursing Home-The Savior-Wheeling Pavilion. After much discussion, the board feels that this is premature, and we will discuss it again at a future date. Discussion on upcoming groundbreaking and a fall dinner dance. Dr. Kioutas reports that Senator Paul Sarbanes is "elated" with our nursing home project and will work to get the GANHC a congressional grant.

April: John Secaras, as fundraising chairman, delivers a report to the Diocesan Clergy/Laity Philoptochos Conference at Saints Peter and Paul Church in Glenview, IL.

April 1: Christine Burbulis, Frances Kuchuris, John Regas, and Peter Regas resign from the GANHC Board in protest of the architect selection process.

April 4: The Hellenic Medical Society fundraiser is held with a portion of the proceeds benefiting GANHC. Nursing home rendering is on display during the event.

April 6: GANHC contracts with Cambridge Realty Capital Ltd. of Chicago to serve as financial consultants for the project.

April 24: John Secaras provides an update during a meeting of the St. John's Philoptochos Society.

April 27: GANHC Board meeting at Annunciation Cathedral. Contract with architect reviewed and approved by attorney Phil Makin. Contract with financial consultants currently under review. Discussion about the upcoming groundbreaking ceremony. Thank you letters have been sent to Frances Kuchuris, John Regas, Peter Regas, and Christine Burbulis, all GANHC board members who resigned in protest of the architect selected. Groundbreaking: 680 invitations were sent out. Shovel donors are those who have donated $100,000 or more. May 12 GANHC Fundraising Committee meeting at the home of John Secaras to plan the groundbreaking and the dinner dance on September 28. It is decided to reduce the minimum contribution level for the groundbreaking to $50,000 so that more supporters can participate.

May 5: Meeting at SSAS to discuss progress. Agenda items: Increasing the size of the lake, adding a floor later, flooding risks, floor plans, skylights, acoustical ceilings, single bedrooms, mechanical rooms, room size, interior design, and marble. The entrance must make an architectural statement.

May 12: GANHC Fundraising Committee meeting at the home of John Secaras.

May 13: John Secaras makes a presentation on the nursing home project to the Assumption Women's Club.

May 17: GANHC Groundbreaking ceremony and celebration at the Wheeling property. More than 250 people are in attendance. Special guests include His Eminence Metropolitan Iakovos; Lee Zaras, governor of the Federation of Sterea Hellas (Roumeli); Gus Christofidis, AHEPA 13th District; Nicholas Zafiropoulos, Consul General of Greece; Rita Mullins, mayor of Palatine; Illinois Senator Adeline Geo-Karis; Cook County Treasurer Maria Pappas; Chris Tomaras; Matt Manavis, president of the Greek-American Restaurant Association; Tom Pappas, president of the GARA board; Bertha Facklis, president of the Hellenic Women's Philanthropic Association Soteria; Georgia Boolookas; Pauline Karalis; Dr. Mary Dochios Kamberos; and Louis Mitchell.

Following the groundbreaking, the GANHC hosts its Annual Meeting at the adjacent Holy Family Wheeling Professional Building, 201 E. Strong St., Wheeling, IL.

May 18: GANHC Board meeting at Annunciation Cathedral. Reports on the groundbreaking event and updates from Cambridge are on the agenda. The total in accounts is $508,702.

May 19: GANHC submits the first status report to the Illinois Health Facilities Planning Board. According to the report, "The project is currently in the final design phase. We are in the process of obtaining financing for the project, as well as the preparation of construction documents to obtain bids from contractors. Since we have not yet begun any construction or pre-construction work or obtained financing, all of the components are yet to be finished and zero percent of the project is complete." The report lists total GANHC assets (including the cost of land and outstanding pledges as $1,590,422.57), an increase of $341,813.33 since the submission of the CON in November 1997. At that time GANHC reported $1,248,609.35.

June 15: GANHC Board meeting at Annunciation Cathedral. Treasurer Anna Manos resigned for personal reasons. John Secaras is nominated and elected to replace her as treasurer. Gus Zografos, a civil engineer, is hired to help with the water problem at the pond. Gus donates the services of his firm Pearson Brown. Weisman Foundation donates $1,500. St. Peter and Paul Philoptochos are planning a fall luncheon to benefit GANHC.

June 21: GANHC engages the services of civil engineers Pearson, Brown & Associates.

July 20: GANHC Board meeting at Annunciation Cathedral. To date, $67,987 of the $12.5 million costs outlined in the CON has been spent. We are informed that the property contains wetlands requiring special authorization. A wetlands engineer is hired to plan to close the "channel" at the property.

July 23: GANHC Board lunch meeting at the offices of Shayman, Salk, Aaronson, Sussholz, & Co., 630 Dundee Road, Northbrook, IL. Instructed SSAS to add the words "Greek-American" to all drawings. SSAS will obtain additional brick samples to provide a range of colors and textures to choose from. They suggest using smooth face stone at the base of the building and not the chiseled face to provide a more Mediterranean aesthetic to the building. SSAS suggests first-floor elevation a minimum of 18 inches above the 100-year flood elevation. The lake area is being expanded to provide compensatory floodwater storage for the area of the site occupied by the new building. The lakes will also be used for stormwater detention. It was decided that a chain-link fence be installed around the lake to prevent residents from wandering into the water. A landscaping architect can help "beautify" the lake. Some tweaks are made to the designs. Discussion on how to go about selecting a contractor and assuring that Greek contractors and subcontractors have the opportunity to bid on the work.

July 23: GANHC Fundraising Committee meeting at the home of Dr. Kioutas.

August 17: GANHC Board meeting at GACS. The board unanimously adopts three motions. One formally confirms the intentions of the board that the facility provides for charity cases and that the policy will be not to evict someone if unable to pay. A second motion requires that two percent of all monies raised through fundraising be placed in a separate account for charity cases, and the third authorizes the opening of a separate account for charity purposes with an initial deposit of $750. We spent $145,017 of construction expenses that fall within the $12.5 million cap outlined in the CON. Representatives from several nursing home management companies presented their qualifications to the GANHC before the start of the board meeting.

September 1: GANHC Board lunch meeting at the offices of Shayman, Salk, Aaronson, Sussholz, & Company. Agenda items include selecting the exterior brick, the status of the interior designer, and discussing potential General Contractor and sub-contractor bidders.

September 21: GANHC Board meeting, Annunciation Cathedral. Account balances: Cash savings: $162,000.18 and CDs $163,558.52. Discussion on the upcoming fundraiser. The committee is leaning towards contracting with Bethany Methodist's Management division to manage the new home. The decision was deferred until after the fundraiser because there is too much that needs to be completed for the event,

September 27: "The Autumn of My Years" dinner dance for the GANHC. The event is held at the Fountain Blue in Des Plaines, IL. Bud Photopoulos is the master of ceremonies. The event resulted in $308,049 in donations and pledges. Dr. Mary Dochios Kamberos pledges $250,000 at the event and others follow suit.

October 19: GANHC Board meeting at Annunciation Cathedral. A report on the September dinner dance and updates on HUD are among the topics. Bank accounts and CDs total $172,845. Payouts to architect and topographer of $323,857 towards our $12.5 million cost per CON. An aviary with birds will be in the lobby and a 20-foot-long fish tank will be on the second floor. There are 538 square feet per bed.

October 27: GANHC selects Design Trends International of Houston, Texas for interior design services.

November: GANHC submits final plans to the Illinois Health Facilities Planning Board.

November 16: GANHC Board meeting, Sauganash Restaurant. Article II (entitled Governing Policy) now has a second paragraph. Bylaws are unanimously amended to include the following statement: "In accordance with the charitable purposes of the corporation, the policy of the corporation will be that upon establishment of our nursing home facility, a provision will be made for charity cases. Further, it will be the policy of the corporation not to evict a resident of the nursing home facility if he/she becomes unable to pay." Contracts for Bethany Management Firm to manage the nursing home and to Design International for interior design are approved.

November 20: Danae Chapter of the Daughters of Penelope hosts a dinner dance to benefit GANHC.

November 24: The GANHC fundraising committee meets at the home of Dr. Kioutas to plan future fundraising events.

December: GANHC goes online with a new website at http://www.ganhc.org.

December 21: GANHC Board meeting at Annunciation Cathedral. In addition to reports on fundraising and the CON process, updates on our financing efforts are reported. Discussion on mattress types, acoustics, lighting, tub rooms, overhead televisions, and positioning toilets on an angle to allow room for a walker. We will have acoustic wallpaper.

1999

January: GANHC Board selects A.J. Maggio General Contractors as the project's general contractor.

January 7: Several GANHC Board members, including all three Johns (Psiharis, Rassogianis, and Secaras) attend the feast day of St. John liturgy at St. John's Greek Orthodox Church in Des Plaines. Following the services, the Philoptochos Society presented a check for $3,350 towards their $10,000 pledge. John Gatsis, a member of the parish council, donated an additional $700.

January 25: GANHC Board meeting at GACS. Discussion on whether a project manager is needed and on a possible telethon. General Contractor bids have been received but are higher than the budget allows. The total project is $12.5 million. The portion allocated to contractors is $8 to $9 million. The telethon is discussed as a fundraiser.

THURSDAY, APRIL 22, 1999

Hellenic American Workers Association makes donation

CHICAGO—When the Hellenic American Workers Association recently dissolved, Athanasios Rikos, president, presented a check in the amount of $3,085.25 to Bill Kakavas, board member of the Greek-American Nursing Home Committee. Pictured, from left, are Rikos and Kakavas.

The *Greek Star*, April 22, 1999. Elaine Thomopoulos collection.

February 15: GANHC Board meeting at GACS. HUD will be in touch with the Village of Wheeling to see if they are capable of issuing bonds. Thus far, Wheeling has indicated an interest. We need to get our own appraiser. At this time GANHC maintains accounts at Atlantic Bank (formerly National Bank of Greece), Cole Taylor Bank, and Broadway Bank. Certificates of deposits are held at Edens Bank, First Chicago Bank, Cambridge Bank, Western Springs Bank, St. Paul Federal Bank, Liberty Federal Savings, and North Shore Community Bank. George Lekas and Gerry Garbis were elected to the board.

March 15: GANHC Board meeting at Annunciation Cathedral. Reports on February 22 meeting with the contractors and architects. The meeting with the contractors included: Helen Georges, Dr. Kioutas, Jim Pirpiris, John Secaras, Tina Spiratos, Elaine Thomopoulos, Theresa Tzakis, and two HUD representatives. Phil Makin, GANHC's attorney, withdrew from the project due to other commitments.

The minutes continue: "A letter was received from CLESE, an organization which is composed of forty different ethnic communities. John Psiharis spoke briefly on CLESE. Since the committee has previously subscribed to CLESE, a motion was made by Jim Kozonis that we subscribe again this year to CLESE at $100 per year. Seconded by John Secaras. All in favor." Cash, checking, and certificates of deposit total $530,108. Bill Kakavas presents a check for $3,085.25 from the Hellenic American Workers Association.

March 26: GARA places $106,000 into the equity account set up by GARA for the GANHC. Sufficient funds to proceed by way of tax-exempt bonds are now available.

April 19: GANHC Board meeting at Annunciation Cathedral. Steve Manta and James Christie are voted onto the GANHC Board. Bill Kakavas offered to host a fundraiser at his home in June 1999. Total savings and CDs are $616,835.

April 30: Members of St. John's Philoptochos Society present Dr. Kioutas with a donation of $6,650, completing its $10,000 pledge. The presentation was made at Norwood Park Home where supporters Peter K. and Sara Ladas reside.

May 1: GANHC contracts with Diversified Management Resources for nursing home management services.

May 24: GANHC Board meeting at Annunciation Cathedral. Among topics discussed: ATT shares given to us by Dr. Kamberos split and we now own 183 shares valued at $10,867. The board decides to retain the shares and enroll in an automatic dividend reinvestment program. The board decides to have twice-per-month meetings since time is of the essence for many of the matters being dealt with.

May 30: Per the GANHC 1999 Audited Financial Statements: Assets of $1,718,671 including $425,000 land, $2,500 restricted cash and deposits, and $518,900 in deferred project costs. Pledged outstanding is $147,801. Revenues: Contributions of $590,395 and $30,432 investment income. Expenses are $65,160 (including $17,331 in property taxes to be refunded).

June 8: Special GANHC Board meeting at St. John Greek Orthodox Church in Des Plaines to approve applying to the U.S. Department of Housing and Urban Development (HUD) to guarantee the loan. Guest Bessie Pantazelos reports that the 13th District Daughters of Penelope released $15,000 of their pledge to GANHC. Tina Spiratos reported the transfer of $307,000 from Soteria on June 3. Father Massouras, Gerry Garbis, John Secaras, and Dr. Kioutas to meet with Metropolitan Iakovos. The Village of Wheeling asks GANHC to pay a portion of the cost for paving the street which is close to the property.

June 28: GANHC Board meeting at GACS. Reports on General Contractor's contract, finances, and public relations.

July 26: GANHC Board meeting at Annunciation Cathedral. James K. Marousis, President of the George M. Eisenberg Foundation for Charities, attends to present a $50,000 donation from the Foundation. The second-floor dining room will be named in honor of the Eisenberg Foundation.

Honorary Chairman
His Grace Bishop Iakovos
Bishop of Chicago

Chairman
Dr. Theo E. Kioutas

Governing Board
Eleni Bousis
Christine Burbulis
Helen Georges
Bill Kakavas
Mary Kakavas
Jean Kaporis
Demetrios L. Kozonis
Frances Kuchuris
Anna Manos
Rev. George Massouras
James M. Mezilson
Toni Panos
Demetrios Pirpiris
Dr. Chadwick Prodromos
John Psiharis
John C. Rassogianis
John Regas
Peter Regas
John Secaras
Eugenia S. Seifer
Christine M. Spiratos
Dr. Elaine Thomopoulos

June 27,1999

Mr. and Mrs. Bill Kakavas
301 Chiltern Drive
Lake Forest, IL
60045

Dear Bill and Mary,

It is with much pleasure that I advise you that your gifts totaling $147,000 have played a major role in our success thus far. The chapel at the Greek American Nursing Home will bear a plaque with whatever names or message you determine. Please let us know in writing what you prefer.

As board members of the Greek American Nursing Home Committee, you both have worked endlessly toward the completion of this humanitarian project. I look forward to the time we can stand together by the chapel and read the inscription you selected.

Sincerely,

Theo. E. Kioutas M.D.

Theodosis E. Kioutas, MD

The *Greek Star*, September 30, 1999. Elaine Thomopoulos collection.

Checks are presented by AHEPA 13th District and Daughters of Penelope. Updates on the contracts with the management firm and Maggio are provided by Tina Spiratos and Gerry Garbis.

August 17: The Illinois Health Facilities Planning Board obligates (approves) the project granting us until August 15, 2001, to complete the nursing home.

Late August: GANHC is advised for the first time that HUD will not accept premium payments and requires us to have a total of $3,631,186 in cash and payments made on preliminary construction costs before it would guarantee our loan for sale of tax-exempt bonds or have $2,783,493 to obtain a taxable mortgage.

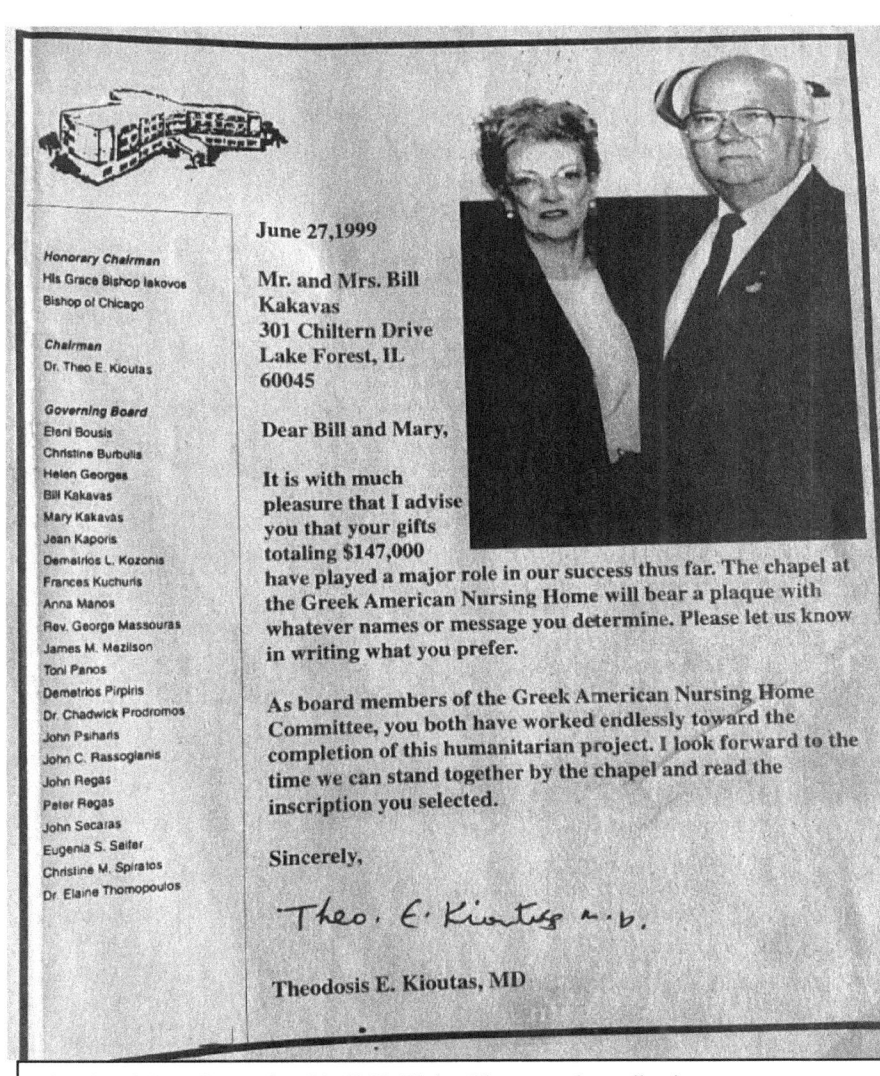

August 30: GANHC Board meeting at Annunciation Cathedral. Treasurer's report: Income received within the last month is $133,476.22. Total funds in all accounts plus ATT stock (183 x $47.50) is $1,068,341. Agenda items include General Contractor Maggio's decision to delay the contractual start date per our request and a discussion on obtaining major donors.

September 20: GANHC Board meeting at Annunciation Cathedral. $285,270 in donations received. Cash balance and payments made on preliminary construction costs totaled $1,938,099 leaving a shortfall of $845,394 for the sale of taxable securities.

September 23: Jim Kozonis resigns from the GANHC Board.

October 21: The dollar amount needed is now $573,538.

October 25: GANHC Board meeting at Annunciation Cathedral. The amount now that needs to be raised is $335,858. The net increase for the month is $271,495. Total accounts are $1,346,375. To be raised by Thanksgiving and HUD will begin to process the loan. George Lekas arranges for a one-half-page article in the *Greek Star* with a photo of Dr. Dochios-Kamberos to announce her magnificent contribution.

November 15: Special GANHC Board meeting at Annunciation Cathedral. The focus of this meeting is on fundraising. The audit is complete. Expenses include $13,785.52 to the Illinois Department of Public Health for a license.

November 20: Greek American Restaurant Association (GARA) hosts a fundraising dinner to benefit GANHC at Crystal Palace Banquets, Niles, IL. A check for $200,000 is presented to the GANHC that evening and Dr. Kioutas and Bill Kakavas accept the donation.

November 22: GANHC Board meeting at Annunciation Cathedral. Planning for the "special meeting" and fundraising are the main topics. Elaine Zacharakis, an attorney in corporate health care, agrees to join the fundraising committee. Treasurer's Report: Total cash and securities on hand as of 11/21 is $1,575,705.80. Construction prepayments acceptable to HUD are $871,560. Total to date: $2,447,271.89. HUD requires a minimum of $2,783,130. The minimum shortfall is $335,858.11.

December 13: GANHC Board meeting at Annunciation Cathedral. The shortfall for HUD is now $142,451. Georgia Photopoulos submits a wonderful letter praising the nursing home project to the *Greek Star*.

December 27: Sotiris Rekoumis hosts a four-hour Radiothon during his radio program to raise funds for the GANHC. In total, 146 callers pledged $82,000 to the GANHC.

December 29: Dr. Theodosis and Mrs. Anna Kioutas host a Holiday reception at their new home for GANHC board members.

2000

January 23: St. Peter and Paul Philoptochos Society host a brunch after liturgy to benefit the GANHC.

January 22: Hellenic Link-Midwest honors the GANHC and Dr. Theodosis Kioutas for efforts to establish a nursing home during a Dinner Dance and Scholarship Awards event at Ambassador Banquets, North Avenue and York Road, Elmhurst. A portion of the proceeds benefits GANHC.

January 24: GANHC meeting at Annunciation Cathedral. The treasurer's report indicates that GANHC has $2,857,524 and exceeds HUD's minimum requirement of $2,783,493. GANHC must now focus on raising another $350,000 to enable us to obtain favorable financing by issuing tax-exempt bonds over conventional financing options.

February 12: Society Ladies of Tripolis host a Millennium New Year Luncheon at Fountain Blue in Des Plaines, IL, with proceeds benefiting the GANHC. Tickets are $25 each.

February 28: HUD issues a firm commitment letter to insure the $11,275,000 loan.

February 28: GANHC Board meeting. Andrew Erkes of Cambridge Realty Group, who is helping us to finance the project, reports that HUD has approved the loan application and will guarantee the loan for $11,400,000. Vote to amend bylaws to increase the size of the board of directors from 20 to 25. Efforts to raise funds to meet HUD's tax-exempt bond requirements continue and $106,000 is still needed to meet the minimum. Tax-exempt bonds will reduce the interest rate by approximately 1.50 percent annually, resulting in an estimated savings of $169,000 per year, and generate up to $600,000 to offset operating losses during the initial lease-up period.

March 5: St. Demetrios of Waukegan Philoptochos Society hosts a *Makaronada* Luncheon after Divine Liturgy. Father John Sardis gives a "moving and inspiring" address about the importance of this project. GANHC board member Theresa Tzakis provides an update on our progress to those in attendance. The event raised $5,000.

March 27: GANHC Board meeting at Annunciation Cathedral. Greek American Restaurant Association donates an additional $106,000 to GANHC. Perry Callas, the bond attorney, briefs us on the process of setting up a tax-exempt bond issue. A cornerstone-laying ceremony is discussed. Inserting a time capsule into the cornerstone is considered. The GANHC will receive $100,000 from Lou Mitchell's estate.

April: Sts. Peter and Paul Philoptochos Society hosts an after-church brunch in the church hall, raising $8,700 for the GANHC. Among others, Dr. Theodosis and Anna Kioutas, and John Secaras represent the GANHC.

April 8: The bond interest rate of 7.9 percent is locked in.

April 17: GANHC Board meeting at Annunciation Cathedral. Treasurer's report: GANHC has $2,143,451, including the AT&T shares which sold for $6,749.88, and the GARA equity account totaling $306,147.50.

May 2-3: Loan agreement for HUD to guarantee our loan is completed.

May 7: General Contractor A.J. Maggio begins the first day of construction.

May 22: Elaine Thomopoulos speaks during a meeting of the Assumption Women's Club to provide an update on GANHC's progress.

May 22: GANHC Board dinner meeting at Costa's Restaurant to celebrate the HUD closing. An update on our closing of the loan agreement which took place on May 2 and 3 is provided. Mr. Maggio, the contractor, has paid the Village of Wheeling $60,000 for various permits after the closing. The company that was digging at the property pulled out and a new excavator needs to be found. Risk hazard and flood insurance are approved and the need for a project manager is discussed.

May 31: GANHC 2000 audited financial statements report: Total assets of $3,672,491 including $425,000 in land, $2,530,231 in restricted cash and deposits, and $593,773 in deferred project costs. Liabilities are $16,200. The pledges outstanding are $57,179. Revenue: $1,543,751 in contributions and $58,120 investment income. Expenses $58,550 (including $15,583 for property taxes to be refunded).

June 5: GANHC Special Board Meeting at Annunciation Cathedral. The main purpose is to approve the selection of a project manager and finalize plans for the June 18 event. The Board, with all in favor, hired Brian Replinger from Greeby Co. for that role not to exceed 14 months.

June 18: The GANHC hosts a Father's Day Picnic and festivities on the nursing home grounds. Despite rain and occasional thunderstorms, the event is a success with hundreds in attendance. The co-chairs of the event are Jim Pirpiris and Gerry Garbis.

GANHC Treasurer John Secaras extends the board's appreciation to AHEPA, the Daughters of Penelope, Philoptochos societies, *topika somateia,* and other fraternal and religious groups for their support and singles out the Hellenic Women's Philanthropic Society "Soteria," Dr. Mary Dochios Kamberos, and the Greek-American Restaurant Association (GARA). He also recognizes Bill and Mary Kakavas for their significant contributions and fundraising prowess.

June 26: GANHC Board meeting at Annunciation Cathedral. A report on the picnic is provided by Gerry Garbis and Jim Pirpiris and future fundraisers are discussed.

July 7: GANHC Board special meeting at Annunciation Cathedral. Agenda item: "The general contractor, Maggio, has advised us that to start building by late summer/early fall he must order steel fabrication at this time...he needs a three-month lead time. We must decide whether to authorize payment for steel before HUD approval. Please attend this important meeting. Your vote is needed!!!!!!"

July 21: GANHC Board meeting at GACS.

July 21: GANHC dinner dance committee members meet at the home of Stella Mash, chairperson, to discuss the "Celebration Dinner Dance."

July 24: GANHC Board meeting at Greek Islands restaurant. The discussion includes a report on the nursing home design. A color chart is passed around to the board members. A neutral color is selected for the elevators with white on the outside. The walls will be a different color on each floor. The first floor will have a homey atmosphere. No decision on color has been made yet but there will be Greek flavor throughout. Dr. Kioutas met with neighbors at the property. They are pleased with the nursing home project and the meeting went well. Discussion on a fall fundraiser. Concrete pouring is in progress. Estimated completion by June 2001.

August 28: GANHC Board meeting at GACS. Construction progress and updates are discussed along with plans for a fall fundraiser. The steel structure is being fabricated and the timetable is for one wing of the building to be erected every month. Underground plumbing for "B" Wing completed and "A" Wing" will be finished by the end of the week. Steel for "A" will be onsite on September 1. The roof is scheduled to be installed in December. We are informed that the late Mr. and Mrs. Peter Ladas left the GANHC a bequest of about $100,000.

September 18: GANHC Board meeting. Location unknown.

September 24: The American Hellenic Society of Berwyn hosts its 40th Anniversary Dinner Dance at the Skylite West, 7117 W. Ogden Ave., Berwyn, IL with the proceeds benefiting GANHC. Tickets are $35 each and music by Stevie "B" D.J.

September 25: GANHC Board meeting at Annunciation Cathedral. Discussion about the November dinner dance. Construction is on schedule. A video or slide presentation will be prepared for the dinner as well as for use in community presentations.

October 15: Order of AHEPA, Chicago Chapter 46 of District 13 “75th Anniversary Celebration Dinner Dance Honoring Dr. Theodosis Kioutas” at Avalon Elegant Banquets, 1905 Elk Grove Village, IL with proceeds to benefit GANHC.

October 17: John Secaras, Mary Secaras, and Ethel Kotsovos represent the GANHC during a meeting of the St. Demetrios of Elmhurst Philoptochos Society. They received a $500 donation and reported there is much interest in the nursing home and that many questions were asked.

October 23: GANHC Board meeting at Annunciation Cathedral. The board discussed an update from Diversified Management (the project managers) and outlined the process. The Village of Wheeling will grant a certificate of occupancy when the project is complete. The papers are then sent to the state. One month for the state to review. Second month for them to visit and inspect. We should be able to open 90 days after the inspection. We need $2 million to open (we have $1.4 million to date). When we open the doors, we need $600,000 and the year after opening $1 million will be needed. We need to train Greek-speaking CNAs. GACS should explore creating a program for this. Approved the purchase of three washers ($5,800 each) and four dryers at $3,700 each, for the laundry room. We need to approve the purchase of physical therapy whirlpool tubs. Dr. Kioutas reports that the whole facility is licensed for skilled care, but these beds can also be used for intermediate care.

November 4: The Hellenic Society of Constantinople hosts its annual dinner dance at Crystal Palace Banquets, 2648 Dempster Ave, Des Plaines, IL. Donation is $60 per person, and proceeds benefit GANHC.

November 5: Gortinia Society has a fundraising dinner dance at Crystal Palace with proceeds to benefit GANHC.

November 11: The Greek American Restaurant Association holds a fundraiser in support of their $200,000 pledge to GANHC. The event is held at Crystal Palace Banquet Hall. Tickets are $40 per person.

November 18: The Laconian Ladies and Misses Benevolent Society unanimously voted to donate $50,000 to the GANHC during a meeting at St. Demetrios Church.

November 20: GANHC Board meeting at St. Peter and Paul Greek Orthodox Church in Glenview. Much of the meeting is spent on the upcoming dinner dance,

November 26: “A Dream in Progress a Celebration Dinner Dance,” organized by the GANHC and held at the Crystal Palace Banquets, 2648 Dempster Road, Des Plaines, IL. The emcee is Allison Rosati of NBC.

PAGE 8

THE GREEK STAR — THURSDAY, JANUARY 18, 2001

Greek-American Nursing Home Crystal Palace fundraiser in excess of $500,000

By John Rassogianis and Elaine Thomopoulos, Ph.D.

Kosmos, kosmos, kosmos was a refrain dramatically, almost prayerfully, intoned by Greek radio host, John Katellis in the not too, too far distant past. Yet these emphatically uttered words marvelously captured the emotion of the big Nov. 26 turnout for the Greek-American Nursing Home fundraiser gala. The theme was "A Dream in Progress" and the site was the Crystal Palace—and it was kosmos, kosmos, kosmos for the nearly 650 guests. Mrs. Stella Mash, chairperson, and her committee would certainly agree with these long ago spoken words used to hype great events in a receptive [illegible].

The capacity turnout and the enthusiasm generated by Allison Rosati, NBC Channel 5 News Anchor and mistress of ceremony made the event one of the main attractions of the year. Addressing the guests, Rosati traced the beginnings and development of the nursing home dream, referring to it as "just a thought, just an idea, just a possibility now a reality," where "families will be caring for families." She continued, "Our members are strong, our hearts are big, our people are generous."

Rosati's presence contributed to an occasion laced with a mix of the serious, the sumptuous, and the sensational, each mood balancing the other, blending in with the musical tones provided by John Liatardakis and his orchestra. Indeed, the melody of words and music that went on inside the Crystal Palace coincided with the magical spirit of the winter theme design by Dean Quintas. Elegant floral centerpieces highlighted crystal vases set up high on each table. Boughs of snow-tipped pine cones cascading from evergreen branches revealed tiny white orchids. Banquet tables were accented by elegantly shaped chairs covered with white covers, carefully tied with over- [illegible]

[illegible] Steve Mash. [illegible]

... quirements to guarantee the building loan at a favorable interest rate. He emphasized, however, that it was not without the help of the community and three special entities—Dr. Mary Dochios Kamberos (with current pledge and contribution for in excess of $800,000), the Women's Philanthropic Society SOTERIA ($330,000), and the Greek-American Restaurant Association (GARA) ($306,000).

Among the evening's surprises, Illinois State Senator Adeline Geo-Karis read a resolution by the Illinois State Senate commending Dr. Kioutas for his lifetime of excellent, responsible and compassionate medical practice, as well as his civic and charitable good works. Pat Michalski, of the state of Illinois Ethnic Affairs Office, presented Kioutas with a book listing all state offices from Governor George Ryan for his outstanding accomplishments. Dr. Kioutas graciously expressed his appreciation but emphasized that the nursing home is a community effort. He thanked the board and the many individuals and organizations who have given their support so generously.

Guests that evening were very generous in making contributions toward the needed start-up operation expenses. All were touched with the $50,000 donated by the Lakonia Ladies Society and presented by Eugenia Stathakis, president, and Beulah Iatropoulos, vice president. In her stirring remarks, Iatropoulos said, "The women that started this organization, our mothers and grandmothers, are long gone. They left us a treasury and a fine membership. We did not squander what they left us. We had to find a cause—the Greek American Nursing Home."

What a wonderful evening! What a great committee: Mary Dennis, Helen Flessas, Bill Kakavas, Harriet Keramidas, Ethel Kotsovos, Frances V. Papas, Betty Quintas, Dean T. Quintas, John and Mary Secaras, LaVerne Stellas and Theresa Tzakis. Photos by Sam Tzakis, John Secaras, George Lekas.

Allison Rosati, NBC Channel 5 News Anchor, mistress of ceremony.

Stella Mash, chairlady; Mr. and Mrs. Nick Dennis; George Lekas, board member.

Helen Georges, co-chairlady; Christine Varnavas.

Eugenia Stathakis, president Lakonia Ladies and Misses Benevolent Society; Stella Mash; Beulah Iatropoulos, treasurer and vice president Lakonia Ladies and Misses Benevolent Society presents $50,000 check, Allison Rosati.

Reservations: Anna Christy, Theresa Tzakis, Harriet Keramidas, Helen Flessas.

John Secaras, treasurer and fund raising chairmanGANHC, Allison Rosati, Mary Secaras.

Reservations: Frances V. Papas, Mary Secaras, Sonya Kalpake.

George Christie and Jim Verros, GARA board member.

Sam Markos, Crystal Palace owner and GARA board member, John Secaras.

Dr. Mary Dochios-Kamberos, mega benefactor; Ethel Kotsovos, Nick Vlachos, Dr. Kamberos' nephew.

John Secaras; Tina Spiratos, board member; Dr. Kamberos; Anna Kioutas; Mary Kakavas, board member.

Dr. Kioutas; Betty Quintas, fund raising committee; Anna Kioutas; George Kioutas; Dr. Katherine Kioutas Katsoyiannis.

Eugenia Stathakis, Beulah Iatropoulos, Lakonia Ladies and Misses Benevolent Society, Kay Stath supporter.

BEGIN A SUBSCRIPTION FOR A FRIEND OR FAMILY MEMBER.
CALL (773) 878-7331

The *Greek Star*, January 18, 2001. Elaine Thomopoulos collection.

Tickets are $75 each. The capacity turnout is nearly 650 guests and over $500,000 is raised.

December 17: GANHC Board meeting at GACS. Treasurer's report: Checking account $350,825.18, an increase of $169,338.24 from the prior month.

December 29: The Hellenic League holds its annual Cotillion with a portion of the proceeds benefiting the GANHC. GANHC receives a donation of $50,000 from the proceeds of the Hellenic League's Crystal Ball and Debutante Cotillion 2000, held at the Chicago Hilton and Towers Hotel.

2001

January 8: GANHC Board meeting at Costa's Restaurant, Halsted and Van Buren. Discussion includes a final report on the "Dream in Progress" fundraiser.

January 22: In an update to the GANHC Board, John Secaras reports that about 35 percent of the construction is completed and $3,114,088 has been paid out to date. A donation of $165,000 in stock by Dr. Mary Dochios Kamberos was received. James Christie, A. Anthony, and Karalis stock are in the process of being sold. $100,000 from the Ladas estate is pending.

February 8: Executive Board-Management Team meeting at GANRC. Agenda items include the status of the building, hiring, south side needs, capital expenditures, insurance, brochure, marketing, grand opening, and board member presence for group tours.

February 26: GANHC Board meeting at Annunciation Cathedral. Discussion on the need to raise further funds for cash flow. One suggestion is a screening of *Captain Corelli's Mandolin.* The fundraising committee will investigate this. The nursing home is 52 percent complete. A new generator is authorized for $39,715. A letter from Baldwin Pianos confirms the donation of a piano to the nursing home by Bill and Mary Kakavas.

March 4: AHEPA 13th District holds a dinner dance at the Diplomat West in Elmhurst, IL. The event honors Greek American veterans and proceeds benefit the GANHC.

March 26: GANHC Board meeting at Sauganash Restaurant. Total funds on hand or in transit are $757,346 plus unpaid pledges of $159,379.

April 23: GANHC Board meeting at St. Demetrios Church. Funds total $750,205. Gerry Garbis provides updates on construction progress. Complaints about the number of visitors on the site. Contractors are concerned about liability.

April 30: A construction update reports that 60 percent of the construction is now complete.

June 4: GANHC Board meeting at Annunciation Cathedral. Vote to amend bylaws. Article IV Section 1. To increase the size of the Board of Directors from 25 to 28. Before the meeting, the board met with Shael Bellows of First Health Care, the new management company, to discuss the terms of our contract. At the end of the fiscal year (May 31, 2001), GANHC had $776,932.29 in our accounts. Pledges due are $106,075.

June 25: GANHC Board meeting at Sauganash Restaurant. GANHC was informed that we need to add 35 additional parking spaces, costing between $65,000 and $75,000. We need to add shut-off valves in each room at an additional cost of $10,513. The new business is to add another section to the bylaws which would provide for honorary board members. These board members would have the same rights as a board member, except to vote on the issues.

July 6: Joint GANHC and First Health Care Associates meeting at their offices, 10700 W. Higgins Road, Rosemont IL.

July 9: GANHC Fundraising Committee meeting at Saints Peter and Paul church. A fundraising dinner dance is planned at Crystal Palace on the Sunday after Thanksgiving. The board narrows the possibilities for the name of the facility to three: Hippocrates Home - a Greek-American Nursing & Rehabilitation Center, (Reverse), Greek-American Nursing & Rehabilitation Center - Hippocrates Home, or Greek-American Nursing & Rehabilitation Center. First Health Care Associates recommends Susan M. Barbian as administrator.

July 20: GANHC and First Health Care Associates Liaison Committee at FHC offices. Agenda items include building status, operating projection, supply bids, medical director and physician team, name and logo, security systems, Wanderguard, parking lot and pond aerator, staff hiring, and Frank Macknick, marketing consultant. Susan Barbian, the executive director, is to begin on August 6.

July 23: GANHC Board meeting at St. Demetrios Church. Financial, insurance, and construction updates are discussed. Checking, money market, CD, and savings accounts collectively hold $663,913 with $145,258 pending reimbursement from our loan. The cost for 20 dozen pieces of silverware and glasses and 240 plates is $9,702. When the generator is installed on July 30, 95 percent of the construction will be finished, and 95 percent of the HUD cap spent. Visitors are encouraged to visit on Saturdays or Sundays to reduce the disruption of the construction process. An additional $62,000 is needed for the paving of the 35 parking spaces, including light poles, and $28,358 for the replacement of part of the fire lane which was undercut. The management company requests $20,402 for additional security cameras.

August 24: GANHC Executive Board meeting. Agenda items include answering services versus answering machine, occupancy timeline, number of Medicare beds, rate setting, advertising for key staff including the Director of Nursing (DON), bumper guards in the parking lot, exterior signs, security after the building is turned over to us and copy machine quotes. Initial residency rates are established.

August 27: GANHC Board meeting at St. Demetrios Church, 2727 W. Winona Ave., Chicago, IL. The agenda includes discussion and updates on construction, First Health Care meetings, marketing, and fundraising. Frank Macnick was hired as marketing director based on the recommendation of First Health Care. Construction Report: Some rooms need re-tiling and walls at the contractor's expense. The telephone line has not yet been hooked up. Many visitors are stopping by the property causing both delays and potential safety hazards. Total cash and reimbursements: $801,256.

September 18: GANHC Board meeting, Sauganash Restaurant. Furniture delivery is scheduled for October 22nd.

September 21: GANHC Executive Committee meeting. Agenda items include security guard bids, Sysco for bids on dishes, charts and chart racks bids, dietician, internal security, sign, logo, and marketing.

September 24: GANHC Board meeting at St. Demetrios Church. Finances, fundraising, and construction reports are on the agenda.

October 5: GANHC Executive Committee meeting, Furniture to be delivered on October 22. Review of various contracts and bids.

October 14: American Hellenic Society of Berwyn hosts its 41st Anniversary Dinner Dance with the proceeds to benefit GANHC. The event is held at Skylite West, 7117 W. Ogden Ave. Music by Stevie "B" and Greek songs sung by Tom Topalis. Donation $35.

October 22: GANHC Board meeting at Saints Peter & Paul Church, 1401 Wagner Road, Glenview IL. Focus on planning for the November fundraiser. Discussion on the technological needs of the facility.

November: St. John the Baptist Philoptochos Society holds its Annual Autumn Membership Tea with over 130 in attendance. The theme of the tea is "Walk Down Memory Lane." Helen Elliott, president of the society, presents GANHC Treasurer John Secaras with a donation of $23,000.

November 16: GANHC Executive Board meeting. Agenda items: Fire Department inspection, George Walgreen proposal, update on security, medical director update, marketing, employee update. Status of the building (third-floor carpeting, cleaning), equipment ordering, computer bids, and dinner dance.

November 19: GANHC Board meeting at St. Demetrios Church. Construction update. Mr. Maggio is not making progress per the timeline and a meeting will be held with him on November 20 to discuss this. If that fails, we may need to pursue legal remedies. Mr. Maggio has seven days to proceed with plans for us to obtain the Certificate of Occupancy. The sprinkler system is leaking, which is not uncommon when first installed. The Wheeling Fire Department inspection passed. Village of Wheeling, Illinois Department of Public Health, HUD, and nurses' organization's inspections are still to come.

November 25: "The Dream Comes True" GANHC Dinner Dance at Crystal Palace Banquets, 2648 Dempster Road in Park Ridge, IL. Dr. Mary Dochios Kamberos is honored as the first "Super Mega Donor." The Invocation and Benediction are offered by Metropolitan Iakovos of Krinis, Presiding Hierarch, and the Diocese of Chicago. Music by the Linardakis Band. A champagne toast kicks off the evening. Sofia Marousis is the General Chairperson and Bette Brown and Theresa Tzakis are co-chairs.

November 30: GANHC-First Health Care Team meeting at FHC. Discussion on hiring progress and building status. Deposit of $1,900 for dishes and silverware. The Greek translation of documents is moving along.

December 14: GANHC Executive Board meeting to discuss the selection of vendors, rearranging furniture, and hiring progress for dietitian and dietary manager.

2002

January 8: GANHC Board meeting at Costa's Restaurant.

January 11: GANHC Executive Board and Management Team meeting at SASS. Agenda items: Status of the building (Springfield, heat, kitchen), status of dishes/food, equipment still needed/bids being obtained (door protection, bumper guards for halls, five microwave ovens), clinical software, hiring (dietitian, housekeeping supervisor, food service supervisor, activities director, nurse, aides), upgraded suites, contracts, admissions report, community relations report, marketing and miscellaneous. We can open one floor with three nurses plus part-time for weekends, two floors require six nurses. Fourteen private rooms.

January 14: GANHC Board meeting at Saints Peter and Paul Church. The final report on the Nov 25 dinner dance is a net income of $214,541. The architects will do a final inspection on January 14th and the Illinois Department of Public Health will conduct inspections on January 17 and 18. Tom Pappas from Market Square Restaurant offers to cater a

Philoptochos Nursing Home Tour Lunch. Activities Director Anna Kourakis, Admissions Director Eleni Karavas, and Housekeeping Supervisor Kathy Hall have started work and are getting things set up within their departments. Volunteers for grant writing are needed.

February 15: The GANHC Board provides a private tour of the new nursing home to Metropolitan Iakovos and area clergy.

February 15: GANHC Board meeting at GANRC. Total cash and reimbursements are $886,458.87. Unpaid pledges are $94,932.56.

February 19: The GANHC Board provides a private tour to AHEPA leaders.

February 22: GANHC Executive Board-Management Team meeting at GARNC. Agenda items: Status of building, health insurance, Monday board meeting, grand opening, the blessing of the building, and tour groups. There will be one Hellenic suite and one presidential suite.

February 23: GANHC hosts 60 members of the St. Demetrios Chicago Philoptochos Society.

February 24: GARNC takes part in the "Passport to the World" event at Wheeling Park District to begin to introduce ourselves to the community.

February 25: GANHC Board meeting at GARNC. Pre-meeting in-service training on how to respond to routine questions from the community regarding the nursing home by Susan Barbian. Government final approvals, stationary logos, and upcoming open houses are discussed.

February 28: GARNC hosts 40 St. John's Greek Orthodox Church Golden Agers for lunch and a tour.

March 3: His Eminence Metropolitan Iakovos and GANHC host Blessing of the Waters (*Agiasmos*) services and a Preview Tour. More than 400 are in attendance.

March 3: The GARNC is profiled in the "55 Plus" *Chicago Tribune* column written by Jane Adler in an article entitled "A Trio of New Facilities is Coming to the Suburbs."

March 6: GARNC hosts 50 participants from our new neighbors, the Wheeling Senior Center.

March 8: GANHC and First Health Care Associates meeting at GARNC. The agenda includes wish lists, ethnic wing, marketing, bids from Code Alert, Wander Guard, and Accutech, and delayed egress on doors.

March 15: GANHC hosts a VIP Grand Opening event with more than 300 in attendance.

March 17: GANHC hosts the Public Grand Opening and Ribbon Cutting. Nearly 500 guests visit and tour the new facility.

March 24: GANHC has a float in the Greek Parade.

March 28: GARNC hosts 30 members from St. John Philoptochos.

April 1: GANHC Board meeting at GANRC. Six admissions, 10 by the end of this week. All Greek. Total funds are $824,335.41 with $114,581.56 in unpaid pledges. Payments were made for landscapers, mattresses, tubs, washers and dryers, occupational therapy equipment, and telephone lines. Employee benefit of one-dollar lunches for two shifts (lunch and dinner) is approved.

April 10: GARNC hosts members of Holy Apostles Philoptochos.

April 22: GARNC hosts a *YGEIA* Health Education Program. Dr. Kioutas is the speaker for the first program of the series. Kioutas introduces Dr. Nicholas Papanos as the new medical director of the center.

April 22: GANHC Board meeting at GARNC.

May 10: GANHC Board and Management Team meeting at GARNC. Census is 24 residents with seven more expected in the next week.

May 20: GARNC presents a "*Ygeia*" Health Education program on stress management by Dr. Demetrios Trakas at GARNC.

May 20: GANHC Board meeting at GARNC. Agenda items include finances, the status of resident admissions, and publicity.

May 28: GANHC-Management Committee meeting at GARNC. The same builder should be used for the campus memorial sign so it will look the same as the other. Census: 33 residents with six planned admissions. The location of the committee office and employee benefits are discussed.

June 9: Midwest District of the Pan Arcadian Federation hosts its annual dinner dance at the Chateau Ritz, 9100 N. Milwaukee Ave, Niles IL. The event raised $20,000 to benefit GANHC.

June 13: GARNC launches a respite care program allowing families to admit a loved one into the facility on a short-term basis to allow caregivers to reinvigorate or plan a getaway.

June 20: Dr. Kioutas and Bill and Mary Kakavas attend a hearing at the Cook County Assessor's office with papers drawn up by Helen Georges and Tina Spiratos documenting that 85 percent of the patients are on Public Aid. It is decided that the Nursing Home will be reimbursed for three years in back taxes.

An invitation to Assumption of the Virgin Mary services at the GARNC. August 15, 2002. John Psiharis collection.

June 24: GANHC Board meeting at GARNC. Reports include financial, fundraising, and resident admissions. The census is 48 (26 Public Aid, 17 private pay, three Medicaid, and two respite). The nursing home is spending $200,000 a month over and above what is collected.

June 17: GARNC hosts a *YGEIA* Health Education Program on dementia with Dr. Katherine Katsoyiannis.

July 3: Independence Day cook-out for GARNC residents and families.

July 12: GANHC Executive Board meeting at GARNC.

July 18: GARNC presents "Family Greek Night," an evening of Greek music and fun at the GARNC.

July 29: GANHC Board meeting at GARNC. The census is 65 residents. The payroll is $150,000 per month. We need $400,000 per month to operate (including $80,000 per month mortgage payments). July private pay billings are $85,000. Pan Arcadians would like to name the small lake "Arcadian Lake," in recognition of their financial support.

July 31: GARNC *YGEIA* Health Education Program presents a discussion on skin cancer by Kathy Culiner, R.N., of the Kellogg Cancer Center at GARNC.

August 15: GARNC hosts church services for the Assumption of the Virgin Mary, *Kimisis Tis Theotokou* in the chapel. Fr. Milton Gianoulis presides. Lunch is served after services.

August 21: GARNC presents a talk on long-term care insurance by George Pentaris at GARNC.

August 26: GANHC board meeting at GARNC. An Honorary Board is established. Senya Kalpake will donate the furnishings for the chapel and earmarked donations for the chapel will be placed in a separate account.

September: Dr. Theodosis Kioutas is honored by Illinois Governor George Ryan for his efforts toward making the dream of the Greek American Nursing Home a reality. John Secaras, treasurer of the GANHC, accepts the award on behalf of Dr. Kioutas. Also, present is Illinois Treasurer Judy Baar Topinka.

September 7: Elaine Thomopoulos provides an update to the Holy Apostles Philoptochos Society during their membership meeting at the church.

September 23: GANHC Board meeting at GARNC. Most of this meeting is spent discussing the critical financial situation.

September 28: The *YGEIA* Health Education program at GARNC presents "How's Your Health? A Senior Fair."

September 28: GARNC participates in the "Memory Walk," a fundraising event held along Chicago's lakefront to raise funds to fight Alzheimer's Disease.

October 12: Holy Apostles Philoptochos Society hosts, the "Touched by an Angel," luncheon and fashion show at Ashton Place, 341 W. 75th St., Willow brook IL. Donations are $40 for adults and $20 for children under 12. Proceeds benefit the GARNC and Gaucher Research Fund.

October 14: GANHC hosts Columbus Day Radiothon from 9:00 a.m. to noon on the Sotiris Rekoumis radio program, WEEF 1430 AM, and $50,000 is raised. Special recognition to Dr. Kioutas, Catherine Fasseas, Chris Tomaras, John Secaras, John Andrew, and Bill and Mary Kakavas for their work on this project.

October 20: American Hellenic Society of Berwyn presents its 42nd Anniversary Dinner at Skylite West. 7117 W. Ogden Avenue. Tickets are $35 per person.

October 24: St. John's Philoptochos Society hosts a monthly birthday celebration at GARNC.

October 28: Students from Plato Academy visit the GARNC to perform skits and recite poems for the residents in observance of *OXI* day. They then spend time engaging in conversation and playing games with the seniors. This visit is in addition to their bi-monthly visits related to their service-learning curriculum.

October 28: GANHC meeting at GARNC. The resident mix is 77 percent Greek and 23 percent non-Greek. Dinner Dance underwriting is $47,000 so far. There are 88 residents and three in the hospital.

November 16: *YGEIA* Health Education program at GARNC entitled, "Oh, My Aching Feet," by Dr. Stavros Alexopoulos.

November 18: GANHC emergency board meeting to discuss nursing home operations and financial crisis. We have collected $17,000 from the Radiothon thus far. Dinner Dance: as of Nov. 10, 2002, there is $50,000 in underwriting and 245 reservations.

November 19: *YGEIA* Health Education program at GARNC entitled, "Alzheimer's, A Family Affair," by Cynthia Bell, director of the GARNC Alzheimer's program.

November 20: Names Day Vesper Services are held in the chapel. Metropolitan Iakovos officiates. Dr. Dochios-Kamberos is honored during a memorial service for her parents.

December 1: GANHC hosts the "Beyond the Dream" Celebration Dinner Dance at the Crystal Palace Banquets, 2648 Dempster Road in Park Ridge. Tickets are $85 per person. Net income $157,686 with 605 tickets sold. The John Linardakis Band performed. Catherine Fasseas chairs the dinner.

December 2: GANHC meeting at the GARNC.

December 3rd *YGEIA* Health Education program at GARNC entitled, "Dealing with Depression During the Holidays," with Colleen Caron, RNC, MS, Alexian Brothers Hospital.

December 16: GANHC Board special meeting. Two finalists for the administrator position are interviewed. After meeting in executive session, the board approved the selection of Burton Behr as the new administrator in an open meeting. Those present, except John Secaras and Tina Spiratos who abstained, approved the hiring. In recognition of her major financial support to GANHC, Dr. Mary Dochios Kamberos was unanimously elected to the board. Accounts receivable is $1.3 million.

December 16: John Secaras resigns as co-fund drive chairman and as a member of the Legal Committee.

December 24: Burton Behr's first day as administrator of the GARNC.

December 31: GANHC hosts a New Year's Eve celebration at McMahon's Arena Restaurant and Steak House, 3315 Milwaukee Ave., Northbrook, IL. The evening features Las Vegas-style Big Band music by Ed Collins and a live Vegas band. Greek music is provided by a disc jockey. Owner Gus

Cappas provides an open bar, champagne, and party favors. Chaired by Eleni Bousis, tickets to the event are $100 per person.

2003

January 2: GANHC Board special meeting at GARNC to discuss GANHC's options in connection with First Health Care Associates, facility operations, and finances.

January 27: GANHC Board meeting at GARNC. Food costs have decreased to $3.72 down from $5.50 per day. Two inspections had no findings. The monthly Pinnacle Report indicates high resident satisfaction rates. Census: 99 residents in the facility, eight in the hospital, and two incomings. HUD inspection reveals the building is in excellent condition so the closing can move forward. The Alzheimer's Unit is expanding and will be known as "The Village." New caldrons in the dining room. Residents will have food served on china with tablecloths on every table and have a choice of two soups.

The Board thanks and recognizes those who came forward to ensure that we met payroll. They were James Christie ($25,000), Dr. Theodosis Kioutas ($25,000), Chris Tomaras ($25,000), Eleni Bousis ($25,000), Demetrios Pirpiris ($10,000), Bill Kakavas ($10,000), Gerry Garbis ($5,000), and John Secaras ($5,000). To date, 605 tickets are sold for $33 each. Net income from the dinner dance, including donations and underwriters, is $156,686. Eleni suggests a gala event at the same hotel and offers to chair the event.

January 28: As part of a *YGEIA* Health Program, GANRC hosts a lecture on glaucoma during Glaucoma Awareness Month by Dr. Christopher Kardasis.

February: The Educational Society of Sellasia presents a $5,000 donation to the GANHC. According to Panos Giannakopoulos, president of the society: "On behalf of the Educational Society of Sellasia and the executive board, it is our pleasure and honor, as an organization, to contribute the amount of $5,000 to be used for the needs of the nursing home."

February 22: GARNC hosts a free program on pharmaceutical assistance.

February 23: GARNC hosts a Doctors' Breakfast to introduce the facility and services including physical therapy, occupational therapy, speech therapy, dementia unit, etc.

February 23: GARNC presents "The Paideia Project: The Golden Age of Pericles," a video presentation and discussion by Professor George Kourvetaris, in the main room of the GARNC.

A flyer for *The In-Laws*, an original play written and directed by Maria Boundas Bakalis, and performed by the St. John Players. March 2003. John Psiharis collection.

February 24: GANHC board meeting at the GARNC. Among the topics discussed is revising the bylaws considering the opening of the facility. GARNC receives an "F-Tag" from the Illinois Department of Public Health. This is a high score and as a result, we are certified for Medicare and Medicaid for two years (rather than the standard annual process). Christine Howard is promoted to the Assistant Administrator position.

March: The Metropolis of Chicago Philoptochos Society contributes $9,250 to the GARNC. Of the total, $6,750 is designated for the altar of the Centre's chapel. The balance is for operating expenses. The funds were raised via the society's annual luncheon held in September. Presenting the donation were Georgia Barris, Philoptochos board president, Mary Ann Bissias, and Joanne Stavrakas.

March 1: GANHC Bylaws Committee meeting at GANHC.

GREEK AMERICAN REHABILITATION & NURSING CENTRE

Dr. Theodosis Kioutas and the Board of the Greek American Rehabilitation & Nursing Centre

Invite You to an

OPEN HOUSE

Sunday, March 16 2-4p.m.

Sunday, March 23 2-4p.m.

"Celebrating the First Year of Operation of the Greek American Rehabilitation & Nursing Centre"

Come see our progress and enjoy Greek entertainment and refreshments. RSVP requested 847/459-8700.

220 N. First Street Wheeling, Illinois

(Milwaukee Avenue 1 block North of Dundee Rd. to Strong Avenue West to First St. South)

Invitation to the GARNC First Anniversary Celebration Open Houses. March 2003. John Psiharis collection.

March 2: GANHC holds a "Celebration Brunch," to celebrate the first anniversary of the opening of the Greek American Rehabilitation and Nursing Centre.

March 6: GARNC continues *YGEIA* Health Education Programs with a lecture by Mary Lewis, Director of the Alzheimer's Department, entitled "Caretaking for Individuals with Alzheimer's/Dementia: Understanding the Illness and Living with the Individual."

March 7, 8, and 9: The St. John Players present *The In Laws*, "a play primarily in English with a Greek theme," written and directed by Maria

Bakalis. The performance is held at St. John the Baptist Greek Orthodox Church and a portion of the proceeds benefit GARNC.

March 16: GANHC hosts the first of two open houses at the GARNC to celebrate its first year of operation with 300 guests in attendance. Among others, the Trovadouri Group of Chicago performs. Free popcorn and a showing of *My Big Fat Greek Wedding* in the third-floor lounge entertained the guests. Complimentary ice cream sundaes are served in the ice cream parlor.

March 23: GANHC hosts the second of two open houses at the GARNC to celebrate its first year of operation with 200 guests in attendance. Among others, the Olympian Dance Troupe performs. Free popcorn and a showing of *My Big Fat Greek Wedding* in the third-floor lounge entertain the guests. Complimentary ice cream sundaes are served in the ice cream parlor.

March 24: GANHC Board meeting. There have been 200 admissions since opening. The current census is 110 with two beds on hold. The open houses had 300 people in the first week and 200 in the second. The census has reached 120 residents. Once bifurcation is complete, GANHC can get a line of credit for $800,000. Funds are urgently needed. At present, 70 percent of gross revenue is paid out for payroll. This percentage will go down once the house is full. James Mezilson and Steve Manta resign from the board and Peter Karhalios is unanimously voted onto the board (motion by Bill Kakavas and seconded by Eleni Bousis).

March 30: The GARNC participates in the Greek Independence Day Parade in Greektown.

April: The American Hellenic Society of Berwyn president Gus Flessor presents Dr. Theodosis Kioutas with a check for $5,100 which is proceeds from their Forty-Second Anniversary Dinner Dance. This donation completes the organization's $20,000 pledge for a room on the second floor. The society was founded by Nicholas Economos, Gustav Rassogianis, and James Papadimitriou and chartered on April 24, 1960, with 58 members.

April 9: State Representative Sandra Pihos sends a letter to Governor Rod Blagojevich appealing for the state of Illinois to pay the outstanding debt owed to GARNC.

April 10: GARNC hosts a *YGEIA* Health Education Program lecture entitled "Normal Aging – How Does It Affect Memory Loss" by neuropsychologist Dr. Michael Mercury.

April 15: GANHC completes bifurcation process.

May 5: GARNC hosts a *YGEIA* Health Education Program lecture entitled "Aging with Grace – Maintaining a Positive Attitude," by Dr. Jack Hayes.

May 5: GANHC Board meeting at GARNC. Dr. Chad Prodromos has resigned from the board but will continue to support us. Eleni Bousis reports on her interactions with Leadership 100 members. She gave about 40 people letters about GARNC. Eleni is appointed chair of the upcoming gala to be held on October 10 at the Westin O'Hare. Mary Kakavas moves to invite Dr. Katherine Katsoyannis to join the board. Gerry seconded. Motion is tabled.

May 10: GARNC presents a *YGEIA* Health Education Program entitled "Hip and Knee Surgery? Get All Your Questions Answered" by Dr. Dan Kuesis.

May 14: GARNC presents a *YGEIA* Health Education Program lecture by Carol Drengenberg on Wellness.

May 27: GANHC meeting at GARNC. The current census is 117 residents. GARNC has receivables of $981,000 and payables of $626,000. Dr. Katherine Katsoyannis is unanimously voted onto the board on a motion by Bill Kakavas and seconded by George Lekas.

June 14: GARNC takes part in the Arlington Park Racetrack "Greek Fest: An Afternoon of Greek Food, Music, and Dancing to benefit the GARNC." Co-sponsored by *Greek Circle Magazine*. General admission payable at the door is $6, and children under sixteen are free. The proceeds benefit the GARNC.

June 28: The Pan Laconian Federation of the United States and Canada presents the Leonidion Award to Dr. Kioutas in recognition of his leadership of the GANHC during their convention banquet at Chateau Ritz Banquets in Niles, Illinois. Tickets are $65 per person.

June 30: GANHC Board meeting at the GARNC.

July 28: GANHC Board meeting at the GARNC. The census is 137 with nine hospitalized. A board committee has been appointed to investigate a line of credit of $800,000, but no less than $500,000. They will visit Cole Taylor, CIB, and New Century Bank to inquire. Committee members are Dr. Kioutas, George Lekas, Bill Kakavas, and Jim Christie.

July 31: GARNC holds a "Celebrate Summer" event. "The patio of the GARNC is transformed into an outdoor café reminiscent of Greece or Greek Town. Enjoy lakeside views as you partake in the festivities. Let your mind take you away to a Greek Island with music including *rembetika* music from 1 p.m. to 5 p.m. featuring Andreas Georgas and the Hellenic Five, performing popular music, from 5 p.m. to 8 p.m."

September 7: GARNC residents celebrate Grandparents Day with a special performance by the Orpheus Dance Troupe.

September 8: GANHC Board meeting at GARNC. The meeting includes a discussion with attorney Maureen McGuire. The current census is 66 residents (23 Medicare and 43 private pay) with 15 hospital patients to be admitted soon. Dietary fees increased by $2 per day.

September 27: GARNC presents a health fair and the Women's Auxiliary presents its first bazaar from 9:00 a.m. – 3:00 p.m.

October 4: GARNC hosts an on-site health fair and bazaar with doctors on hand for questions or concerns. The craft bazaar is run by Friends of the Centre Auxiliary to help raise funds for the center.

October 5: GANHC hosts the "Our Accomplished Dream Dinner" fundraising dinner dance at the Chateau Ritz Banquets, 9100 Milwaukee Ave., Niles, IL. Cost $100 per person. Chaired by Eleni Bousis and co-chaired by Chris Tomaras and Peter Karahalios. John Davis of WBBM-TV Chicago is the master of ceremonies.

October 27: GANHC Board meeting at GARNC. George Lekas moved, and John Rassogianis seconds a motion to raise room rates as follows: Current residents/semi-private will increase from $145 to $155 per day starting January 1, 2004. For admittances after November 1, 2003, rates will be $165 per day starting January 1, 2004. Current private or Village residents will be increased from $165 to $175 per day on January 1 and $185 effective January 1, 2005. For new residents coming on November 1 or thereafter, the rate for private and memory care will be $185. There will also be charges for incontinence, oxygen, and isolation. All in favor, motion carried.

November 20– 21: His Eminence Metropolitan Iakovos of Chicago and the GANHC observe the "Feast Day of our Chapel, the Presentation on the Theotokos into the Temple." Vespers on Nov 20 at 6:00 p.m. Hierarchical Divine Liturgy on Nov. 21 at 9:00 a.m.

November 25: Several GANHC board members attend the James R. Thompson Center Holiday Tree Lighting Ceremony with Illinois Governor Rod Blagojevich and First Lady Patti Blagojevich.

December 2: GANHC Board meeting at GARNC. The census is 160 residents with 24 Medicare, 48 private, and 86 Public Aid. The board decides not to renew the contract with RXPERTS, which had been handling pharmacy services for the facility, due to higher prices and poor service. A decision is made to bring the accounting functions "in-house." With some bills and pledges pending, it is expected the Benefit Dinner will net $130,000. The Board approves a negotiated settlement with First Health Care to exit our agreement with them.

December 31: GANHC has account balances of $313,369, including $2,050 earmarked towards the purchase of a bus, $5,652 in the chapel account, and $2,104 in the charity account.

2004

February 9: GANHC Board meeting at GARNC. The Greek-American Nursing Home Auxiliary, consisting of resident families and community volunteers, has raised $2,050 earmarked for the purchase of a bus.

February 26: "GARNC celebrates February as Heart Health Month. Dr. Bruno Cortis, cardiologist and author of 'The Spiritual Heart' and 'Heart and Soul,' speaks on how to uncover the healing power of a spiritual heart. Learn how to heighten your chances for longevity and vibrant health by understanding the relationship between stress and your heart. In this practical seminar, you will learn the links between stress and cardiovascular disease and learn stress release techniques."

March: GANHC announces that Dr. John C. Sarantopoulos was appointed director of "ReGenesis," the Department of Physical Medicine and Rehabilitation (PM&R). Dr. Sarantopoulos, a physiatrist, will oversee an entire floor dedicated to the needs of rehabilitating and recuperating individuals.

March 1: GANHC Bylaws Committee meeting at GARNC.

March 30: Social workers from Northwest Community Hospital tour the nursing home and have lunch in the dining room afterward.

April 3: Brunch with the Easter Bunny in the first-floor activity room sponsored by the nursing home auxiliary.

April 5: GANHC Board meeting at GARNC. We expect to achieve the break-even point of 167 residents within the next few months. Bylaws are discussed. In the absence of Dr. Kioutas, Helen Georges appointed a nominating committee to prepare a slate for the election of officers. They are John Secaras, Elaine Thomopoulos, Bill Kakavas, George Lekas, Mary Dochios-Kamberos, and Peter Karahalios. Based on Bill's report that there is much food being wasted, a motion is unanimously approved that all volunteers receive free meals. We will consider free meals for employees later.

April 25: GARNC Open House celebrating the second anniversary of the center. Special tours of the Memory Loss Village, Neighborhood Long Term Care, and ReGenesis Rehabilitation Center are showcased. Entertainment is provided by the Macedonian Dance Troupe.

April 28: Dr. Van Stamos, an orthopedic surgeon, presents a lecture for those contemplating hip or knee surgery at the GARNC.

April 28: GANHC meeting at GARNC. New bylaws are adopted. Conflict of interest and financial disclosure policies are enacted.

The board unanimously votes to make Dr. Kioutas an Honorary Chief Executive Officer as follows "A lifetime personal position is hereby created for Dr. Theodosis Kioutas who was President of the GANHC from inception in 1985 to 2004. The Honorary Chief Executive Officer will be a mentor and consultant to the officers and Board of Directors of the GANHC. The Honorary Chief Executive Officer when present at a meeting of the Board will have the right to cast one vote." John Secaras reports that it will cost about $700 for a portrait of Dr. Kioutas, and a collection is taken from board members.

April 30: GANHC Nominating Committee meeting at GACS.

May 20: Dr. Katherine Katsoyannis, GANHC Board member and geriatrician at GeriCare Ltd., presents a lecture in conjunction with Older Americans Month entitled "Questions and Answers on Memory Loss," at the GARNC.

May 22: George Reveliotis, an attorney specializing in real estate taxes and seniors, speaks during an Older Americans Month lecture at the GARNC.

May 24: GANHC Board meeting at GARNC. Elections are held with the following assuming office: Eleni Bousis, president; Peter Karahalios, vice president; Demetrios Pirpiris, second vice president; Gerald Garbis, treasurer; George Lekas, assistant treasurer; Theresa Tzakis, secretary; and Christina Spiratos, assistant secretary.

May 28: GARNC hosts a lecture on "Preventative Medicine and Anti-Aging Techniques" by Violet Bawolsky of Ancient Healing and Jerry Kolcan. It is an Older Americans Month lecture.

June 5: GANHC committee meeting morning at GARNC. Meetings of several committees occur simultaneously.

June 13: GANHC Annual Meeting and Reception at GARNC.

June 14: GANHC Board meeting at the GARNC. The board discusses unpaid payroll taxes of $500,000 for FICA and $50,000 in state taxes that we just became aware of. A nominating committee to consider new board members is established: John Secaras, chairman, John Psiharis, Tom Pappas, George Lekas, and Christina Spiratos are members. Elaine Thomopoulos presents a plan that she and Harry Tompary discussed to evaluate the operations of the nursing home.

July: GARNC participates in a Greek Heritage Night with the Chicago Fire.

July 12: GANHC Board meeting at GARNC. James Angelopoulos and Jean Kaporis were removed from the board per their wishes. Father George Massouras will step off the board to become the GANHC liaison with His Eminence. Upon recommendation of the nominating committee, Faye Pantazelos of New Century Bank and Gus Bahramis, C.P.A., are elected to the board. The board hires a security company to provide overnight security. The board preliminarily approved the quote of $5,880.36 for the Wall of Honor plaque. This is without the 517 names that will appear on the plaque. The board authorizes the creation of a website for up to $1,000.

July 22: Greek Night at the GARNC for residents and their families. A Greek band performs, and tables are set up behind the patio and in front of the lake. Wine and appetizers are served.

August 2: GANHC emergency board meeting on finances at GARNC. There are $811,000 in back taxes owed to the IRS and the state including FICA payments. A wide-ranging conversation includes a discussion on several cost-saving and revenue-collection measures including moving to in-house physical therapy from the outsourcing that had been done. A security guard is employed and on his first day catches an employee punching someone else's timecard. The employee was fired immediately. We will be short $170,000 for August due to delayed invoicing and state payments.

August 9: GANHC Board meeting at GARNC.

August 25: GANHC officers (Eleni Bousis, Peter Karhalios, and Gus Bahramis) meet with the Internal Revenue Service to discuss GANHC's FICA tax delinquency.

September 13: Eleni Bousis and John Psiharis meet with Michelle Milewski of Midwest Bank to explore refinancing options for the nursing home.

September 20: GANHC Board meeting at GARNC. Board members undergo mandatory HIPAA training before the meeting. Resident care and finances were discussed.

October: Elaine Thomopoulos resigns from the GANHC Board of Directors.

October 10: GANHC Benefit Dinner at the Westin Hotel-Chicago O'Hare.

October 11: GANHC Board meeting at GARNC. The current census is 173 residents with 88 Public Aid, 59 private pay, and 25 Medicare.

October 18: GANHC Fundraising Committee meeting at GARNC. Agenda items: December 2 Holiday Raffle Dinner and March 12 Gala Dinner Dance.

October 20: GANHC emergency board meeting at GARNC to discuss the IRS letter and administrator position.

October 27: GANHC Search Committee meeting at GARNC.

October 30: GANHC Search Committee meeting at GARNC.

November 10: GANHC Board meeting at GARNC.

November 14: GANHC hosts a "Community Forum" at the Chateau Ritz to report to the public on our finances. Agenda: Prayer, president's letter, accounting report, treasurer's report, Mr. Gus Bahramis, and closing statements.

December 2: GANHC Holiday Razzle Dazzle Christmas Raffle Dinner benefit at Wellington Banquet Halls, 2121 S. Arlington Heights Rd, Arlington Heights, IL. The Grand Prize is $3,000. There are 300 tickets available for $125 each. Tickets sold: 122. The event raised $15,200. Hosted by the GANHC with the assistance of the Greek American Centre Auxiliary. Co-chairs: Mary Kakavas and Bette Brown, Auxiliary President.

December 13: GANHC Board meeting at GARNC. The census is 175. We have accounts receivable of over $900,000 and still more owed by the state that is past due. The need to strengthen collection efforts was discussed as was the need to get an accounting staff in place and functioning.

2005

January 10: GANHC Board meeting at GARNC. The resident census is 164 with 17 Medicare residents. Savings of 32 percent in laundry expenses.

February 21: GANHC Board hosts "A Special President's Day Dinner," honoring philanthropic organizations that have supported us.

March 4: Anna Vissi, Jimmy Damon, Robin Simone, and John Davis visit the GARNC and perform for residents. The surprise visit occurs the day before they are to headline the GANHC Mardi Gras Gala.

March 5: The GANHC Mardi Gras Gala is held at the Westin O'Hare. The event features renowned singers Anna Vissi, Jimmy Damon, Ellen Karis, and Robin Simone. CBS News journalist John Davis serves as master of ceremonies. The Gala chairlady is Gina Christie. Vicky Palivos chairs the silent auction and Jim Pirpiris is the chair of sponsors. Eleni hosts Anna and her two bodyguards throughout their stay. The event raised $262,930.

March 14: GANHC Board meeting at GARNC.

April 11: GANHC Board meeting at GARNC. Agenda: Refinancing, health insurance, new board members (Thomas Skallas – attorney, Tom Diamond, Jack Mitsakopoulos, Peter Kopsaftis, Chris Tomaras, and Dr. George John

GREEK AMERICAN
REHABILITATION &
NURSING CENTRE

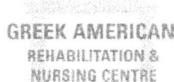

The Greek American Rehabilitation & Nursing Centre

**Invites You to
Join in the Quarterly
Medical Advisory Discussion**

Wednesday, July 13, 2005
7:00p.m. Refreshments & Discussion

220 N. First Street • Wheeling, Illinois
(One block north of Milwaukee & Dundee intersection, turn west at Strong Street-Starbucks to First Street south.)

**As a Community Developed Center,
We Invite You to Share Your
•Suggestions •Expectations
•Protocol •Concerns**

**Please respond to Perrie Veremis Hayes
at 847/459-8700 x13 by July 8, 2005 or fax your response.**

Our Home, is Your Home

Yes, I will be at the medical advisory discussion. Kindly fax your response to 847/465-9957.

Name________________________________

Address______________________________

City______________ State__________ Zip__________

Telephone________________ Fax________________

Email________________ www________________

Quality Care with Genuine Hospitality

220 North First Street • Wheeling, IL 60090 • 847-459-8700 • FAX: 847-465-9957

Invitation to a GARNC Quarterly Medical Advisory Discussion. July 13, 2005. John Psiharis collection.

Sianis), and community picnic. The census is 163 residents, 24 Medicare, and five holds.

May 9: GANHC Board meeting at GARNC.

May 17: GANHC Board meeting at GARNC.

May 24: GANHC Board meeting at GARNC.

May 26: GARNC hosts a lecture by Mark Florek of MAGA Ltd., entitled "Straight Talk on Long-Term Care Insurance."

May 29: GANHC hosts a Memorial Day Picnic. Live music by the Hellenic Five. The raffle for the event has 462 of the 500 tickets sold and raises $231,000. "Join the residents, families, and friends in a Memorial Day Picnic that will unite the past and the future. Enjoy '*Elliniki parea and kefi!*' We will be having a raffle drawing for a brand-new car, airline trips, cash, and other great prizes."

June 13: GANHC meeting at GARCC. The census is 163, 26 are Medicare, and six are in the hospital. Tom Skallas, based on a recommendation of the nominating committee, is unanimously elected to the board. Bill and Mary Kakavas resign from the board.

July 13: GARNC hosts a Quarterly Medical Advisory Discussion for the community. Refreshments and discussion. "As a community-developed center, we invite you to share your suggestions, expectations, protocols, or concerns."

July 19: GANHC board meeting at GARNC. Census is 166 with four in hospital. Nicholas Pishos, Effie Galetsis, Toula Dernis, and Timothea Papas were elected to the board.

August: GANHC formalizes the relationship with the Greek Orthodox Metropolis of Chicago. The Metropolis will ensure weekly services in the chapel from a local priest at no cost.

August 9: GANHC has accounts payable of $1,282,630 down slightly from the $1,563,585 owed on June 3rd.

August 22: GANHC Board meeting at GARNC. The census has risen from 154 to 175 residents. Medicare residents are up to 25. Conversion of the fourth floor into a 68-bed Alzheimer's/Dementia unit commenced.

August 27–August 28: GANHC has a booth at Chicago's two-day Greektown Festival. Board members take shifts to staff the booth.

September 19: GANHC board meeting at GARCC. Census 166. The name of the home was changed to Greek-American Rehabilitation and Care Centre (GARCC) by a 13 to 2 vote.

October 17: GANHC meeting at the GARCC. Agenda items include the treasurer's report and committee reports (legal, refinancing, medical, operations, nominations, food/kitchen, and public relations).

October 4: Jewelry designer Doris Panos hosts a fundraiser to benefit the GANHC at the Neiman Marcus Michigan Avenue Store. Appetizers donated by U.S. Foods.

November 21: GANHC meeting at the GARCC.

November 23: A portion of the proceeds from a concert featuring Alkeo and Dionisiou and organized by George Katerinis, held at the Congress Theater, are donated to the GANHC.

December 7: AHEPA Smoker to benefit the GANHC. Chateau Ritz. Gerry Garbis, event chairman. Tickets for the evening of dinner, gambling, and raffle are $25 each.

2006

March 4: GANHC Gala.

May: John Psiharis resigns from the GANHC Board at the end of his term.

October 4: GANHC hosts a golf outing at Kemper Lakes Golf Club in Long Grove, IL.

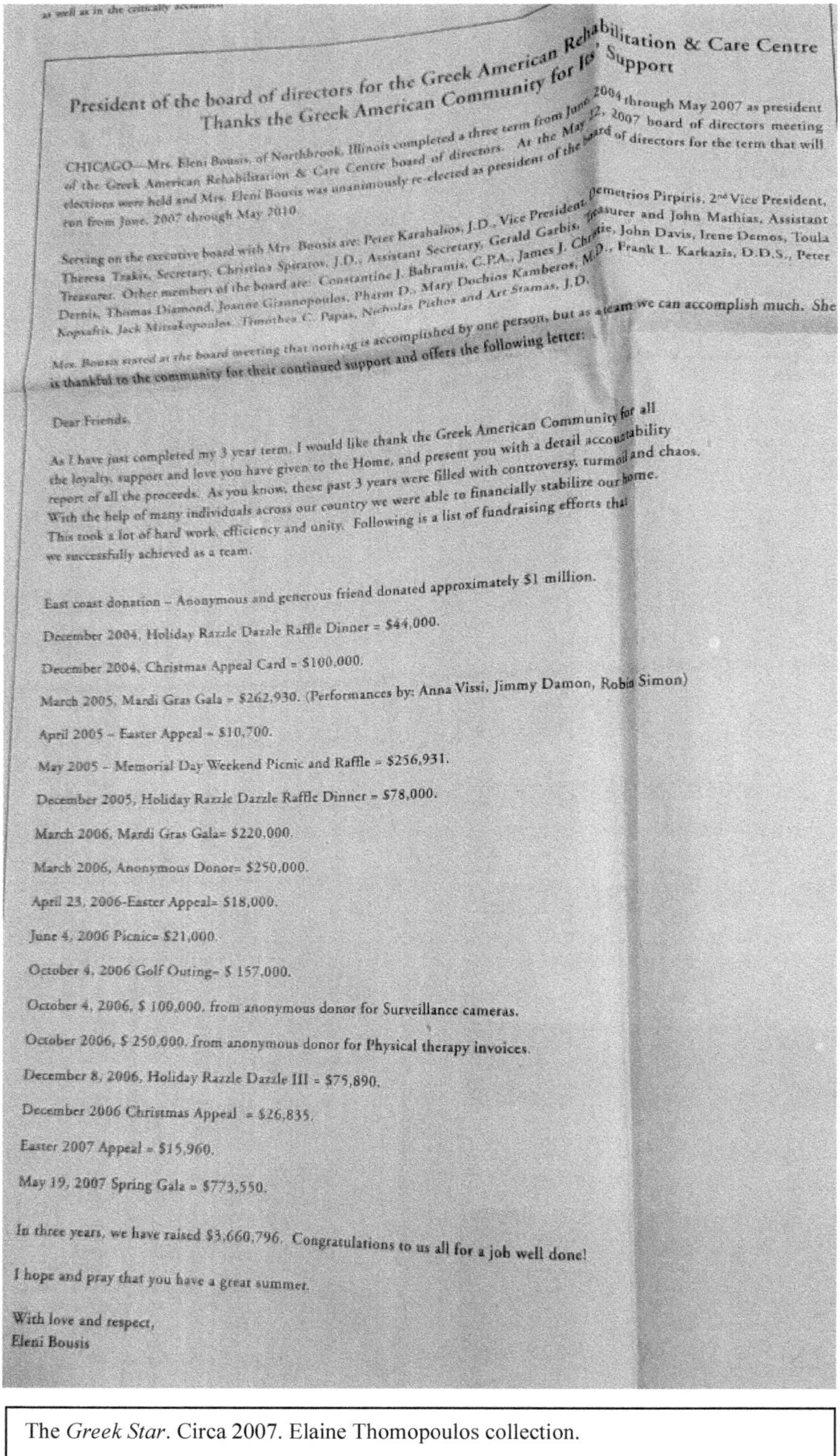

as well as in the critically acclaimed

President of the board of directors for the Greek American Rehabilitation & Care Centre Thanks the Greek American Community for Its' Support

CHICAGO—Mrs. Eleni Bousis, of Northbrook, Illinois completed a three term from June 2004 through May 2007 as president of the Greek American Rehabilitation & Care Centre board of directors. At the May 12, 2007 board of directors meeting elections were held and Mrs. Eleni Bousis was unanimously re-elected as president of the board of directors for the term that will run from June, 2007 through May 2010.

Serving on the executive board with Mrs. Bousis are: Peter Karahalios, J.D., Vice President, Demetrios Pirpiris, 2nd Vice President, Theresa Trakis, Secretary, Christina Spiratos, J.D., Assistant Secretary, Gerald Garbis, Treasurer and John Mathias, Assistant Treasurer. Other members of the board are: Constantine J. Bahramis, C.P.A., James J. Christie, John Davis, Irene Demos, Toula Dernis, Thomas Diamond, Joanne Giannopoulos, Pharm D., Mary Dochios Kamberos, M.D., Frank L. Karkazis, D.D.S., Peter Kopsaftis, Jack Mitsakopoulos, Timothea C. Papas, Nicholas Pishos and Art Stamas, J.D.

Mrs. Bousis stated at the board meeting that nothing is accomplished by one person, but as a team we can accomplish much. She is thankful to the community for their continued support and offers the following letter:

Dear Friends,

As I have just completed my 3 year term, I would like thank the Greek American Community for all the loyalty, support and love you have given to the Home, and present you with a detail accountability report of all the proceeds. As you know, these past 3 years were filled with controversy, turmoil and chaos. With the help of many individuals across our country we were able to financially stabilize our home. This took a lot of hard work, efficiency and unity. Following is a list of fundraising efforts that we successfully achieved as a team.

East coast donation – Anonymous and generous friend donated approximately $1 million.

December 2004, Holiday Razzle Dazzle Raffle Dinner = $44,000.

December 2004, Christmas Appeal Card = $100,000.

March 2005, Mardi Gras Gala = $262,930. (Performances by: Anna Vissi, Jimmy Damon, Robin Simon)

April 2005 – Easter Appeal = $10,700.

May 2005 – Memorial Day Weekend Picnic and Raffle = $256,931.

December 2005, Holiday Razzle Dazzle Raffle Dinner = $78,000.

March 2006, Mardi Gras Gala= $220,000.

March 2006, Anonymous Donor= $250,000.

April 23, 2006-Easter Appeal= $18,000.

June 4, 2006 Picnic= $21,000.

October 4, 2006 Golf Outing= $ 157,000.

October 4, 2006, $ 100,000. from anonymous donor for Surveillance cameras.

October 2006, $ 250,000. from anonymous donor for Physical therapy invoices.

December 8, 2006, Holiday Razzle Dazzle III = $75,890.

December 2006 Christmas Appeal = $26,835.

Easter 2007 Appeal = $15,960.

May 19, 2007 Spring Gala = $773,550.

In three years, we have raised $3,660,796. Congratulations to us all for a job well done!

I hope and pray that you have a great summer.

With love and respect,
Eleni Bousis

The *Greek Star*. Circa 2007. Elaine Thomopoulos collection.

INDEX

H

R

S

X - Y

Z

www.ingramcontent.com/pod-product-compliance
Lightning Source LLC
Chambersburg PA
CBHW060654060526
44119CB00076B/248
9798989072422